YOU SHALL BE MY WITNESSES

by

FRED FIELD GOODSELL

AMERICAN BOARD OF COMMISSIONERS
FOR FOREIGN MISSIONS

Boston   1959

Printed in the United States of America

YOU SHALL BE MY WITNESSES

TO
THE HUNDREDS OF AMERICAN BOARD
MISSIONARIES I KNOW PERSONALLY AND
TO THE MEMORY OF THE THOUSANDS
WHO HAVE GONE BEFORE

INTRODUCTION

The American Board of Commissioners for Foreign Missions is by no means the largest agency of the sort in America today. But it is the oldest. It was the pioneer. Organized in 1810, it was incorporated in 1812 under the broad title it still bears, to indicate that it was already serving several denominations in other areas beyond the Congregational Churches of New England among which it took its rise. These other Christian bodies have long since evolved their own societies to the same end. But the title stands unchanged as a reminder that this Board was first in the field for the continent and a pledge that its motivation at home and its policies abroad shall never be in any narrow sense denominational.

First in the field, the American Board has in consequence been the first to confront the novel developments and unforeseen problems arising for Christians of all names and creeds in the vast expansion of the project of proclaiming the gospel persuasively around the globe, by all sorts of services ancillary to the spoken word, through a century and a half marked by more rapid and extensive changes than any prior period in human history. For many of these changes, especially in interracial relations and the emergence of backward peoples into free nationhood, the missions movement is ideologically responsible to a degree hardly as yet recognized.

For a thousand years after the ends of the territories contiguous to the old Roman roads had been reached, unknown seas and the iron curtain of Islam estopped the urge of evangelism, except for brief and sporadic incidents, until the Age of Exploration culminated in the eighteenth century in charted seaways for regular two-way traffic, and made possible a secure service of supply for far outposts of Western religion and commerce alike. Promptly there followed an explosion of these rival drives in the Western soul. Their subsequent interplay, often in conflict, sometimes in unhappy alliance, forms one of the most fascinating and revolutionary episodes in the annals of mankind.

In all these events, redrawing the contours of the world and producing, among other consequences hardly anticipated at the outset, dynamic new units of the World Church, the American Board has perforce had a part. And, because it sits loosely to any control by the domestic councils of the Church body with which it is chiefly connected, so that it is free to take directly such measures as may be recommended by its own experience and insights, it is at least possible that this Board has been somewhat more resilient to novel conditions in its fields, less bound by stereotypes where fresh procedures are called for, than some of its sister bodies. That opinion is often strongly expressed by national Christians in other Churches in what are still called mission lands. We of the American Board should like to think that it is so.

At any rate, the history of this Board is a significant chapter in the account of the modern world mission of the Church. But it has never been written with due detail. In view of two pressing considerations, the officers and counsellors then in tenure ventured a few years since to sponsor such an undertaking. One of these considerations was the approach of the Board's one hundred fiftieth anniversary, in 1960. The other was the retirement of the Board's first Executive Vice-President, Dr. Fred Field Goodsell.

When the Constitution of the Board was revised to provide that among its secretaries one should be first among equals, a sort of Prime Minister, with administrative oversight of the Board's increasingly extended and complicated operations, it was recognized that this innovation was hazardous. By common consent there was only one man on the Board's roll who could be counted on to make it succeed. That man was Dr.

Goodsell: not only in the full sense a Christian and a scholar, but an experienced executive, a master of forceful tact, and a man who combined engagingly a conservative temperament with daring originality of mind. Hence, after a signal career of more than twenty years in the Near East, he was called back to Boston to lead the Board. For nineteen years thereafter he stood at the helm. He brought the ship prosperously through troubled waters, and proved beyond cavil that from now on there must always be a captain.

An Armenian millionaire in California, who had studied under Dr. Goodsell in Istanbul, once remarked to me, "Dr. Goodsell should not have been confined to the Church. He is a statesman with vision, and a diplomat. He should have been Secretary of State." I knew what he meant, but I was glad he had not had his way. Dr. Goodsell has shown that the Church is not confining; and few Secretaries of State have had as wide and lasting an influence as his.

With the Sesquicentennial approaching, Dr. Goodsell on the point of retiring, and the American Board lacking a competent narrative of its course thus far, we felt that he should be drafted for that undertaking. Reluctantly he consented at least to explore the resources for such a narrative. It soon appeared that they were far in excess of what could be organized, digested, and reported within the time limit assigned. For the full history, with all its factors displayed in due perspective, we must still wait. We trust that its achievement may be pursued under the same masterly direction.

Meanwhile, however, our Elder Statesman has produced this volume of interpretation. In it, upon an historical framework, are set in clear light the meanings and trends which have emerged thus far in the career of understanding, sympathetic, creative world ministry for Christ to which the American Board has been dedicated from its inception.

The flame kindled in a Massachusetts haystack long ago has spread far and grown brighter since its sparks began to fly. We trust that this reflective survey of its paths may prove illuminating, not only to the generation of Congregational Christians now responsible for the American Board's continuing advances, but also to Christians in general, concerned as all Christians must be for the peaceable conquest of the hearts of all men by the love of God in Christ Jesus our Lord.

RUSSELL HENRY STAFFORD
Moderator of the International
Congregational Council

Columbia, Connecticut
August 1959

CONTENTS

FOREWORD   xiii

CHAPTER ONE   A Rich and Varied History   1

        TWO   The Beginnings   5

      THREE   Fields, Methods and Stages of
                    Mission Activity   13

       FOUR   The Primary Purpose — Evangelism   33

AN INTERLUDE: I The Church in Angola   41

       FIVE   Enlarging the Concept of Missionary
                    Service — Education   49

        SIX   Enlarging the Concept of Missionary
                    Service — Medical Missions   64

      SEVEN   Enlarging the Concept of Missionary
                    Service — Social Action   82

AN INTERLUDE: II The Board Confronts
                    Social Issues   89

      EIGHT   Mission and Church: Relationships   99

       NINE   The Board Confronts Doctrinal Issues   110

        TEN   The Ecumenical Spirit of the
                    American Board   124

     ELEVEN   The American Board and the
                    Congregational Churches of the
                    United States of America   138

     TWELVE   The Woman's Boards — Their Vision
                    and Strength   154

AN INTERLUDE: III The Sustained Glow of the
                    Field Work of the Woman's Boards   174

   THIRTEEN   The Enlistment and Training of
                    Missionaries   182

   FOURTEEN   The Home Office   197

    FIFTEEN   The Story of the Treasury I   208

    SIXTEEN   The Story of the Treasury II   227

  SEVENTEEN   The Past is Prologue   240

                        APPENDICES

         I   Bibliography   257
        II   "Papers" and "Instructions"   272
       III   Toward a Theology of Mission   275
        IV   Christ and Culture   285
         V   Record of Missionary Appointments   287
        VI   A Graph Relating to Income   292
                          INDEX

FOREWORD

This volume is designed to serve as an interpretation of the History of the American Board of Commissioners for Foreign Missions from its organization in 1810 to the present time. For one entirely unfamiliar with the history of the Board it may also serve as an introduction. To those discerning friends whose interests and work have brought them into close association with the Board and its officers and missionaries, at home or abroad, it is hoped that it will throw additional light at various points on the nature of the task confronting the Board throughout its history.

The centers of gravity in an authentic and comprehensive history of the Board lie in its fields overseas. What goes on "over there" is of even greater importance than what goes on in the home office or among the churches and friends who provide the financial support and the American personnel, important as that aspect of the enterprise undoubtedly is. It is hoped that in time an account can be written of the origin and development of the Christian movement in each major field in which American Board missionaries have invested their lives. Such accounts, for instance, would include the history of the Church of South India and the founding and rise of the Kumiai churches and the beginnings of the United Church of Christ in Japan and the Christian movement among the Zulus of South Africa. This volume does not undertake that task. It rather lays the groundwork for a comprehensive history.

The source materials at the disposal of a historian of the American Board are ample. The archival correspondence since 1810 consisting of over 2400 bound volumes of letters to and from the home office, are on permanent loan in Houghton Library of Harvard University. Other items, including manuscripts and books, and the carefully kept minutes of the Prudential Committee are in the working library of the Board at 14 Beacon Street, Boston, or in the library of Andover-

Newton Theological Seminary at Newton Center, a suburb of
Boston. All these records constitute an amazing and well-nigh
inexhaustible mine for research. It must be confessed that
inadequate use of this material has been made in the preparation of this volume.

The writer is indebted to many friends and colleagues for
suggestions and help in various forms. It would be most
appropriate and satisfying to mention the names of all the
persons to whom I am indebted. I must not fail to mention
especially Miss Mary A. Walker, the librarian and archivist of
the Board whose help has been graciously and efficiently
rendered at all times, and Mr. Armstrong Hunter of the
Cabinet Press of Milford, New Hampshire, whose skillful and
soulful assistance has far outrun the bounds of duty. Mrs.
Richard Winkfield merits praise as a patient and competent
stenographer and typist. I am indebted to Mrs. Loy Long
for work on the Index. To the members of the Advisory
Committee on the American Board History Project, I wish also
to express my sincere thanks.

FRED FIELD GOODSELL

Boston, Massachusetts
August 1, 1959

YOU SHALL BE MY WITNESSES

1

A RICH AND VARIED HISTORY

The history of the American Board of Commissioners for Foreign Missions may be likened to a well-cut diamond. It reflects light and color from several facets.

One facet of the history is the story of dedicated men and women who heard the voice of God and responded, "Here am I, send me." The record of their service and heroism is inspiring and instructive; without their sensitivity and obedience there would be little to report. From such a point of view the Board's story is best told in autobiography and biography. Not many full length biographies of those who went abroad or of those who manned the home base have been written.[1] Many more should have been written.

Another facet of the Board's history is the story of the development of churches around the world. From this point of view the history focuses on the planting, nurture, and maturing of indigenous churches overseas. The "mission" as a unit of foreign workers in any area is all-important at the outset and for varying periods, depending on the insight and devotion of the "sower" as well as the nature of the "soil" with which he works. But eventually the mission decreases as the indigenous churches develop and reach up toward maturity. Board history from this point of view adds new chapters to Dr. Luke's book of the Acts of the Apostles. Churches have come into existence in many lands, and the brethren overseas have a story to tell of what God has done for them in Christ.

Or, one may view the history from the point of view of education. Congregationalists in New England have always prided themselves on their intelligence and intellectual efforts.

[1] See biography section in Appendix I: Bibliography.

They rebel against forms of Christianity which insult their minds. They believe in schools and in the early years often went to extreme lengths of suffering and sacrifice to provide them for their children. So it has come about that across the world American Board missionaries have regarded the school and the printing press as essential means for the proclamation of the Christian Gospel. In a sense the history of the Board has been a struggle to provide education and to train leaders for Christian communities, which in turn have been expected to move steadily toward higher levels of intelligent living and significant action.

Or yet again, the history of the American Board may be studied in the facet of service. The concept of what constitutes "mission service" has broadened and deepened through the years since the Board was founded. It has ranged from what might be regarded now as a narrow view of the relation of the Christian Gospel and human need to the contemporary view that nothing that promotes human welfare is alien to the purpose of the Christian mission.[1] The foreign mission movement was once described as "the world-wide application of the Golden Rule."[2] Famine, poverty, disease, suffering, the ruin to life and property resulting from man-made or natural catastrophe — all these have touched the heart and prompted the missionary to action. How philanthropic service has been conceived and developed is one key to American Board history.

Another aspect concerns international relations. In this field the missionaries of many boards have pioneered. American Board missionaries were the first to explore some parts of the world — including Patagonia, Eastern Asia Minor, parts of Africa, and Borneo — and thus opened lands to the trade, travel and diplomacy of the West. Until the 1860s few Americans except missionaries lived abroad, and the ambassadors of Christ were in a worthy sense ambassadors for their nation, too. In turn, the missionaries were interpreters of distant lands and

[1] See Paul A. Varg, *Missionaries, Chinese, and Diplomats*, (Princeton, N. J., Princeton University Press, 1958) for an exciting story of the development of the philanthropic motive in Christian missions.
[2] C. H. Patton, *The Business of Missions*, (New York, Macmillan, 1924), pp. viii, ix.

people to their fellow citizens at home. How America regarded the rest of the world, and how the rest of the world regarded America, was and is to large measure dependent upon the missionary enterprise.

Or, the American Board may be considered from the point of view of its part in American church history. For a time the American Board was the only foreign mission society in America. It received support from other than Congregational churches. Through the American Board hundreds of missionaries and millions of dollars were devoted to the service of Christ overseas by churches of several denominations. In time other foreign mission societies were organized, most of them denominational in character, and the American Board was led to rely increasingly on the Congregational Christian churches. Thus the Board has been a factor in American church history. In this aspect, too, it shines.

Finally, the history of the American Board may be studied from the point of view of Christian cooperation. The activities of the Board in its early years were cooperation incarnate. In time denominational cooperation sagged. Now, particularly in the last generation, Christian cooperation has again been regarded as imperative. The movement toward cooperation and unity has grown steadily in recent years; in many countries there are large *united* churches. India, Japan, the Philippines and other lands have been proving grounds for twentieth-century Christianity. Christian leaders overseas have said:

> We believe that unity of the churches is an essential condition of effective witness and advance. In the lands of the younger churches divided witness is a crippling handicap. . . . While unity may be *desirable* in the lands of the older churches, it is *imperative* in those of the younger churches.[1]

Each of these facets suggests a point of view from which a history of the American Board might be written. All histories

---

[1] Norman Goodall, editor, *Missions Under the Cross*, (New York, Friendship Press, 1953), p. 234.

are partial; as one historian puts it, "the highest truth of history will always transcend a statement of fact."[1] Particularly is this true of any history as rich and varied as that of the American Board. Nonetheless, the following pages are an attempt to explore and interpret several facets of the Board's varied history — a history which in many respects is unique and in a real sense is as wide as the world.

---

[1] Allan Nevins, in *The Saturday Review*, Feb. 6, 1954, p. 8.

2

THE BEGINNINGS

The Colonial period of American history was over by 1783, the year of the treaty with Great Britain. For the next three generations most Americans were busy with the problems of developing a genuine democracy and of settling their expanding heartland. Neither in this period nor in the period between the Civil War and the First World War did Americans have a mind to explore on a grand scale and understand fully the world of which they were a part. The British navy was in effect America's first line of defense against major assaults from abroad — except when Britain herself chose to attack in 1812. American pioneers in the realm of international relations were for the most part a few merchants and sailors and, after 1812, Christian missionaries. For many years these contrasting classes were almost the only representatives of unknown America in many parts of the world.[1]

The Christian missionaries were representatives of elements in a young, vigorous America who were serious about the Protestant Christian faith. The blessings which God had showered upon the thirteen colonies, especially in New England, constituted in the minds of these Christians an obligation

[1] Herman Melville's writings, *Typee, Omoo, Moby Dick,* once again popular in our day, describe well the life of sailors and merchants in this era. His picture of missionaries will hardly commend itself to those who know the facts. He professes to be for missions in the abstract but sees little to commend in the Mission to the people of the Sandwich Islands. "Not until I visited Honolulu was I aware of the fact that the small remnant of natives had been civilized into draught-horses, and evangelized into beasts of burden. But so it is." "To read pathetic accounts of missionary hardships, and glowing descriptions of conversions and baptisms taking place beneath palm trees, is one thing; and to go to the Sandwich Islands and see the missionaries dwelling in picturesque and prettily-furnished coral-rock villas, whilst the miserable natives are committing all sorts of immorality around them, is quite another." He lightens his judgment slightly with the remark that "the present deplorable condition of the Sandwich Islands is by no means wholly chargeable against them [the missionaries]. The demoralizing influence of a dissolute foreign population, and the frequent visits of all descriptions of vessels, have tended not a little to increase the evils alluded to. In a word, here, as in every case where civilization has in any way been introduced among those whom we call savages, she has scattered her vices, and withheld her blessings." The reader of Melville alone would hardly get the balanced view of missionaries which Melville himself professes to give. Quotations in this note are from the first edition of *Typee: A Peep at Polynesian Life,* (London, John Murray, 1846), pages 250 to 254.

to evangelize the neighboring Indian tribes and, as the frontier was pushed further westward, all Indian peoples. As the result of a spiritual revival which swept college campuses in the late seventeen-hundreds, new missionary passions warmed the hearts and minds of many college students. The God of Christianity was the God of creation, the Lord of the earth. He must be made known, they said, not only to Indian tribes in North America but also to the entire non-Christian world.

Williamstown — The Haystack

Among those who felt this way were several students at Williams College in western Massachusetts. Calling themselves The Brethren, they met often to talk of the state of the world and their part in it, to pray for the world's peoples and nations. One day they were walking in the fields near Williamstown, discussing and praying, when a storm suddenly broke. They took refuge from it in the lee of a haystack. As the rain fell they continued their discussions and prayer. When the storm was over, they made their way back to their college rooms. But something had been changed within their hearts. While meeting at the haystack they had resolved to become America's first foreign missionaries. "We can do it if we will" became their cry.

That was in 1806. Andover Theological Seminary, founded in 1807 as a Trinitarian seminary in opposition to Harvard's Unitarianism, became the training center for the missionary candidates when several "Brethren" enrolled as theological students at the end of their Williams College course. The foreign mission movement got under way with the organization in 1810 of a church-affiliated foreign mission society, the American Board of Commissioners for Foreign Missions. But we are getting ahead of the story.

The young men of the Haystack Prayer Meeting (as the haystack event came soon to be called) were scanning world horizons. Samuel Mills, their inspiring and inspired leader, had heard of the work of the Connecticut Home Missionary Society

among the Indian tribes to the West. His father had told him of
the pioneer mission work of John Eliot in the sixteen-hundreds
and of David Brainerd in the seventeen-hundreds. He had
heard also of William Carey of England who had gone to
India in 1793 as a missionary of the newly-organized Particular
Baptist Missionary Society in England. He had heard of the
organization of the ecumenically-minded London Missionary
Society in 1795, largely as a result of an appeal from Carey
after he had reached Calcutta.

The Meeting at Bradford

These things Samuel Mills knew — and he told his fellows.
They pondered them, and at length determined to talk with
the gentlemen of the General Association of Congregational
Ministers of Massachusetts which was meeting in Bradford,
Massachusetts, in June, 1810. So the young men from Andover
Seminary went to Bradford, and spoke of their concern. They
presented the needs of the Indian tribes west of the then
United States and also of the people of the great land of
India. They sought the counsel as well as the support of
their "Reverend Fathers" as they pressed for positive action
leading to the launching of an actual mission.

The ministers at Bradford were impressed with the enthusiastic faith and commitment of the young men of the
Haystack and the new Seminary, but being practical and
experienced pastors they shook their heads in doubt, not
over the faith but over the fancy that imagined such an enterprise as was envisaged could be carried forward without adequate planning. There was no desire to quench the burning
torch, but there was every desire to proceed soberly and
with good hope of success.

The main conclusion reached at Bradford June 29, 1810,
was to follow the method in common use in the Commonwealth of Massachusetts at the time, namely to appoint "Commissioners" to look into the matter presented by the young
men, and to take the necessary steps with as much wisdom

as they could muster. Nine commissioners were appointed: "His Excellency John Treadwell, Esq., Rev. Timothy Dwight, Gen. Jedidiah Huntington, and the Rev. Calvin Chapin, of Connecticut; Rev. Dr. Joseph Lyman, Rev. Dr. Samuel Spring, William Bartlett, Esq., Rev. Samuel Worcester, and Deacon Samuel A. Walley, of Massachusetts."[1] These were the original American Board of Commissioners for Foreign Missions.

Farmington — The First Annual Meeting

A scene helps to tell the story. Five of the commissioners appointed at Bradford gathered around a small table in the living room of the pastor of the Congregational church in Farmington, Connecticut, September 5, 1810. Rev. Noah Porter, the pastor, was invited to sit with them for their first annual meeting. Of these men, four were ministers of local churches. John Treadwell, the governor of Connecticut, was the only layman. Three laymen and one minister of the group appointed were not present. Those who had gathered discussed and adopted a constitution of fourteen articles. They elected officers for the following year, including a Prudential Committee of three members. They provided for certain other details. They prepared an "Address to the Christian Public" to enlist that public's support.

The Farmington gathering faced two major questions: Where? and How? The young men at Bradford had asked whether they should "direct their attention to the eastern or western world." As the Commissioners considered this question they prudently "VOTED, that the Board highly approve the readiness of the young gentlemen at Andover to enter upon a foreign mission; and that it is advisable for them to pursue their studies, till further information relative to the mission field be obtained, and the finances of the institution will justify the appointment."[2] In the Constitution which was prepared and adopted at the first meeting no specific

---

[1] American Board of Commissioners for Foreign Missions, *Annual Report*, 1810, p. 11. In subsequent footnotes, Annual Reports will be referred to by the letters AR, with year also indicated.
[2] AR, 1810, p. 13.

fields were mentioned. The Commissioners simply provided in Article II that "the appointment of missionaries, their destination, appropriations for their support and their recall from service, when necessary, shall be under the exclusive direction of the Board." In their "Address to the Christian Public," however, the Commissioners spoke of "the millions on our own continent and in other parts of the world, to whom the Gospel has never been preached," and the willingness of the "young men of good reputation for piety and talents . . . to go into any part of the unevangelized world where providence shall open the door."

Worcester — The Second Annual Meeting

The second annual meeting was held in Worcester, Massachusetts, when seven members gathered on September 18, 1811. The Prudential Committee reported on their correspondence with the Directors of the London Missionary Society to whose annual meeting they had sent one of the four Andover volunteers, Adoniram Judson, to inquire specifically about fields and measures. The upshot of this consultation was the hope expressed by Secretary George Burder of the London Society that "they may proceed with all convenient dispatch, from your shores to those of India." The Prudential Committee in the light of this suggestion said: "Though at present the Eastern world appears to hold out the most favorable prospects for missionary efforts; yet the Committee presume, that this Board will not lose sight of the heathen tribes on this Continent." The Prudential Committee's report continues:

> The Eastern world . . . presents most extensive fields for missionary labors; fields which appear to be fast whitening for the harvest. All . . . are full of people sitting in darkness and in the region and shadow of death, and by experiments already made, it has been abundantly evinced that it is by no means . . . vain . . . to attempt to spread the Gospel of salvation among them. . . . The most favorable station for an American mission in the East would prob-

ably be in some part of the Birman [sic] empire. The
population of that empire is great and somewhat advanced
in civilization; the character and manners of the people are
perhaps as favorable to the reception of the Gospel as will
be found in any part of the heathen world; and what
deserves particular consideration, they are not within the
limits of the British empire and therefore not so much
within the proper province of British [Mission] Societies.

The Prudential Committee called attention to home mission
fields as well, speaking of the "many tribes of men in pagan
darkness" who seemed to call for "a very tender and serious
attention" by American mission forces. The Committee therefore proposed that "as soon, and upon as extensive a scale as
their means will admit" missions should be established "in the
East" and "upon some place within the territories of the Indians
of this continent."

Later in the year a second "Address to the Christian Public"
was prepared and widely distributed. The Address stated
that "at their late annual meeting [the Commissioners]
resolved to establish, as soon as practicable, a Christian
mission in the East, and another in the West. In the East,
their attention will be directed to the Birman empire; and in
the West to the Caghnawaga tribe of Indians." The Address
pleads for interest and support, and indicates that the mission
was an expanding one. One sentence suggests efforts yet to
come: "Prophecy, history and the present state of the world
seem to unite in declaring that the great pillars of the Papal
and Mohammedan impostures are now tottering to their fall."

The Mission is Launched

Some months were still to pass before a mission was actually
launched. There was still organizational work to be done. But
the Committee kept at it, and in February 1812 the first missionaries were sent overseas.

The missionaries were eight in number: Rev. and Mrs.
Adoniram Judson, Rev. and Mrs. Samuel Newell, Rev. and

Mrs. Samuel Nott, Rev. Gordon Hall and Rev. Luther Rice. All the men were ministers, graduates of Andover Theological Seminary, ordained by a council in the Tabernacle in Salem, Massachusetts, on February 6, 1812, shortly before their departure for their mission. The Judsons and the Newells sailed for Calcutta, India, on the *Caravan;* Messrs. Hall and Rice, and the Notts on the *Harmony* for the same port. The ships reached their common destination, the *Caravan* June 17, the *Harmony* August 8, 1812. The mission was under way.[1]

Hartford — The Third Annual Meeting

The Board's third annual meeting, held at Hartford, Connecticut, September 16 and 17, 1812, brought together twenty-four corporate members from eight states[2] to hear reports and to discuss the future of the enterprise they now sponsored. The Board was now officially chartered; the Commonwealth of Massachusetts through its General Court had passed an Act of Incorporation signed by the then Governor, Caleb Strong, on June 20, 1812. The Act had authorized William Bartlett and Samuel Spring of Newburyport, Joseph Lyman of Hatfield, Jedidiah Morse of Charlestown, Samuel Worcester of Salem, William Phillips of Boston, John Hooker of Springfield and their associates to function as an incorporated body by the name of the American Board of Commissioners for Foreign Missions. The "associates," it is explained in the records, were Messrs. Treadwell, Dwight, Huntington and Chapin, all of Connecticut, as originally appointed by the General Association of Massachusetts.

The Act of Incorporation provided for membership of the Board. Section 5 said that any "annual meeting may elect by ballot any suitable persons to be members of said Board, either to supply vacancies, or in addition to their present number." Section 8 provided, in quaint terms, "that not less than one

[1] See Chapter 2 of William E. Strong, *The Story of the American Board*, (Boston, Pilgrim Press, 1910), for an account of the first mission. Look out for the misprint on page 18; the date should be 1812, not 1813.
[2] Connecticut, Massachusetts, New Hampshire, New Jersey, New York, Pennsylvania, Rhode Island and Vermont. AR, 1812, p. 37.

third of said Board shall at all times be composed of respectable laymen, and that not less than one third of said Board shall be composed of respectable clergymen; the remaining third to be composed of characters of the same description, whether clergymen or laymen." Evidently it did not dawn upon the male minds of that day that women might qualify for membership in such an august body! Devout women rose up in their collective might several decades later.[1]

The Hartford meeting also heard a good deal of discussion on types of missionary work to be undertaken in addition to the mission to India already launched. Four types of field called for missionary activity: (a) peoples of ancient civilizations, (b) peoples of primitive cultures, (c) peoples of the ancient Christian churches, and (d) peoples of Islamic faith.[2]

There was a feeling of urgency at the Hartford meeting. It was felt that the mission should be extended soon, even though funds in hand were insufficient and despite the fact that the mission to India had been undertaken without full financial resources. There was a vision of a world in darkness, with multitudes of people doomed if they did not hear the Gospel of Jesus Christ. There was an atmosphere of dedication to the task at hand, that is, to sustain the pioneers now half way across the world as they translated into deeds the professions of Protestant Christians in America.

---

[1] From time to time throughout the Board's history the question of membership has been studied and reviewed. Through the years the basis of membership has been broadened to include many persons known to be interested in the work of the missionaries, or persons who represented bodies from which might come candidates for mission service or financial support. In 1830, for example, the twenty-first annual meeting in Boston was told that 90 persons had been or were members of the corporation, 66 of whom, from 15 states and the District of Columbia, were living. Twenty-eight were present at the meeting. Membership then consisted of two groups beside the regular corporate body: corresponding members (there were 21 in 1830) and honorary members (there were then more than 600). Corresponding members were elected from among persons, "clergymen and laymen, residing in different and especially in distant parts of the United States, and in other lands . . . who though it be no part of their official duty to attend its meetings, or to take part in its votes or resolutions, yet when occasionally present, may assist in its deliberations, and by communicating information and in various ways, enlighten its course, facilitate its operations, and promote its objects." Honorary members were of two classes, ex officio, and those making a personal contribution at any one time — $50 in the case of clergymen and $100 in the case of laymen. Honorary members were given the privilege of attending meetings of the Board, and of assisting in its deliberations, but without the right to vote. Ex officio honorary members were presidents of auxiliary societies which had contributed at least $1000 a year to the work of the Board. AR, 1830, pp. 3-6.
[2] But see below, pp. 27 and 28, for a fifth type of field which was soon to emerge.

3

FIELDS, METHODS AND STAGES OF
MISSION ACTIVITY

The five young men who were ordained at Salem February 6, 1812 were soon on their way to India as American Christian international pioneers. They opened the way for others. They set in motion a series of events which, paralleling those started elsewhere by men of other nationalities,[1] were greatly to influence the course of the history of Christianity. They were a part of the spiritual awakening which made the nineteenth century "the great century" of Christian expansion.[2]

The first missionaries had a double objective. They desired to preach the Gospel of Jesus Christ to those who had not heard it and thereby offer a way of escape from eternal damnation. They also desired to plant churches and to nurture them toward Christian maturity. In time the goal of mission endeavor came more and more to be defined in the latter terms — to plant, nurture and aid in the growth of indigenous churches in various parts of the world.

The mission was begun, and its impetus led to the establishment of many other missions. A list of those missions indicates the extent of the movement for which the American Board of Commissioners for Foreign Missions has been sponsor and responsible agent. Divided into the four categories mentioned in chapter two, those fields were:

Missions Among Peoples of Ancient Civilizations:[3]

MARATHI (1813), India. A mission among the Marathi-speaking people of western India, headquarters in Bombay.

---

[1] Especially William Carey of England. See J. B. Myers, *William Carey*, (New York, Revell, 1887).
[2] Kenneth Latourette, *A History of the Expansion of Christianity*, (New York, Harpers, 1943), Vols. IV, V, VI.
[3] Figures indicate date of initial effort. Capitals indicate that Board work still continues.

CEYLON (1816). A mission to the Tamil people of Jaffna at the northern tip of Ceylon.

Canton (1830), China. A mission begun in response to a request of British missionary Robert Morrison, maintained until 1866 when it was transferred to the Presbyterians, re-opened in 1883 and discontinued in 1922.

Siam (1831). Transferred to the American Missionary Association in 1850.

Jews in Constantinople (1832). Transferred to the Mission to the Jews of the Free Church of Scotland in 1847.

MADURA (1834), India. A mission among Tamil-speaking Indians in South India, centered around the great city of Mathurai (formerly spelled Madura).

Singapore (1834), Malaya. A temporary mission, opened by personnel from Canton during the Opium War of 1834. Closed in 1843.

Madras (1836), India. Work in this southeastern India city was left to other boards with the death of Rev. Miron Winslow, 1864.

Amoy (1842), China. Transferred to the Foreign Mission Board of the Dutch Reformed Church of America in 1857.

Foochow (1847), China. Closed in 1950, one year after the Communist occupation of China.

Arcot (1851), India. Like the Amoy mission, transferred to the Foreign Mission Board of the Dutch Reformed Church in 1857.

Shanghai (1854), China. American Board personnel resident in Shanghai aided union enterprises in Shanghai. Closed in 1950, one year after the coming of the Communists to power.

North China (1854). A major mission of the American Board with headquarters at Peking. Closed one year after the 1949 Communist occupation when all missionary personnel withdrew.

JAPAN (1869). A mission which is now part of the Church of Christ in Japan, historically centered around Osaka, Kobe, and Kyoto.

Shansi (1881), China. Incorporated into the North China Mission in later years, headquarters at Fenchow. Closed in 1950, one year after the Communist occupation of China.

South China (1883). The reopened Canton mission (see above).

Shaowu (1918), China. A mission in the city of Shaowu, upriver from Foochow, for many years a special interest of the Christian churches. Closed in 1950, one year after the rise of the Communists to power in China.

Missions Among Peoples of Primitive Cultures:

American Indians (1817). During the period 1817–1883 missions were conducted among Indians, especially the Cherokees, Chickasaws, Choctaws and the Dakotas. All told fifteen tribes were evangelized, located in what is now Tennessee, Kentucky, Georgia, North Carolina, South Carolina, western New York, Ohio, Arkansas, Missouri, Oklahoma, North Dakota, South Dakota, Minnesota, Oregon, Washington.

Sandwich Islands (1820). The Board sent many missionaries to Hawaii, earlier called the Sandwich Islands, turning responsibility over to the indigenous Hawaiian Evangelical Association in 1863. Assistance from the American Board in finance and personnel continued to a very limited and decreasing extent until 1908.

Cape Palmas (1833). Missionaries of the Board attempted to establish a base at Cape Palmas on the Guinea Coast in Northwest Africa. When they withdrew in 1843, some of the work was transferred to the American Protestant Episcopal Board.

Sumatra and Borneo (1834). The first missionaries to Sumatra were struck down by cannibals. The Netherlands Government gave their successors permission to pioneer in Northwest Borneo. In 1838 the survivors transferred to Amoy, China.

South Africa (1835). A mission was established among the Zulus; later on other points were occupied in what became the Union of South Africa and Portuguese East Africa (Inhambane). This Mission continues.

Gaboon (1843). After the Cape Palmas Mission was closed, pioneer work was begun at Gaboon, West Africa. In 1870 this was transferred to the Presbyterian Board.

Micronesia (1843). A mission to the Polynesians in the Marshall and Caroline Islands. For some time the Gilbert Islands were occupied but that mission was transferred to the London Missionary Society in 1917.

Angola (1880). Portuguese West Africa. After pioneering, a mission was established among the Ovimbundu, a major tribe of the Colony.

Southern Rhodesia (1893). A mission to the Ndau people in the Rhodesian Highlands.

Missions Among Peoples of the Ancient Christian Churches:

Ottoman Empire (1820). Missions among the Armenians, Greeks, Bulgarians, Syrians, Assyrians and other Christian minorities in the Ottoman Empire, all of whom belonged to one or the other of the ancient Christian Churches, were begun in 1820. Work continues among Armenians and Greeks.

Mexico (1872). Mission directed especially to Mexican citizens alienated from Roman Catholicism. The American Board field is in northwestern states with institutional cooperation in Mexico City.

Spain (1872). Mission directed especially to Spanish elements alienated from Roman Catholicism. American Board fields were in northern and northeastern states with institutional work at Madrid. In 1933 responsibilities were transferred to an interdenominational committee.

Italy (1872). Mission begun as an experiment which was terminated after two years, leaving field to other agencies already at work.

Czechoslovakia (part of Austria) (1873). Mission directed to Czech people alienated from Roman Catholicism. Work transferred to local Protestant body in 1932.

PHILIPPINE ISLANDS (1903). Mission directed to people alienated from Roman Catholicism after the Spanish-American War. The large southern island of Mindanao was assigned to the American Board as its special field by Protestant Council. Cooperation with Union Theological Seminary at Manila, and with Silliman University at Dumaguete on the island of Negros. This mission is part of the United Church of Christ in the Philippines (Presbyterian, Disciples, Evangelical United Brethren, Congregational Christian, and autonomous Filipino churches).

FRANCE (1946). A "Mission of Fellowship" to war-stricken European people, centered in Chambon-sur-Lignon in Haute Loire, France.

Missions Among Muslim Peoples:

TURKEY, Arab, Persian and Turkish Muslims (1820). Mission directed to all peoples of the Near East, including large Arab, Persian and Turkish populations. Syria and Persia Mission units transferred to Presbytarian Board U.S.A. in 1871. The Mission among Turkish Muslims continues, and since 1915 the American Board has undertaken some responsibilities in Syria and Lebanon, in most cases in cooperation with the Presbyterian Board.

THE PHILIPPINE ISLANDS (1903). Mission to all people on the large southern island of Mindanao, including large Moro Muslim population.

* * * *

The Board settled down early to the long pull amidst vast populations. Roughly speaking, by 1820 each of the types of fields envisaged in 1812 had been occupied and by 1869 the question of major fields of effort was fully decided. Each mission called for individual treatment. Hence strategy and methods differed. A global mission had been begun; a variety of activities was called for and relevant plans were developed.

It will be of interest to describe briefly the patterns of development of the church in each of the four types of mission field. We shall look for a moment into the situation of the early churches in India, China, and Japan; among peoples of primitive cultures; in Orthodox and Roman Catholic countries; and among Muslim peoples.

The Church in India, China and Japan

Westerners may well stand in awe of the achievements of Oriental civilization. Humility is the appropriate attitude in the presence of such structures as the Temple of Heaven at Peking, China, or the Daibutsu at Kamakura, Japan, or the Taj Mahal at Agra, India. Equally fitting is willingness to learn and the desire to understand and appreciate the scriptures which the Oriental religions have produced. A fair question is: What can the West teach the East?

Christian missionaries, again and again, have felt that they go to the people of these ancient civizations for what seems on the face of it a preposterous errand: to share with them religious insights. But the thoughtful missionary is soon forced to realize that if he has a mission, it is not based upon human achievements, it does not flow from venerable religious teachers, it is not to be culturally classified as Western or Hebrew or Greek. It is *sui generis*. It is something given, not acquired. It is something many of whose aspects are beyond though not opposed to human understanding. The thoughtful missionary begins to understand in depth the meaning of Paul's words: "The word of the Cross is folly to those who are perishing but to us who are being saved, it is the power of God. . . .Has not God made foolish the wisdom of the world. . . .We preach Christ crucified, a stumbling block to Jews and folly to Gentiles, but to those who are called, both Jews and Greeks, Christ the power of God and the wisdom of God. For the foolishness of God is wiser than men, and the weakness of God is stronger than men."[1]

The correspondence of missionaries in India and Ceylon with Board secretaries prior to 1885 is heavy with descriptions

[1] I Corinthians ii, 18-25.

of the degradation of the masses of the people around them. Not only ignorance, poverty and disease but also superstition, magic, corruption and cruelty appalled the stoutest hearts. The word "heathen", fallen into deep disrepute today, seemed almost too decent to be applied to masses of humanity living like beasts. The lengthy "instructions" which Board officials in America at times gave new missionaries on the eve of their departure failed to prepare them for the human degradation they saw in lands of the ancient civilizations.

The missionaries tackled their task with more faith than knowledge. They were soon to discover by the method of trial and error where they could hopefully begin. Like Paul in ancient Athens they could point to temples and scriptures whose very existence, though in ruins or desuetude, seemed to condemn the beastliness of the masses of the people. But their progress was slow, very slow, slower than Christian enthusiasts in their homeland had dreamed it would be. The "wisdom of the East" was hard to locate and was not germane to the Gospel of Christ. An intellectual approach was out of the question in most cases. The Hindu, Buddhist and Confucian concepts of God were in striking contrast to the personal God apprehended through Christ. These concepts had, as it were, crystallized or sterilized religious thinking.

By and large, it was discovered that friendliness expressed through loving concern for the poor and the sick, eagerness to learn and listen, patient endeavor to satisfy human curiosity, unwillingness to take offence, calmness under provocation and persecution, a disposition to be content with what seemed at first meager results — these characteristics of the missionary were in demand among Oriental peoples. The language of love and goodwill had to be mastered and used constantly.

The Church Among Peoples of Primitive Cultures

American Board history can contribute richly to the topic: How the Church grows among peoples of primitive culture. American Indians, Hawaiians, Micronesians, Zulus, the Ovimbundu, the Ndau and other tribes have found values in the New Testament which have modified and revitalized but not destroyed their cultures. In many cases churches which had been formed, all too often on Western patterns, later underwent thorough indigenization in structure and relationships without losing their essential Christian character. In other cases, notably in Angola (Portuguese West Africa) among the Ovimbundu, churches from their very beginning stood well within the framework of the local culture. In some respects social and cultural adjustments were easily achieved. But tribal traditions and community folkways usually are too strong to permit much radical change.

In all cases religious doctrine is naturally a battleground. Ethics are another. But time and time again, the Western visitor, be he missionary or thoughtful tourist, is impressed with the relevance, reality and power of the new-found faith among peoples turning away from animism. The outstanding, overpowering fact of the Gospel is the fact of Christ. His luminous figure shines in the pages of the Gospel. He draws fear-ridden hungry souls to himself, not as a Jew but as a man — a man who reveals the love and integrity which are at the heart of the universe. No one has the right to predict or to attempt to control the process by which the Holy Spirit forms and informs the Church among any particular tribe or group. Humanly speaking, there have been many mistakes, crises and even disasters in the birth and nurture of the Church among peoples of primitive culture, but the fact is that God in Christ appears to be at work in every situation.

Evangelical Churches in Orthodox and Roman Catholic Countries

Historically the American Board has been the servant of those who have wished to preach the Christian Gospel to all mankind according to the insights of the Protestant Reformation. It is true to say that the dominant effort has been to enlighten all men as to the real nature of the Gospel, and to do this with kindly regard for all who acknowledge a common goal. The origin of the Board deep in the experiences of the evangelical revival of the late eighteenth century in America gave it a positive emphasis. Missionaries were sent to build up and not to tear down. The mood was thoroughly friendly in approach to all peoples, even though it was inevitable that in the declaration of the truth as they understood it, error should be branded as error.

One hundred and fifty years ago America was predominantly a Protestant country. Roman Catholicism and Eastern Orthodoxy were little known. It was not long, however, before missionaries of the Board came into contact with Romanism and Eastern Orthodoxy. Missionaries in the Sandwich Islands from 1820 onwards did all they could to prevent the incursion of Roman Catholic priests in the conviction that both their doctrine and their practice would be harmful to native Hawaiian society. In the Near East before ten years had elapsed after the arrival of the missionaries in Jerusalem, Beirut, Smyrna and Athens in the eighteen twenties, missionaries became aware of the potential opposition of the Orthodox churches — chiefly Armenian and Greek. It could not have been otherwise. Both Armenian and Greek hierarchies quite understandably looked with disfavor upon these American Protestants. "Why have they come? We have the truth," the long-established Churches said.

The Armenians, ardent nationalists and a minority in the Ottoman Empire, discovered the potential value of contacts with the missionaries. They were, unquestionably, among the most alert and progressive elements in Turkey. Commercially and intellectually, their leaders were eager for Western civilization. They were interested in what the missionaries had to say and do. The first concern of the missionaries, namely to translate the Bible into modern Armenian, created excitement. Missionaries began to preach and to read the Bible publicly in a language the people could understand. Schools were started. Reform movements among the Armenians profited by the activities of the missionaries. The Armenian Orthodox Church authorities became suspicious. Before two decades had passed there were excommunications and other efforts to repress the new trends with the result that a Protestant Evangelical Movement came into being and Protestant Armenian Churches were formed. The missionaries had sought to revitalize not to divide the Orthodox community and Church. But their efforts inevitably created dissension. The Protestant movement acquired momentum and operated from several centers, one of the most influential being the city of Aintab in Cilicia, now Gaziantep in Turkey.

The beginnings of Protestantism among adherents of the Greek Orthodox Church paralleled the Armenian developments but with much less response and with even greater difficulties. The Bulgarian Evangelical Churches developed into sturdy Christian agencies in an environment more friendly than the Greek but less widespread than the Armenian.

Emphasis should be placed upon the most important fact in the modern history of the Orthodox Churches and their relations with Protestant movements. The Orthodox Churches of the Near East had been forced by the advance and power of Islam into the role of national guardians. The Church was the last stronghold of national life and traditions stemming from the early centuries of Christian history. The bonds within which the Christian minorities lived were very onerous. The Orthodox communities literally owed their continued national existence to their Church. This created a Church which as a church had become static and an end in itself. Such a Church almost lost its sense of mission as a Christian body. To a large extent it exchanged its spiritual function for a political one. The arrival of the missionaries challenged this position. The Church of Christ exists, ideally, to preach the Gospel and to be the means of inspiring new life in Christ for all men. The missionaries assumed that even under difficult political circumstances, the Gospel could transform men and society. By and large, the Protestant Churches which came into existence in Greece, Bulgaria, Asia Minor and Syria were centers of vital religious life and outlook in contrast to the formalism and rigidity of the Orthodox Churches. This function the Protestant churches have continued to fulfil even under changing political circumstances. The impact of the Protestant movement upon the Orthodox Churches and communities is to be measured by the remarkable development within those communities themselves.

The story of the impact of Protestant missions upon Roman Catholicism differs in two respects: the severity of opposition encountered, and slower growth.

Very early in its history the Prudential Committee demonstrated its interest in the peoples of Central and South America — areas where Roman Catholic missionaries had been pioneers and guides since the early fifteen hundreds. The revolutions in the early eighteen hundreds which had unseated Spanish and Portuguese colonial governments had created republics which were symbols of freedom. North Americans were not oblivious to these developments. It was quite natural, therefore, that the Prudential Committee in 1823 announced that it had "taken measures to ascertain the religious and moral state of the southern and western countries of South America with a view to missionary labors . . . "[1] On July 25, 1823 John C. Brigham and Theophilus Parvin were sent to Buenos Aires. Their object was stated to be "to circulate Bibles and Tracts, and to ascertain the religious and moral state of" people in South America. Again in 1832 the Prudential Committee sent a mission of inquiry, this time to Patagonia.

Neither of these missions of inquiry resulted in action.

Fifty years later in 1872, work among Roman Catholics in Latin America was begun "in accordance with what is felt to be the wishes of the great body of churches acting through the American Board."[2] At this time, however, attention was

---

[1] *View of the Missions of the ABCFM,* November 1823, (leaflet in American Board archives, AB 90-Z-10), p. 2.
[2] AR, 1872, p. 84.

also riveted on the religious situation in Spain where in 1868 a revolution had taken place, marking the beginning of a new era. From the suppression of the nascent Reformation in Spain in 1570 until 1868 there had been no toleration of dissent from Romanism. "As late as 1861, the secret study of the Scriptures subjected the offenders to imprisonment and condemnation to the galleys, and subsequent civil disability."[1]

For ten years prior to 1872 many churches in America had been stirred by the events in Spain and in Latin America. An organization called the American and Foreign Christian Union had been formed to combat the machinations of the Romanists at home and abroad. A considerable number of Congregational churches had contributed to the funds of this Union but in 1871 these churches withdrew and presented a memorial to the annual meeting of the Board in Salem, Massachusetts, asking the Board to extend its work to nominally Christian countries.

The Prudential Committee consequently undertook to establish missions in Mexico, Spain, Austria (Czechoslovakia) and Italy. The story of these missions cannot be given here. Suffice it to say that after two years of experimental effort, it was deemed inadvisable to add another Protestant mission to those already operating in Italy. The mission in Czechoslovakia achieved some success by the formation of a body of evangelical churches which is active and vital to this day (1958), twenty years after the withdrawal of all American Board personnel. The mission in Spain, ably led by Rev. and Mrs. William H. Gulick, through many vicissitudes, resulted in the organization of a small number of evangelical churches which in 1885 joined with other groups in forming the Iberian Evangelical Union. Three years later this Union merged with "the Spanish Christian Church" to create the Spanish Evangelical Church in which all divisive denominational terms, formulas and titles were avoided so far as possible, a large degree of autonomy being left to the

[1] AR, 1872, p. 85.

individual churches and missions. This is the body which at Amsterdam in 1948 was received into the World Council of Churches as a charter member. All American Board personnel withdrew from Spain in 1928, except the members of the faculty of the International Institute for Girls at Madrid, now an entirely independent institution. The churches formed by the Mission in Mexico continue to grow and to witness effectively under recurrent difficulties.

The Church Among Muslim Peoples

It has taken literally centuries for Christians and Muslims to forget the bitterness of the Crusades of the Middle Ages and many there be in both communities who have not yet denounced that heritage of hate and misunderstanding. Historians of culture sometimes repeat the aphorism: "The perversion of the best is the worst." When analyzing some cultural transition or reversal the Christian in Muslim lands may be tempted to turn that saying in this fashion: "Misrepresentation of the best can be the most difficult to retrieve."

The plain fact is that Christianity and Islam have so much in common that the real differences leap into colossal significance. The differences lie mainly in the realm of doctrine, though the central historical fact of the crucifixion of Jesus is denied by Muslims.

The American Board sent its first missionaries to the Near East in 1819. The commission given to them embraced all the peoples of that great area, Muslim, Christian and Hebrew. Those early missionaries were indeed explorers. Few had heard of Raymond Lull or Henry Martyn, men who had given their lives to declare God's love to the Muslims of the Near East. Few were prepared by study of Muslim history or of the Qur'an. This ignorance was measurably true of missionaries mingling with the Jewish people in the Near East and also with adherents of the various branches of the Orthodox Christian Churches of that area. But their ignorance of the dominant Muslim peoples was most costly.

It is not surprising that after a few years the missionaries with their passion for evangelism followed the lines of least resistance in their approach. The Armenians, the Greeks and the Jews showed some interest in the newcomers. Before long the "Mission to the Armenians" and the "Mission to the Jews" were designated as distinct units. The Greeks were less responsive. The Muslims — both Arabs and Turks — maintained their traditional exclusiveness, an attitude forcibly underscored by governmental authority as well as by community customs.

It was not till well on in the nineteenth century that some missionaries in the Near East made a sustained effort to pierce the walls of pride and prejudice between Christians and Muslims erected by the forces of hate during Crusader days and their aftermath. The New Testament, later the Old Testament, were translated into Arabic, Turkish and Persian. The Arabic version of the Bible was done so well that it won the admiration of many Arab scholars.[1] Some other pieces of literature in Arabic and in Turkish were produced and available for distribution but for the most part remained unnoticed.

The correspondence of those missionaries most aware of the walls of separation between Muslim and Christian in the Near East is burdened with the agony of failure and of hope deferred. The developments of evangelical work among the Armenians and Greeks brought some encouragement to those missionaries who had a heart for the Muslims. Political events and war throughout the nineteenth century intensified and complicated the relations between the Christian minorities and American missionaries on the one hand, and Muslim rulers and peoples on the other.

But beyond all more or less superficial contacts, Christian missionaries among Muslims have come to understand better the nature of what some Westerners call "the impenetrable wall" between peoples of Christian and Muslim faiths. The

[1] See Eric M. North, *The Book of A Thousand Tongues*, (New York, Harpers, 1938), pp. 54, 55.

few individual Muslims — Arab, Turkish, Persian, Indian — who have confessed Christ have only served to highlight by their witness and suffering the relative impenetrability of Islamic culture and religion by Christian witness.

Efforts inspired by love and loyalty have continued. Missionaries have witnessed great changes in the texture of Muslim society due to the terrific impact of Western civilization, including world wars, during the last fifty years. The Muslim mind is changing rapidly. In its search for truth, Christian missionaries are standing by, seeking God's will and direction, and are rendering such services to acknowledged need by school, hospital, the printed word, and personal friendship, as point to Jesus Christ as the Way, Truth and Life.

*　*　*　*

Four different types of mission field which were early encountered and entered by the Board have been noted. It was not long before a fifth type of challenge appeared, and a new field developed. This type may be called atheistic secularism — a mission field not defined geographically but found almost everywhere.

Secularism has had its heyday in the twentieth century, though it was present in many places in embryo in the nineteenth. It is strong in the so-called Christian countries of Europe and North America. It is defined by one Christian scholar as "that characteristic of our world according to which life is organized apart from God, as though God did not exist."[1] Secularism was first recognized as a major opponent of Christianity at the Jerusalem Conference of the International Missionary Council in 1928. At that conference Dr. Rufus Jones, the great Quaker theologian and philosopher from Haverford College in Pennsylvania, led the assault on the newly identified foe. He was impressed that in some respects the twentieth century is a post-Christian era. He and others pointed out that the struggle between light and darkness in the world was no

[1] John C. Bennett, *Christianity and Our World*, (New York, Association Press, 1936), p. 1.

longer so much the conflict of Christianity and non-Christian
religions but rather the conflict of religion and the secular state
of mind. Strangely enough, the Jerusalem Conference lent
strength to the argument by stressing the values in the non-
Christian religions on the conviction that these religions were
declining in vigor, authority and outreach. Such a decline — if
it were indeed true — was due to the baleful influence of
secularism in the world.

The American Board long ago recognized the viciousness
and subtlety of the acids of modernity, as Walter Lippmann
called them in *A Preface to Morals*. The Christian community
in every land is subject today to the erosive action of these
acids. The Christian church, weak or strong, is called where-
ever it is "to live and give life in a world shaken to its foundations" by secularism in various forms.[1] Accordingly, the
Board has fostered "missions of fellowship", rehabilitation
projects, accelerated interchange of leadership, international
and interracial seminars and other measures aimed at strengthening the churches in all lands against the common foe.

Stages of Mission Activity

Effort in this fifth type of field has not diverted but has
strengthened work in other major fields of interest. The principal efforts of the Board continue among peoples of ancient
civilizations in Japan, India, Ceylon; among primitive peoples
in Micronesia, Africa (Zululand and Union of South Africa,
Southern Rhodesia, Angola) and Pagan tribes in the Philippine
Islands; among peoples of ancient Christian Churches in the
Philippines, Mexico, the Near East; among Muslim peoples in
the Near East and part of the Mindanao area of the Philippine
Islands. But patterns of mission activity now evolving to meet
the challenge of secularism are operative in each field.

It is interesting to note that in all areas where Christian
missionaries work several distinct stages of mission enterprise
may be traced and described. This is true of the Christian

---

[1] John R. Mott, ed., *World Mission of the Church*, (New York, International Missionary
Council, 1939), p. 13.

effort among people of sophisticated or simple culture, in city and in town, East and West, North and South. The stages are four in number, and may be called the pioneering stage, the training stage, the fellowship stage, and the ecumenical stage. It will be well to explain each of these briefly.

(1) *The Pioneer Stage.* The five young men ordained in Salem were the forerunners of hundreds of missionaries sent to Ceylon, Hawaii, South Africa and West Africa, the Near East, Siam, Borneo, and South China — all before 1865! These were the pioneers, and they were made of stern stuff, both physical and spiritual. The Board that sent them had to feel its way in developing its policies and principles. The early missionaries were surrounded by masses of people speaking strange languages, eating strange foods, observing odd superstitions and customs, subservient to many social and religious traditions at variance with the Gospel the missionaries hoped to communicate.

The first task of the pioneers was to establish house and home and to provide for their daily needs. Next they had to learn the language, translate the Bible, open elementary schools, set up simple printing plants, conduct Christian worship, establish good relations with governmental authorities, become acquainted with all sorts of tribal and community customs and modes of thought. The early missionaries sought to win friends — as many as they could. But the initial steps took time. Years, in some cases a generation, were required before the mission might emerge from the pioneer stage of life. Words cannot adequately describe the patience, courage, perseverance, ingenuity and wisdom and devotion required of the pioneer missionary. No wonder the incidence of death among the pioneers was high and that outstanding success came to only a few.

(2) *The Training Stage.* As missionaries made friends and became established, a nucleus of a Christian community was gathered. Often the written or the printed page was the magic tool for creating friendship and multiplying useful human con-

tacts. Likewise but somewhat later simple medical treatments opened hearts and homes to the meaning of the Christian Gospel in very practical and understandable terms. The first fruits were very precious in the eyes of the missionaries. The dawning consciousness of what Christ could mean to a non-Christian individual or home was greeted by heart-moving gratitude to God, poured out in prayer, song and continued service and in long letters home. As soon as practicable a group was formed to constitute a training class or school for the preparation of catechists, preachers and teachers. It was inevitable that many of the first adherents to the Christian way of life and thought of God should enter the employ of the missionaries, some of them in the homes, many of them in the schools, dispensaries and chapels of the missions. New standards of conduct, new customs, new ideas, new ambitions became characteristic of those who responded to the new opportunities for physical and spiritual well-being while stubborn hostile opposition often arose to harass native Christian and foreigner alike.

The training stage — in every mission area — may be said to have continued until a community of converts and adherents was formed with its own more or less well qualified leaders in many types of Christian activity. The length of this period varied with the political, social and religious circumstances of the people or area, as well as with the indefinable genius of the people. Humanity is basically the same the world over, but superficially, as anthropologists agree, the time schedules of development toward maturity vary widely.

(3) *The Fellowship Stage.* During the pioneer and the training stages of missionary activity the missionary stands in the center of the picture and is the dynamo of all enterprises. This situation begins to change when the mission wisely and increasingly places more and more responsibility upon indigenous leaders and the local churches. The aim of the mission has been to establish self-governing, self-supporting, self-propagating local churches. This is of necessity a gradual,

sometimes a very gradual, development. Before the middle of the nineteenth century, Secretary Rufus Anderson in American foreign mission circles, following more or less the lead of Henry Venn of England's Church Missionary Society, laid unforgettable emphasis upon this three-point formula for growth in every field. But from the beginning it was understood that nothing could be counted success which failed to contribute to the growth and stability of an indigenous Christian community at the heart of which is the Christian Church. The goal was churches moving toward autonomy, financial independence and missionary outreach.

The fellowship stage of growth begins in earnest as the missionary recognizes himself and is recognized by others as a colleague but no longer a director, much less a master of Christian action in an area. Local churches have formed associations or councils or conferences which plan and prosecute the work of the Christian movement. In some cases, united churches are formed, as in India, China, the Philippines, Japan and to some extent in Mexico. The movement toward cooperation and for unity grows by leaps and bounds. Churches in all areas seek the goal of world Christian fellowship.

(4) *The Ecumenical Stage.* Nationalism is a powerful force in the twentieth century. It has been in the making ever since the American and French revolutions of the late eighteenth century. It affects all aspects of life in every land, even the most remote and secluded. Communism appears as a great social and economic heresy with its roots in Western civilization but with its fruits of strife and false hopes scattered around the globe. These two forces — Nationalism, Communism — are related positively or negatively to the still greater force of world Christian brotherhood, the ideal toward which across the centuries the Christian Church has been moving with halting steps and slow. What one recent writer calls The New Reformation is in progress at this moment of history.[1] It is a time of Christian cooperation in study, work, and mission, re-

[1] Truman B. Douglass, *Preaching and the New Reformation,* (New York, Harpers, 1956).

gardless of past traditions, national backgrounds, stages of development. The International Missionary Council, formed in 1922, and the World Council of Churches, constituted in 1948, are the two great associated channels of this reformation, the true goal of which can be envisioned by those who possess and are possessed by faith, hope and love of New Testament quality. The fact that these two bodies are merging is a very significant sign of the times.

We may therefore recognize the present stage in the growth of the world Christian community of which the American Board and its associated churches abroad are vital parts, as the ecumenical stage. Never again, we confidently hope, can the Christian church be plunged into the dark ages of isolation and fragmentation, even though the road ahead may be centuries long and perversely hard. Of course the issue is in God's hands. With others we pray, "Thy will be done on earth as it is in heaven."

American Protestant Christianity has proclaimed the Christian Gospel and helped to establish Christian communities in many lands. It has been empowered to do this by the vigor of American life, which for a century and a half has sustained the effort of missionary endeavor. Today American Protestants greet churches of many lands and races as they seek to strengthen the fellowship of a world Christian community. The Christian forces of America share in what one writer-statesman calls "the fourth consensus" — the consciousness of the reality of world community.[1] This is the world-view of tomorrow in which all Christian missionaries will share. Indeed, they are called of God to hold the world together in a beloved community which in diverse times and diverse places they pioneered and help to create.

---

[1] Chester Bowles, *American Politics in a Revolutionary World,* (Cambridge, Harvard University Press, 1956).

4

THE PRIMARY PURPOSE — EVANGELISM

It is not easy for Congregational Christian folk in the middle of the twentieth century to understand the flaming evangelical passion of some Congregational ministers and laymen and missionaries of the early nineteenth century. Those pioneers were on fire to preach Christ crucified and risen, with a view to producing genuine individual conversions to Christ, his thought of God and his way of life. For the most part modern folk are mystified by the vagaries of old-time religion. They scorn sentimentalism. They do not get excited over religion. Revivals on the old-time pattern are not features of Congregational church life today. Congregational Christianity seems to have "cooled off" in recent generations.

From the beginning the American Board has been an evangelical movement, itself the product of the evangelical revival of the early nineteenth century. It was organized for a purpose which was often explained as three-point program: to preach the Word, to translate and distribute the Bible, to promote the study of the Bible. Such a program fulfilled our forefathers' concept of evangelism. They held, by and large, to what one modern writer[1] calls "the simple Gospel": "God so loved the world that He gave His only begotten Son. Christ died for our sins. He loved me and gave Himself for me. Believing, we have life in His name. There is joy and peace in believing. Accept this. Confess Jesus Christ as Lord and Savior and go in peace."

Evangelism was "the personal proclamation of this Gospel by word of mouth, whether from a pulpit or from individual to individual." Our forefathers were evangelists, dedicated

[1] Norman Goodall, writing in *Frontier*, London, January 1958, pp. 66-70.

to the purpose of preaching the Gospel so that those who had not heard it might be offered a way of escape from eternal damnation. Said the Board in 1811: "The object [of our work] is the salvation of men; the furtherance of the great purposes for which the Redeemer came down from heaven."[1] The missionaries sent out in early years were aflame to serve that object.

Difficulties were soon encountered. The missions acquired property. To manage the property required time and attention. The missionaries discovered the dire poverty of undeveloped peoples. They became concerned about the physical as well as the spiritual needs of men. Where preaching was effective, churches were gathered — and they must then be guided and sustained. It was felt necessary to open schools and at times to devise means of providing suitable employment for Christian converts. All these and other concerns, worthy as they might be, distracted minds from the main objective.

Even within the objective, priorities struggled with one another. Mission administration, training of local leaders, translation of the Scriptures and printing Christian literature (including textbooks for elementary schools and theological training classes) preoccupied mission groups and individual missionaries. At times the simple evangelistic objective was buried in a multitude of related though lesser involvements.

There were times when the American Board encouraged activities other than those dealing directly and strictly with the evangelistic purpose as first conceived. There is the famous passage in the Board's instructions to the first group of missionaries sent to the Sandwich Islands in 1819, for example:

> Your views are not to be limited to a low or narrow scale; but you are to open your hearts wide, and set your mark high. You are to aim at nothing short of covering those Islands with fruitful fields and pleasant dwellings and

[1] AR, 1811, p. 29.

schools and churches; of raising up the whole people to an elevated state of civilization.[1]

Occasionally there had to be reminders of what was after all the central object of the Board's work. In 1834 the Board emphatically stated, that "this Board regard the preaching of the Gospel, by the living voice, as the great business of our missionaries; that the preparation and circulation of the Scripture and tracts is next in order; and that the establishment and instruction of schools, and other labors directly aimed at the amelioration of society, should always be kept strictly subordinate to the others."[2]

Yet as the years went on mission churches developed and "the great objective" became gradually redefined. To build the church became as important an object as to preach the Word. The indigenous churches were to be established, and once established they were to be urged toward self-government, self-support and self-propagation. It was felt, of course, that the churches would themselves assume the tasks of evangelism and thus work toward the spiritual transformation of the environing population.

As the new definition of the goals of mission endeavor developed there came to be, as we shall see in coming chapters, a changed attitude toward educational, medical and social service activities as worthy mission concerns. These became highly regarded objects of missionary effort, though in the eyes of some they interfered with the evangelistic task of building the native church.

*   *   *   *

Board administrators in Boston maintained a little more psychic distance from the actual operations on the fields, and sought to maintain perspective on the mission program overseas. They were aware of the pitfalls into which they themselves would have fallen had they been field workers rather than mission administrators far away. But they tried to look

---

[1] *Instructions from the Prudential Committee,* (Boston, Samuel Armstrong, 1819), p. ix.
[2] AR, 1834, p. 23, quoting a vote at the annual meeting of the Board.

at all tasks and problems in the light of the object of planting
and nurturing churches which one day would be independent,
indigenous, and mission-minded. That day was slow in coming. On the field there were usually good reasons why things
happened as they did; in Boston, however, there was some
impatience with delays on the field. At times a secretary
felt constrained to speak out and hold high once again the
great object for which mission endeavor was felt to exist:
the life and growth of the Christian Church. Such a speaking
out occurred at the annual meeting of the Board in Springfield, Massachusetts, in October 1862. The speaker was Dr.
Rufus Anderson, vigorous and alert chief executive of the
American Board.

Dr. Anderson read a paper on the state of the churches
overseas. He was disturbed that the churches in mission
fields were not taking root more rapidly and that their leadership was not passing quickly enough into the hands of well-
trained national leaders. He stressed the fact that only
thirty of the more than one hundred and seventy churches
connected with the missions of the Board had ordained
native pastors. The Ceylon, Mahratta (Marathi) and Sandwich Islands missions each had four. The Madura mission
had six. The four missions in the Near East had eleven.
There were no native pastors in the Africa and China missions. Why, he asked, after thirty, forty, even fifty years
should there be so small a number of responsible indigenous
pastors in the mission areas?

Dr. Anderson exonerated the Prudential Committee, the
secretaries and the missionaries — at least he partially exonerated the missionaries! The Prudential Committee had long
since stressed the fact that missionaries should be evangelists, not pastors. The secretaries in season and out of season
had impressed upon the missionaries the strategic importance
of the native pastorate. The missionaries had acknowledged
that the vitality and strength of the native churches were the
proper measure of their success. Why was it then that so few

native men had reached the status of ordained pastors in full charge of churches?

Dr. Anderson gives several possible answers to this question. First, he says, the obstacles in the way of success in this direction have existed, first, in our inexperience; second, in the want of precedents to guide us; third, in ideas and habits the missionaries necessarily took with them from their native land; fourth, in the really unavoidable fact that we began educating our native ministry prior to any proper development of native churches, and of course before we could know exactly what we wanted; fifth, in certain unavoidable errors in our higher education, shared by the Prudential Committee equally with the missionaries, whereby our candidates for the ministry overseas became too strongly exposed to the temptations of higher wages in the business of the world; sixth, in the absence, resulting from the causes just mentioned, of a well-defined and settled purpose among the missionaries, to assign the native churches to the pastoral care of a native ministry; and seventh, in the consequent fact, that until within a few years, the native preachers were not educated avowedly for the pastoral office, and therefore were not in expectation of it.

But this battery of reasons apparently does not quite satisfy Dr. Anderson. So he sets forth another view which some hold — that *married* missionaries tend to create station-churches of which they become pastors and the leadership of which they do not relinquish soon enough. "It is a fact that two-thirds of our churches are station-churches and that few of these have yet any other pastors than the missionaries." This not only militates against creative and expansive work in the total field, it too often "insures perpetual pupilage and dependence," for the native churches and preachers. Or the pioneering native preacher is "drawn away by the allurements of the surrounding world."

It is fascinating to trace Dr. Anderson's thought as he deals constructively with the problem from this point. He underscores two points. There must be *well-defined prospects* and *well-understood expectations*. "The laws governing the human mind are everywhere the same. The fixed relation between 'demand and supply' can no more be safely disregarded with the graduates of Batticotta (Ceylon), Pasumalie (Madura), Lahainaluna (Hawaii), Abeih (Syria), Bebek (Turkey) and Seir (Persia), than it can be with graduates of our American Colleges . . . . This will require untiring effort on the part of the missionaries. It will be more troublesome . . . . As among the Galatians, [native pastors] will sometimes become 'bewitched' and will more or less 'bewitch' their people . . . . But there is no shorter, no easier, no better way to reach the great result at which we aim. Never, otherwise, shall we obtain a permanent, reliable, effective native ministry, and never succeed in establishing Christianity in any of the unevangelized nations."[1] In other words, men trained for the Christian ministry must be employed as ministers and given full responsibility for their parishes.

A Contemporary View

Despite Dr. Anderson the problem continues to perplex the missionary. How does one keep the great objective clearly in view and serve it effectively?

Every interpreter of the facts regarding the rise of the younger churches during the modern Protestant missionary movement should take note of the views of Roland Allen as expressed in two books: *Missionary Methods: St. Paul's or Ours*, published in 1913 and *The Spontaneous Expansion of the Church and the Causes Which Hinder It*, first published in 1927. Allen writes as an Anglican to Anglicans but with the conviction that his major contention applies to all missionary effort. He takes it for granted that the main purpose of the Christian mission is to plant the Church in all the world. This purpose he insists can be achieved by communicating the Gospel to those who will listen and then placing upon

[1] AR, 1862, pp. 17-22.

them immediately complete responsibility for all that should be done in consequence of their having heard and responded to the Word. He takes as his pattern the expansion of the Church in the first century of the Christian era. "The early Church sent out missionaries but it established no missions: we establish a Mission and give it a certain permanence whilst yet we always speak of it as something passing. The consequence is that we get at once a confusion of thought and a conflict of action. The Mission is to establish the Church; but it establishes itself, and exists over against the Church. This is not Biblical."[1] Confusion and failure follow in most cases from this wrong start, insisted Mr. Allen. He has very interesting things to say about questions that inevitably rise from this radical position. For instance, he develops his view of how to sustain, if indeed a missionary is concerned to sustain, the Christian standard of morals. Furthermore, he develops his view with which most missionaries would agree that education, social reform and philanthropy do not constitute a proper foundation for the Christian Church but are expressions of its Christlike concern for the life of human beings. His downgrading of our modern passion for organization is undoubtedly a wholesome warning. Many of his blunt criticisms of mission policy need to be taken to heart and held in mind as actual encounters with non-Christian forces and people develop. The life and growth of indigenous churches demand periodic, soul-searching self-examination by those responsible for Christian witness and fraternal counsel. Such examination should result in purification, readjustment, renewed dedication to the great objective. Allen's writings fulfill a worthy purpose in this respect.

But this takes us to another subject, which will be explored in a later chapter. Suffice here to say that mission activity, like any other institutionalized activity, needs to be reexamined from time to time in the light of its primary purpose or great objective.

[1] Roland Allen, *The Spontaneous Expansion of the Church*, (London, World Dominion Press, 1949), pp. 170, 171.

The Present Position

The American Board's position regarding evangelism in recent years has been marked by its amplitude. The witness of the social center, the clinic or hospital, the school — the selfless service of missionary and national Christian — has been felt to be important as well as the witness of preachment and word. Men are to be won to Christ, and the Board has felt that even a quiet Christlike deed may be an effective means. Considerable scope is left to the individual missionary. The Prudential Committee is careful to look into a candidate's background and experience for evidence of stability and a growing, vital faith. Finding that, the Committee trusts the missionary's judgment — in counsel with his colleagues — as to how he may best communicate his faith to those with whom he comes in contact. Freedom to do what is felt to be needful is permitted the accepted candidate. He must have some skill along a line of desired service within a mission, and that skill hopefully will provide him with opportunities to communicate his faith and sense of values. Yet the missionary is a personal God-directed force in his community, a witness in a unique way to what God has done and is doing for him and society through Christ.

An Interlude: I
THE CHURCH IN ANGOLA

The Christian Mission in 1880 among the Ovimbundu entered a virgin field of primitive culture. Ancestor worship including animistic features was their religion. The bonds of tribal kinship were very strong. The Ovimbundu have been a virile people for centuries. Customs and ideas which Christian missionaries naturally called pagan but which anthropologists would examine without condemnation made the tribe a first-class laboratory for an attempt to discover how Jesus of Nazareth, the Christ of the Gospels and the Epistles, might become a part of their life and thought. Paul preached Christ and him crucified to the pagans of his day. Sanders and Bagster, Currie and Ennis preached the same Christ to these untutored folk of the African Highlands, and behold! they understood!

The nefarious slave trade made slave traders of the Ovimbundu. Not until the Portuguese and other slave merchants began to take Ovimbundu young men to sell as slaves, did the leaders of the tribe hesitate to raid and steal and sell their fellow Africans from more remote regions. This experience left a scar on the souls of the Ovimbundu. Compelled to turn from their trade in slaves and ivory and rubber, they had to seek more humane means of livelihood.

The Portuguese authorities at first were inclined to use the missionaries as tools to extend their rule further into the interior. That did not last long or work out very well, for the missionaries had the welfare of the people at heart.

How shall we preach Christ to these simple, crude but virile, wary wanderers on life's way? What can Christ do for them?

Does he have meaning for human beings who challenge Western ideas of human decency and achievement? The missionary pioneers pondered questions like these. But as they pondered they marched straight forward into the lives of their newly discovered friends, learning their language, eating the same kinds of food, discovering human worth and character beneath the austere surface. They found that fear — stark, awful fear — dominated their lives: fear of enemies, seen and unseen, fear of disease, fear of natural catastrophes, fear of anything unfamiliar. It was not extremely difficult to communicate an idea which would challenge the reign of fear.

Before long one chief began to understand. Here and there a village caught on. Simple remedies to fight the fever, better houses to afford greater security, tools and seed for finer crops, simple books to record their language and make reading possible, songs and music to add delight to tribal ceremonies, schools where children learned both letters and manners — all these and many other avenues led into the hearts and minds of multitudes.

From 1880 to 1900 a Christian community came into existence among the Ovimbundu. The missionaries chose promising leaders and gave them special in-service training as teachers and pastors. As a family or two in a village became Christian, they drew apart from the rest of the village and formed an entirely new center. These new centers of Christian habitation multiplied. Bush schools were maintained and humble places of worship were provided in which the visiting pastor or missionary could speak of the God of love whom Christ reveals and where Christian worship could be a daily concern.

One of the pioneers, still among us though in retirement, Dr. Merlin W. Ennis, was asked to describe his approach as a Christian missionary to the Ovimbundu people. He began by saying that, in his opinion, no people has had a monopoly of God. Our Heavenly Father has revealed himself in some degree to every race. It is for the missionary, first, to be sure what he wishes to communicate as the heart of the Christian Gospel, then to discover as best he can the nature of the religion of the people to whom he would communicate the Gospel. In doing this the missionary should avoid all negativism. He should refrain from condemning the religion of any people, he should refrain from exclusive emphasis upon sin, he should be careful not to impugn the ideas or efforts of other missionaries, Protestant or Roman Catholic. On the other hand, he should seize every opportunity to interpret the Gospel in terms of an answer to human need, not excluding the need of forgiveness, but including vastly more than a backward look. Christ came that man might have life. Life grows more meaningful for the Ovimbundu as they understand the life and teachings of Jesus. There is the lure of life in a community where education, work and health, neighborliness and honest, peaceful relations with all mankind are seen to be vital concerns of religion.

In early years in Angola, in various circles Dr. Ennis was quite naturally asked why he had come to Angola. What is your business? He made the reply: My business is to bring to you the Word of God. This immediately raised the question: What is the Word of God? This gave the missionary the opening he desired. He began to answer that question by referring to the Fourth Commandment of the Decalogue: "Honor thy father and thy mother." His exposition of this as one aspect of the Word of God met with approbation. The Ovimbundu people honored their ancestors. They used symbols, for instance, to remind them of ancestors whom they revered, a bow and arrow for a man, a hoe and a basket for a woman. They did not pray to these symbols, but to those who had used them during their life time. The significance of other commandments was also discussed in the light of Ovimbundu standards of community welfare. The Ovimbundu often said they were under obligation to right wrongs they had committed. This was an open door to further explanation of God's word to men.

From discussions centering around themes like these, Dr. Ennis made constant use of the teaching of Jesus. He found, for instance, that the story of Zacchaeus greatly interested the people. They were impressed by the fact that Zacchaeus was handicapped by his small stature. The tortoise with all its characteristics was the Ovimbundu symbol of inferiority. So they were particularly interested to see how well this handicapped person was treated by Jesus. The parables of Jesus also made communication of truth a relatively easy process.

One problem the missionary had to face promptly was the work of the witch doctors. The belief in magic was deep-seated except among the witch doctors themselves! They knew their tricks and trade were selfish and deceitful! A shrewd Christian soon learned to despise the performances of the witch doctors, even though he understood how often it was fear and despair which drove the people into their clutches. Only as faith in a loving Heavenly Father took root could hope and joy abound.

By the time of the Mission Jubilee in 1930 thousands of evangelical Christians throughout the area looked to several great centers for Christian fellowship and guidance — Bailundo, Chissamba, Kamundongo, Dondi, Elende, Galangue, Chilesso. These centers were the headquarters of parish churches, each with several pastorates. At first these centers seemed widely separated. Gradually the sense of community grew. This resulted in an annual meeting of delegates and leaders from each area — all Ovimbundu Christians. The "Mission" made up of Canadian and American missionaries had met separately each year. By 1948 it seemed desirable that the church group and the mission group should meet together to discuss common concerns. After a few years of experiment with integration, in 1953 the Mission as such disappeared and the Church Council was formed, bringing complete integration with strong Ovimbundu leadership. A constitution was projected. This provided for a well ordered, cooperative enterprise, not only in evangelism but also in education, the press, and medical service. The Church Council was fully launched in 1957 as the responsible body for evangelical Christian work among more than 300,000 Ovimbundu people.

Dr. H. C. McDowell gives one a meaningful glimpse of the nature and task of the Christian community at Missao do Elende where he and his wife entered so fully into the life of the people in a large section of Angola. He writes under date of November 25, 1957:

Before the spell of the recent Annual Meeting of the Elende Church and Mission wears off I want to share something of its spirit with you. During the year there had been more defections than usual, and we were a bit downcast. And then a real thrill!

Many of you will recall that when Ruth [Mrs. McDowell] and I left the States in 1947 it was due to personal convictions that identification with the Umbundu Church, particularly at this stage of its development, presented an overwhelming challenge. During the intervening years we have kept to that course. There are many of us under the same compulsion. It is a continuing task, and will extend through the long years ahead, but it is comforting to see in our day evidences of real growth, not only in numbers but also in Christian perception and dedication.

Working with a Church that has full responsibility, not only for usually accepted tasks of the Church, but also the whole field of education and health, is a completely absorbing venture. This is not true for all of Africa. Many governments provide proper schools, or make substantial grants to mission schools; also medical assistance programs are maintained. Such aid as Portugal is able to give directly to Africans is channeled through Roman Catholic missions. This means, in practice, that our folk have to do for themselves as best they can — with such help as the Protestant missions offer.

Education is the new password in Africa, but as everywhere it is expensive. Our folk pay fees, and under stress of rising costs, advancing standards, etc. it has involved periodic increase in fees; and now being quite beyond the economic level even the astounding sacrificial spirit of the people can no longer cope with them. This year it was the same story, the schools simply had to have more

money. After considerable discussion a proposal was
adopted whereby fees would not be further raised, but
that the church itself would assume direct responsibility,
keeping under constant study the essential needs of the
schools and meeting them from its annual contributions
even before salaries, etc., were paid. They immediately
made available 10.000$00 angolares ($340.00) to meet
present emergencies. It warmed our hearts to hear pastors
and others say, 'We are also parents. There are thousands
less favorably situated than we. Our church is the agency
through which we can level off this heavy load, and we
must set an example regardless of personal sacrifice.' I do
not know what this will lead to, but for the moment at
least my spirits are high. There must be a future for such
people!

An even more delicate proposal related to fees of various sorts that over the years have crept into the church
structure. The people are undergoing a terrific experience;
at a below-subsistence level they are forced into a money
economy. One understands the desire to get a little more
money from every conceivable source, and especially from
this education that was acquired at such great sacrifice.
Also there was a natural carry-over from native culture
where every step of everything required a gift. From the
village catechist to the pastor himself there simply "grew"
a network of fees and emoluments. However, such a procedure easily gets out of hand, precedents get established,
and it becomes increasingly difficult to preclude an under-
current of resentment, lack of confidence in leadership,
suspicions, and a creeping lethargy. Some of the church
leaders have long since sensed the dangers. After considerable soul-searching, it was decided to end the whole
procedure. Serious effort was made to separate the plainly
'bad' but in the end they decided that the situation required drastic action. This may sound a bit flat, but for
the Umbundu Church it was revolutionary.

For many years, we have felt that the missionary can
be quietly and unobtrusively helpful in this whole business of money — not the dispensing of some foreign gifts

but having one's good offices freely accepted in the handling of their own funds. My only duly constituted and elected job in the Elende Church is that of chairman of auditors. We conceive of ourselves as engaged in a huge adult education venture, where all of us share in a continuous in-service training process. And the word continuous in that sentence is used advisedly, especially for missionaries. We have just completed tabulations of gifts to the church totalling $6630.00. When you consider that 13,000 people from 430 villages gave the money you begin to appreciate the job involved. Add to that the established school fees, donations to medical work, etc., and the total is around $17,000.00. Gifts from people who average $.17 a day when they can find a *paying* job! The experience of the Church, not only in Africa, is that unless integrity in money matters, however small, is built into the Church, the Gospel after wonderful triumphs might become quite impotent as it wrestles with an emerging money economy among terribly poor people.

Well, I had thrills! Now I must tell you about Ruth's thrill. Early in the year she concluded that more had to be done for the children. Not knowing where sufficient funds would come from, she began a pre-natal and children's clinic. What has developed is much more than that designation implies. Between 300 and 350 children, under three years of age, from surrounding villages, are brought to the Hospital by their parents on Thursday mornings. They are given a daraprim (anti-malarial) tablet, cod-liver oil, orange juice, and milk. They are regularly weighed, and are checked by the Doctor from Dondi on his occasional visits. A chart is kept of each child. There is a religious service especially prepared for mothers and children. There are fitting health talks and demonstrations, especially preparation of foods. Expectant mothers have their day, and an adequate little maternity ward is provided. There are some interesting side-effects. It is a gala social occasion for the women; notes are compared on children and innumerable other choice morsels passed around. It is a year-round school for the women, and they are always present. The difference in the tots is amazing, and brings great satisfaction. It is relatively expensive business, but thus far Ruth has managed. . . .

And so the church grows — in Angola, Portuguese West Africa.

5

ENLARGING THE CONCEPT OF
MISSIONARY SERVICE — EDUCATION

It seems strange that New England Congregationalists, responding to the challenge of college students to undertake Christian missions overseas, should have hesitated to make education one of their main objectives. Yet that is the fact. It was years before the American Board considered education — particularly higher education — a really worthy mission enterprise. Where education was undertaken in the early days it was solely as a means to the great objective of evangelism, understood as vital, oral preaching of the Word and study of the Bible. If schools would lead to conversion or to the establishment of a Christian community at the heart of which was the Church, then schools should be undertaken. Children should be taught to read the Bible so that the Bible might become familiar to them and their parents and their friends. Redemption was the goal. The idea of secular education for life in a secular society was anathema to the pioneers. Art and science had their place in life, but their function was wholly subservient to evangelism and the growth of the Christian community.

This was the early view, and there were those who argued it even as late as 1876. One of them was Professor (later President) Seelye of Amherst College, who protested against education as a proper method of mission work in these words:

> It is admitted on all hands that the apostolic method was that of direct evangelization. The apostles did not plant schools. They preached the Gospel and planted churches, and, so far as we can learn, they left all questions of education to adjust themselves as the new spirit which followed their labors would direct. . . . If we should go

to the heathen as Paul did, determined not to know anything among them save Jesus Christ, and him crucified,
attempting no schools for the unconverted, but establishing these only to train those who have become Christ's
disciples for the new work, in the new relations of life unto
which they are called, speaking wisdom among them that
are perfect, I cannot but believe that the number would
be immeasurably increased of those whose faith should
stand, not in the wisdom of men, but in the power of God.
. . . In Christian or unchristian lands, therefore, the teaching of schools is alone valuable when applied to cultivate
the understanding of those whose wills are already converted, or when penetrated through and through with the
preaching of Christ, and him crucified, to those still dead
in sin.[1]

The reason for this view of education lay in the intellectual,
moral and spiritual climate of New England in the late eighteenth and early nineteenth centuries. Harvard College, the
fountain of wisdom and the pride of the clergy of New England, had ceased to be loyal to the Trinitarian concept of God
and had "gone liberal" in 1805 with the election of Rev. Henry
Ware of Hingham, Massachusetts, as Hollis Professor of Divinity. It became clear then to conservative Christians that education was not necessarily good, that it might lead to a denial
of the divinity of Jesus Christ, and this would surely lead to
atheism and disorder. The view became established among
Congregational and other traditional people that conversion
and not education, evangelism and not learning, faith and not
knowledge, were alone the power of salvation.

Among the early missionaries this view was widely held.
In time it began to change. The first American Board missionaries to Hawaii and Ceylon discovered that scientific
knowledge was an effective tool with which to combat the
superstitious beliefs and magical practices of the native peoples.
Ignorance seemed the enemy of Christian ideas. Education
would banish ignorance.

---

[1] Julius H. Seelye, *Christian Missions*, (New York, Dodd, Mead and Co., 1876), p. 140.

The Ceylon Mission's Recommendation

The development of educational ministries in Ceylon is an example of how American Board thinking changed.

As early as 1823, the Ceylon Mission, then hardly seven years old, carefully prepared and signed a document which they entitled a "Plan for the Mission College." The document was sent to the American Board in Boston and gave rise to much discussion. It is a cogent statement and contains a carefully thought-out program. It is found in an appendix of an annual report of the Board.[1]

The preamble to the document ran:

"Knowledge is power." This maxim, so justly celebrated and so steadily kept in view by the philosopher and statesman, is not less practical or important to the Christian philanthropist. When those who are engaged in meliorating the condition of their fellow men have knowledge, or the means of disseminating knowledge, they have the power of doing good. To extend the blessings of the most favored countries of Europe or America, to almost any section of the globe, we need only carry thither the literary and religious institutions of those countries. Whatever may be said of the influence of soil, climate, or even government, upon national character and happiness, it cannot be doubted that these depend principally upon causes more exclusively intellectual and moral. Man is an intellectual and religious being; and under the combined influence of pure science and true religion, and of these only, he attains the real dignity of his nature. Hence Christianity, whose office it is to raise man to that elevation from which he fell, and lead him onward to that high destiny for which he was created, does not disdain to seek the aids of learning.

It was generally agreed that elementary schools were essential in every mission field. People, especially children, must be taught to read so that the Bible in vernacular versions would be an open book to them and through them to their parents

[1] AR, 1824, Appendix III, pp. 149-163.

and friends. But there was no such consensus regarding higher education. The opponents of higher education felt it would involve hazards of various kinds. Students would be absorbed with the English language and its treasures of literature and science and diverted from evangelistic efforts. There would be manifold temptations for such students along the line of government service or other secular activities. The missionary was called to preach the Gospel in the vernacular, to promote the reading and study of the Bible and to gather and to nurture groups in Christian churches.

The men in Ceylon took an opposite view. They set forth the immediate objects of the proposed college:

1. To impart a thorough knowledge of the English language, as the only way to unlock the treasures which that language contains.

2. The cultivation of Tamul [sic] literature, which is necessary in order to oppose idolatry most successfully, and in order to raise up a reading population.

3. The study of Sanscrit by a select few, from among those who may be designed for native preachers.

4. To teach Hebrew, and in some cases Latin and Greek, to those native preachers who may be employed as translators of the Scriptures.

5. To teach, as far as the circumstances of the country require, the sciences usually studied in the colleges of Europe and America.

These men had glimpsed wide horizons. They did not propose to limit Christian education to the narrow boundaries of the baptized Christian community. To them it seemed important to provide higher education so far as possible for all promising students in a thirsty land. Referring to a group of 105 boys and twenty-eight girls in school, they said:

They are all, according to their age, instructed in the first principles of Christianity and in Tamul literature. . . .

Such as have been longest under instruction are now so far advanced as to be able, with proper helps, to prosecute successfully the higher branches of Tamul learning; to enter upon the Sanskrit; or to apply themselves to European literature and science, as might be found expedient, to fit them for service under government, for teachers of schools, for interpreters, for translators; or if pious (as some are hopefully so already) for native preachers.[1]

The upshot of the plan for a mission college in the Jaffna area was that on the foundation of the "Central English School" begun in 1823 with thirty-six students, the Mission established Batticotta (Vaddukoddai) Seminary in 1825.[2] Half of the building fund was raised locally. For thirty years the Seminary continued its work satisfactorily. Six hundred ninety-three students had been enrolled. The course of study quite naturally was based upon college standards in America with such adjustments to local conditions and culture as seemed desirable.

But grave doubts were rising back home. As reports came from Cyrus Hamlin at Constantinople, from missionaries at Bombay and Madura in India, as well as from the Jaffna peninsula, the Prudential Committee became more and more concerned. The missionaries everywhere seemed to be pressing for higher schools and for wider use of the English language.[3]

The Deputation of 1854-1855

Facts like these led the Prudential Committee to ask the Board to appoint a deputation to go to India, Ceylon and the Near East to study each situation on the spot and to make specific recommendations. This was the famous Deputation of 1854-1855. Dr. A. C. Thompson, a member of the Prudential Committee, and Secretary Rufus Anderson spent fifteen months on the fields. The results of their study and recommendations were "revolutionary," said Cyrus Hamlin. Secretary Anderson

[1] Op. cit. p. 151.
[2] "Seminary" — this name was preferred to "College," though it meant the same.
[3] Later (in 1877) Cyrus Hamlin wrote a classic statement as to the importance of the use of the English language in schools in mission fields. See Cyrus Hamlin, *Among the Turks*, (New York, Robert Carter, 1878), pp. 282, 283.

maintained "the vernacular theory of education" as over against the view that English should be taught and instruction given in English as well.[1] It was the vernacular system which the deputation recommended.

One striking episode in this great debate was the impasse between Cyrus Hamlin and Rufus Anderson. Hamlin, appointed in 1838, had fostered a "seminary" at Bebek, a suburb of Constantinople, and wished to develop it into a school of college grade. He was encouraged in this by some of his fellow missionaries, opposed by others. When the Deputation visited Constantinople Hamlin faced Anderson and their points of view met head on. Hamlin admitted later in his memoirs: "My relations with the secretaries and the Prudential Committee have always been cordial, even when we differed. Between Dr. Anderson and myself there was no interruption of personal friendship and confidence, only neither of us could bend the other."[2] The disagreement went so far that Hamlin resigned from the American Board in May 1860. He said:

> I could not conscientiously continue as an educator in the service of the Board, after Dr. Anderson's revolutionary system of vernacular education had been decided upon. I had four objections to his system: — 1. It is unphilosophical, not true to human nature, to the wants and capacities of the mind. 2. It will make the Protestant pastors inferior everywhere to the Jesuit missionaries, who all speak foreign languages, and have the Papal history of the Church by heart. 3. It would cause great and general dissatisfaction in the Armenian Protestant community, and heartfelt cooperation would cease. 4. It would injure universally the prestige of the mission to take the back track on education.[3]

It sharpens one's sense of the critical nature of this great debate to read Hamlin's version of the sequel and its wider reverberations:

---

[1] Rufus Anderson, *Foreign Missions — Their Relations and Claims*, (New York, Scribners, 1869), p. 100.
[2] Cyrus Hamlin, *My Life and Times*, (Boston, Pilgrim Press, First Edition 1893, Sixth 1924), p. 415.
[3] *Ibid.*, p. 414.

All the results that I anticipated were realized, and many more. The system, moreover, utterly broke down and passed off the stage, after doing untold mischief. Dr. Anderson was a man of great power, and his errors were proportionably injurious. President Martin B. Anderson, of Rochester, New York, by his eloquent and powerful reasoning saved the Baptists from adopting the same fatal system, although their chief secretary and President Wayland warmly championed it. He was a remarkable man, and his power over the Baptist Church was deservedly very great. He kept Baptist missions from the great setback from which our missions suffered.[1]

Furthermore, it shows the nature of the healing processes of time to note that Secretary Anderson devotes a few gracious paragraphs to Robert College which Hamlin founded, when he wrote in 1871 his monumental volumes on the American Board and the Oriental Churches.[2]

In his memoirs Dr. James L. Barton makes the statement that even in 1885 when he went to the Near East as a missionary of the American Board, "the general impression entertained [in America] was that the missionary was a preacher of the Gospel of Jesus Christ and in that impression he had discovered no place for higher education."[3]

It is indeed difficult for twentieth-century Christians to understand the attitude toward higher education on the mission field which, as Dr. Barton implies, was dominant in Board circles prior to 1885. But there was emerging in America a new force favoring positive and energetic efforts in the interests of overseas educational institutions capable of producing leadership for churches and communities. Dr. Barton says:

> There was no delusion that higher education would or could take the place of preaching the Gospel. . . . It could in no measure take the place of the Church, but it was seen to be an absolutely necessary auxiliary of the Church.

[1] *Ibid.*, p. 414.
[2] Rufus Anderson, *History of the Missions of the American Board of Commissioners for Foreign Missions to the Oriental Churches*, (in two volumes, Boston, Congregational Publishing Society, 1872), pp. 450-454.
[3] J. L. Barton, Memoirs, (manuscript in American Board archives, AB 55, B 28), pp. 192, 193.

The Church without such educated and intellectually trained indigenous leaders would necessarily remain a weak Church, chiefly under the domination of foreign missionaries, while an adequately trained Christian native force would prepare the way for a strong and aggressive Church from which the missionary would be gradually eliminated.

Education, in other words, was recognized as part of an enlarged concept of evangelism.

Dr. Barton's Position

As a Board secretary (in 1894) Dr. Barton was thoroughly convinced of two things about higher education on the mission fields of the Board. First: Christian higher education is "absolutely essential to the permanent success of the foreign missionary enterprise." Second, the cost of higher education abroad "ought not to depend upon the contributions taken in the churches for the support of foreign missions and evangelical operations. . . . The vast majority of the givers to mission boards did so with evangelism clearly in mind. They gave 'for the preaching of the Gospel to the heathen.' . . . [Many of them] were not able to send their own children to college. It did not seem right to take their sacrificial offerings to give the youth overseas a collegiate training. It seemed right to use their donations for theological training schools . . . but not for the training of men and women many of whom will never enter direct Christian work. It seemed to the Secretary that some way should be opened to secure a new and independent constituency for the direction and support of the Higher Educational Work of the Board."[1]

Developments Overseas

For ten years Secretary Barton studied all aspects of the work of the Board as he fulfilled his onerous administrative duties in cooperation with the Senior Foreign Secretary, Judson

[1] *Ibid.*, p. 198.

Smith. Then in 1903 he embarked upon a serious study of the higher educational work of the Presbyterian Foreign Board and the American Board. He found that they were sponsors for twenty-six collegiate institutions which had developed in twelve foreign countries: South America (three countries), Mexico, Japan, China, India, Ceylon, Turkey, Persia, Bulgaria and Spain. These institutions had over five thousand students, taught by 106 American teachers and many times that number of instructors of native origin. It was estimated that the constituency for whom these colleges offered the only higher educational privileges numbered at least one hundred million people. Ten of the sixteen collegiate institutions most closely associated with the American Board had theological departments for the special preparation of a native ministry.

The fact that sixteen collegiate institutions had pushed their tiny heads through somewhat unpropitious soil prior to 1903 proved to Secretary Barton and others that there existed an irrepressible urge within communities overseas, an urge for light. The clamant voices of students in many countries would not be denied.

The story of Jaffna College in Ceylon and the community before and after the visit of the Thompson-Anderson Deputation of 1855 is an excellent case in point. Batticotta Seminary after thirty years of successful operation was closed in accordance with the recommendation of the Deputation.[1] The very next year (1856) the alumni of the Seminary and their friends established Batticotta High School under purely indigenous management. The people who had long sat in darkness had seen a great light and they did not want it put out! Three years later the Mission insisted that a theological training institution was an essential item in their program even though all instruction were to be given in the vernacular according to the recommendations of the Deputation. These were but the preliminary steps. Enthusiasm for a real college could not be suppressed. In 1872 Jaffna College as such was founded and began opera-

[1] See above, pp. 53, 54.

tions. The Training and Theological Institution was removed to a neighboring village, Tellipallai, and Jaffna College remained at Batticotta. In 1877 a Board of Trustees of Jaffna College Funds in the United States was formed and incorporated under the laws of the State of Massachusetts.

Each of these "sixteen collegiate institutions" sought to make a strong case with Secretary Barton. He studied them with great care. Four of them were already under the immediate direction of separate boards of trustees though closely affiliated with the American Board. These four were:

JAFFNA COLLEGE, Ceylon, founded by Marshall Sanders in 1872, with a background of fifty years of educational effort.

CENTRAL TURKEY COLLEGE, Aintab, Turkey, founded by Tillman C. Trowbridge in 1874 on the basis of local indigenous management with a trustee body in America.

EUPHRATES COLLEGE, Harpoot, Turkey, founded by Charles H. Wheeler in 1878 as the result of pleas and pressure from the growing Evangelical Armenian community in Eastern Asia Minor.

DOSHISHA UNIVERSITY, Kyoto, Japan, founded in 1875 by Joseph Hardy Neesima, a remarkable Japanese Christian who had studied at Amherst College and Andover Theological Seminary. His educational venture in Japan began in 1875, but did not acquire university status until 1912.

The other twelve were directly under the control of and dependent for financial support upon the Board or related boards in America.

These twelve institutions were:
Collegiate and Theological Institute, Samokov, Bulgaria
Kobe College for Girls, Kobe, Japan
Central Turkey College for Girls, Marash, Turkey
Anatolia College, Marsovan, Turkey
American College for Girls, Constantinople, Turkey
International College, Smyrna, Turkey
Pasumalai College, Pasumalai, South India
North China College, Tungchow, North China

Foochow College, Foochow, Fukien Province, China
International Institute for Girls, Madrid, Spain
Amanzimtote Seminary, Adams, Natal, South Africa
Collegio Internacional, Guadalajara, Mexico

The Rise of the Higher Education Fund

On the basis of his study Secretary Barton developed a long range plan to secure funds. He made a great point of the fact that added annual income of $5000. a year for each institution would relieve the regular budget of the American Board. The chief features of his plan were these:

First, create a select home-base constituency for higher educational institutions in mission fields. In public addresses, articles, brochures and correspondence stress the fact that through Christian higher education alone, able indigenous leaders in all worthy avenues of life can be produced, a *sine qua non* in the effort to nurture a Christian church and community that ultimately will become independent, self-governing and self-propagating.

Second, secure sooner or later for each mission college a separate, independent, incorporated board of trustees in America whose supreme interest and purpose would be the conduct and support of its own college abroad. Such a board would be able to prepare and circulate its own literature and make cogent appeals to special groups and individuals. "Many would be interested in the whole higher educational program who were not givers to or interested in so-called evangelical missions . . . the educational program would appeal for larger sums than the churches are accustomed to give for missions."

Third, secure American Board approval for a financial campaign for these sixteen collegiate institutions to be conducted with the cooperation of the Prudential Committee but without burdening the regular promotional agencies of the Board. In setting up this financial campaign, Secretary Barton outlined these goals:

a. Added annual income of $5000. for each of these institutions.

b. An endowment of at least $100,000. for each institution. The statement was made that this endowment "would make secure the future of a collegiate institution that is influencing an entire race or country and that must stand at the foundation of all wisely conducted mission work."

Secretary Barton took advantage of the rising tide of interest in foreign missions among the Christian laymen of America. The Business Committee at the Board's annual meeting in Cleveland in 1907 presented a series of resolutions based in part on the following statement: "Whereas, there has recently been inaugurated in this country a Laymen's Missionary Movement, interdenominational and international . . . committees are already at work in several denominations planning to organize the men for larger giving . . . " Resolution No. 9 read as follows: "Resolved, That we urge upon laymen of means the importance of endowment for our collegiate and theological institutions in the East, upon which depends so fully the advance, self-support, and self-propagation of the direct and permanent work of evangelization."[1]

On December 31, 1907 the Prudential Committee spread the following vote on its minutes: "The plan submitted by Secretary Barton was approved, namely, that the Prudential Committee at once set about the securing of a Fund amounting to $2,000,000. for the permanent endowment of its Collegiate and Theological institutions. . . . "[2] Secretary Barton says that "the Prudential Committee took a long stride in advance when it appointed a subcommittee . . . upon 'The Higher Educational Work of the American Board'" with Colonel Charles A. Hopkins, chairman, the Honorable Samuel B. Capen, LL.D., Prof. Edward C. Moore, D.D. and Francis O. Winslow as members. Dr. Barton was secretary of this committee. They formulated their plans and went to work. An illustrated brochure of one hundred pages was published, setting forth in considerable

---

[1] AR, 1907, pp. x, xi.
[2] ABCFM, Minutes of Prudential Committee, 1907, Vol. XXIX, p. 96.

detail the work of eighteen colleges, two having been added to
the original list: St. Paul's Institute at Tarsus, Turkey and
Foochow Girls' College, Foochow, China.

During the next few years the personnel of Secretary Barton's Committee changed. Prof. Moore became chairman, and
Arthur Perry, George A. Holland, Raymond Calkins, members.
Secretary Barton continued to give the enterprise dynamic
leadership. In 1912 a second edition of the brochure was published. On page twenty-six appears this statement: "It is grati-
fying to report that before the close of 1911 the American
Board had received $1,112,000. towards the $2,000,000. endowment besides $100,000. that was sent directly to the college to
which it was given, $157,000. for new sites and buildings, and
$100,000. in addition pledged, to be paid when it will complete
the $2,000,000. sought. . . . One million dollars of this sum,
named 'The D. Willis James Foundation' was provided by Mrs.
D. Willis James and Arthur Curtiss James."[1] There followed a
statement of "immediate and pressing demands" for building
and equipment of thirteen of the institutions.

Dr. Barton pressed forward in the endeavor to reach the goal
of $2,000,000. for higher education but he and the Board were
soon engulfed by the First World War and the raising of endowment funds was of necessity laid aside. With the coming
of the Armistice in 1918, Dr. Barton had become so involved
in the sufferings of millions of Armenians in the Near East,
especially orphans, that he was chosen to head up the efforts
of the Armenian and Syrian Relief Committee in America and
later the Near East Relief and the Near East Foundation. This
huge task[2] along with other duties as senior foreign secretary
of the American Board demanded his full time until his retirement in 1927. He continued to be associated with the Near
East Foundation until his death in 1936.[3]

The Higher Educational Work Endowment Fund as visual-

[1] Mr. D. Willis James had been a corporate member of the American Board for thirty-six
years. Three of those years he had served as Vice-President.
[2] Over one hundred million dollars were raised for relief work in the Near East.
[3] James L. Barton, *Story of the Near East Relief, an Interpretation, 1915-1930,* (New
York, The Macmillan Company, 1930).

ized by Secretary Barton and his colleagues did not attain its goal of two million dollars. It served, however, through the drear nineteen-thirties and the war-rocked nineteen-forties as a beneficent, stabilizing force on behalf of the Board's higher educational interests. It relieved the Board's current budgets of many an item related to higher education which would otherwise have been unmet or severely cut. The income of this Fund since its inception had been divided year by year according to the recommendations of a committee familiar with the specific needs of all the higher educational institutions and their personnel. The following figures show the status of the Fund in the years indicated and the income available for use:

Year	Capital Fund	Income	
1911	1,112,048.00	21,292.68	
1921	1,158,483.42	57,964.24	
1931	1,178,810.71	59,182.19	
1941	1,621,544.71	45,462.49	
1951	1,183,807.26	75,920.47	(16 months)
1957	1,313,325.15	65,581.46	

Toward the end of his life Dr. Barton in his years of retirement noted the status of the colleges for which he had planned and labored. He had been prevented from completing his plan for these colleges or for those that remained closely affiliated with the American Board but all his friends were well aware of the success which had attended his effort to make higher education a major concern of the Board. He had breathed new life into the whole enterprise.

The Unfinished Task

It is appropriate today to focus attention on the unfinished task of the American Board in relation to higher education. There is no question now among the Board's constituency as to the importance of higher education as a genuine part of the missionary enterprise. Likewise there is no question as to the bitter financial need of such institutions as are still related to the Board, or have been newly related.[1] It is not inappropriate to suggest that the fulfillment of Secretary Barton's dream of an adequate, mobile Fund under the direction of the Prudential Committee is one of the urgent, unmet goals of the present day. Our educators abroad greeted with deep joy the initiation of the Higher Education Fund Campaign, 1958-1960, with its goal of $7,500,000 to be put at the disposal of institutions of higher learning associated with Congregational Christian Churches in America and around the world.

One can sense the urgency not only of completing the two million dollar fund for higher education which Dr. Barton began but for doubling its goal in order to meet with a greater measure of satisfaction the clamant calls for financial assistance. And not only this. The elements of the educational policy which the Board adopted as Dr. Barton surveyed the needs from 1903 to 1911 might well be re-studied along with the Lindsay and Padelford Commissions' reports[2] with a view to emphasis upon new aspects of the task which have emerged as conditions on many fields have changed. Such issues as the formation of a united plan and policy for regional effort involving consolidation in some cases, expansion in others, call for careful, renewed consideration.

---

[1] Such as Pierce College in Greece, Ahmednagar College and Lady Doak College in India, Southern Christian College at Midsayap and Dansalan Junior College in the Philippines, Japan International Christian University and several theological schools in India, Africa, Lebanon, Mexico, the Philippines and Japan.
[2] *The Christian College in India*, (Lindsay Commission), (London, Oxford University Press, 1931). *Christian Education in Japan — A Study*, (Padelford Commission), (New York, International Missionary Council, 1932).

6

ENLARGING THE CONCEPT OF MISSIONARY
SERVICE – MEDICAL MISSIONS

The Board's plans at the outset excluded medical missions as known today. As we have seen, the concept of missionary service in the early days stressed evangelism almost exclusively. Early missionaries were expected to have some knowledge of medicine, in order to maintain their health, but as in the case of education, it was several years before the appropriateness of trained physicians for mission work in the various missions was acknowledged.

Even so, it is of interest to note that the Board sent out physicians as missionaries even in the early years. Dr. Thomas Holman was sent with the first group of missionaries to the Sandwich Islands in 1819. He was followed by Dr. Abraham Blatchley in 1823, Dr. Gerrit P. Judd in 1828, Dr. Dwight Baldwin in 1830, Dr. Alonzo Chapin in 1831, Dr. Thomas Lafon in 1836, and Dr. Seth L. Andrews in 1837. Dr. John Scudder was sent in 1819 to the Ceylon Mission. Between 1820 and 1836 eight physicians were sent to missions among the American Indians. In 1834 two physicians, Dr. Newton Adams and Dr. Alexander E. Wilson, were sent to South Africa, the former to accompany missionaries to Zululand on the coast, the latter to accompany those going to the Transvaal in the interior. Dr. Peter Parker was sent to Canton, China, in 1834. Dr. Asa Dodge reached Syria the same year and Dr. Asabel Grant joined the Nestorian Mission in 1835. Dr. Dan B. Bradley and Dr. Stephen Tracy pioneered in Siam 1834-1836, and Dr. Mather B. Hope and Dr. Dyer Ball in Singapore 1836-1838. By 1860, fifty-two physicians had been sent to the field, ten to the Sandwich Islands, three to Ceylon, thirteen to the Ottoman

Empire, four to Africa, six to India, two to Siam, two to Singapore, nine to the American Indians, two to China, one to Micronesia. Of these fifty-two, twenty-two were ordained ministers.

The Early View

It was the view of many of the Board's supporters that the chief function of these physicians was to look after the health of the missonaries. There had been such sad loss of life among the early missionaries that friends were deeply disturbed.[1] But if their responsibility was thought to be the health of missionaries, it is clear that they could not be blind to the medical needs of the nationals among whom they dwelt. Their Hippocratic oath bound them to attempt to alleviate human suffering wherever they could. Some of the early physicians divided their time between medical and evangelistic work. Dr. John Scudder, for example, went to Ceylon with the understanding that he would study theology on the field and ask to be ordained to the Christian ministry by his colleagues in the Mission. Dr. Asa Dodge in Syria was instructed that "medical skill was to be used only as a means of furthering the spiritual objects of the mission."[2] Dr. Peter Parker in Canton was reminded that "our aim and yours is the soul's salvation. We send you and you go to offer pardon and sanctification to men perishing in ignorance and sin . . . you will, if practicable, make frequent excursions into the country, relieving the bodily distress of the people, distributing Christian books, and preaching the word of life."[3]

Medical missions had to make their own way, as it were, and prove their value. The Puritan concept of what is essential in the process of communicating the Christian Gospel to any non-Christian cultural group had to yield to expansion upon experience. Through the service and influence of American physicians the value of Christian witness in the healing ministries of medical personnel became an unanswerable argument for

[1] AR, 1839, pp. 29, 30.
[2] AR, 1832, p. 156.
[3] G. B. Stevens, *Life of Peter Parker*, (Boston, 1896), p. 82.

medical missions. The argument was supported by Jesus' own example, of course. He "went about . . . teaching . . . preaching . . . and healing every disease." (Matthew 4:23). Occasionally it was given play in letters written by the physicians themselves.

Dr. Scudder's Letter

Dr. H. M. Scudder (son of Dr. John Scudder of Ceylon), who served at Madras, India, 1844-1857, wrote in 1851 a long letter to Secretary Anderson stressing "the importance of medical knowledge to those who are laborers among the heathen." The Secretary comments: "Dr. Scudder's testimony is entitled to a very respectful consideration on such a subject; for in addition to the example and experience of his honored father, he has himself pursued a course of medical study, and has tested his theory in actual practice. What he says, therefore, ought not to be regarded as mere speculation."[1]

Dr. Scudder's letter shows how earnestly medical men were striving to establish medical service as an essential part of the missionary program. He rather laboriously yet with deep sympathy for the suffering and misguided millions, marshals and supports in detail eight basic reasons for his attitude and conclusion. The headings of his paragraphs are as follows:

1. The union of preaching and healing harmonizes with the example of Christ and the early disciples.

2. The missionary, if a physician, obtains thereby a happy introduction to the people.

3. The physical benefits which the missionary physician confers make the people more ready to hear his spiritual message.

4. The missionary physician attracts to himself a daily assembly of adult hearers.

5. The missionary physician draws many females within the sphere of his labors.

6. Medical practice wins for the missionary a position of authority fitted to subserve his higher office as a preacher.

[1] *Missionary Herald*, April 1852, p. 102.

7. The missionary's character as a physician brings visitors (non-patients) to his house.

8. The missionary physician has peculiar opportunities for manifesting Christian affection.

Dr. Scudder gives a picture of his own medical service at the time (1851) in these words:

> My dispensary has been attended from far and near. I have two male assistants, one a native, and the other an East Indian. I prescribe, and perform the operations. They do the work of preparing, weighing out and administering the medicines. In this dispensary the Gospel is daily proclaimed. Mrs. Scudder finds a very interesting field of labor in connection with it. She and Mrs. Lackey generally spend some time every day in religious conversation with the women who come for medical aid.

Occasionally, however, such a view suffered setbacks. The famous Deputation of 1854-1855 which visited India, Ceylon and the Near East acknowledged the usefulness of missionary physicians but said in so many words that their main duties were to care for the health of missionary families and to convert souls through their ministry of healing. Shortly before that Deputation went abroad the Prudential Committee had gone on record[1] as opposed to the plan of supporting hospitals. When the Deputation surveyed Dr. Samuel F. Green's medical establishment in Ceylon, they found that he was not only directing a hospital but that he had translated many medical books into the Tamil language and had trained nineteen young men as physicians. The Deputation agreed that this work might continue provided the Board was not asked to support it!

This attitude of the Deputation echoed what had been said to the missionaries in Bombay in 1821: "preaching the Gospel is their highest employment, as it is the divinely appointed method, by which sinners are usually brought to the knowledge and obedience of the truth."[2]

---

[1] John S. Chandler, *Seventy-five years in the Madura Mission,* (Madras, American Madura Mission, 1909), p. 232.
[2] AR, 1821, p. 14.

The Turning Point 1885-1920

From the eighteen fifties to the eighteen eighties the case for medical missions was being strengthened by practical experience. At the seventy-fifth annual meeting in Boston, October 13-16, 1885, the turning point in the policy of the Board regarding their value was registered. Secretary Judson Smith addressed the assembly on "The Future Work of the American Board." He referred to medical missions in these words:

> The work of the medical missionary has assumed increased importance during the last two decades of our history; and in many fields, like China and Japan, the physician exerts a Christian influence only second to that of the ordained missionary. Educated women are finding in this form of professional service new and inviting fields of usefulness, and are thus adding greatly to the bulk and force of the Christian influence exerted by our missions. The conditions of the first proclamation of the Gospel are in some measure renewed; and a skillful and sympathetic ministry to the bodies of the sick and infirm in numerous instances opens the heart and conscience to the supreme gift of salvation. This arm of our missionary force we shall increase, as Providence opens the way, until the special demand is substantially met; and we rejoice to note the increasing number of Christian physicians, men and women, who are offering themselves to this noble service.

After Secretary Judson Smith's favorable testimony as to the value of the medical arm of missionary service the Board placed new emphasis upon it. This new emphasis was underscored by some remarkable testimonies which Secretary Alden assembled from medical missionaries and published in a sixty-page booklet in 1894 under the title "The Medical Arm of Missionary Service." Fourteen physicians reported from their fields in Africa, Turkey, India, China and Japan. Two questions spearheaded inquiries to which replies came: What is the place appropriately occupied by medical work as a missionary agency? Has medical work any perils on the spiritual side as related to the secularizing of missionary work?

The replies were very persuasive. Instead of quoting fragments from many sources the following impressive statement of Dr. W. L. Thompson from Mt. Silinda, Southern Rhodesia might well be pondered:

> Still I have seen enough of the ignorance and superstition and the resulting useless and cruel practices of the heathen of this land to convince any one, it would seem, that the Golden Rule requires us, and that the spirit of the Good Samaritan must impel us, to seek to enlighten and help them in this as in their other needs.
>
> I fully recognize that their great need is of a change of heart, and that this must come through a view of the Lamb of God and a knowledge of his dying love. But how is this to be brought to them? It is not enough that we tell them of Christ's love. The story will seem but an "idle tale" to them unless they see that love exhibited in living form before their eyes. In what other way can we so readily do this as in relieving their physical sufferings? As we look at them, living in their wretched huts with scarcely any clothing, they seem to us to be destitute of all things, but this is not their view of their condition. In regard to these things they are well satisfied. Should we give them clothes they would not look upon it as an act of charity, for they feel no need in this line. They would not feel that we were sacrificing anything for their good, for they look upon us as possessing inexhaustible wealth. They would simply consider that we wished to win their favor, probably for some selfish end. But in regard to their physical sufferings they feel a need; they often suffer hopeless of relief, and if relief can be given, they feel that this is something to be thankful for, that they have been befriended. They become more ready to listen when spoken to of their greater needs and the provision which has been made for them.
>
> Then many of the most debasing and ensnaring superstitions are connected with their theories and treatment of

disease, and to meet these superstitions it is desirable that one should clearly understand the subject with which they are connected. So firmly is the belief in some of these superstitions fixed in their minds that it often occurs that one who has professed Christianity for years, and has appeared to "run well," feels impelled, when some sickness or calamity comes upon him, to seek help from some of these supersititious rites. Nor is this so strange when we think how much superstition still finds place in Christian lands and even among Christian people of those lands; but there it is limited by public sentiment to less obnoxious forms, while here it rules as a cruel tyrant. The belief in witchcraft is very firmly established. When one becomes sick, some one must be to blame. The offender must be "smelt out" and when discovered is most cruelly treated. How can such a superstition be better met than by showing them — placing before their eyes — the agent of disease, showing how it may be introduced into animals with the same deleterious effects that it produces in human beings; that its growth and development are as definite and regular as is that of the corn in their fields, the ticks on their cattle, or the intestinal worms with which they are all familiar?

Closely related to overcoming faith in superstitions is the gaining of confidence in the missionary and his message, and here the influence of skillful treatment of their sick is of great importance. Not only does a right use of medical skill convince them of our kindly regard, but the triumphs of modern medical science often have the impression of miracles to them. And why may they not legitimately serve a similar purpose to these poor heathen that the miracles of Christ and his apostles did to those whom they taught and do to us? Christ doubtless delighted in the relief of physical suffering when consistent with spiritual good; but it seems equally certain that he had a much higher object in view in the performance of miracles — to draw the attention of men to the great truth he had to offer them and to convince them that he spoke with authority: "If ye believe not me, believe the works."

Aside from this object it seems doubtful whether miracles would ever have been wrought merely for the relief of physical suffering. Why should not the miracles of modern medical science help to accomplish these same great ends for the heathen world?

The relevancy of the above considerations should, it seems, be established by the fact that in the absence of the medical missionary all missionaries in this land feel compelled to treat disease. If they have never given any attention to the subject of medicine, they are led to do so at once upon entering upon mission work. All such work, if skillfully performed, is found useful, and of course the greater the skill employed (other things being equal) the more good may be looked for; while in like manner, the results of unskillful efforts may be prejudicial to the cause.

It is suggested that medical mission work "may have its perils on the secular side." It would seem to me that if there is danger here, it must be in the fact that men who are not really consecrated to securing the highest good of those for whom they labor may be more liable to be attracted to this than to other departments of missionary work, though it is certain that this danger is not confined to this department of work.

All the replies to Secretary Alden united in urging more vigorous prosecution of medical missions, calling for additional funds and an increase in the number of thoroughly trained and thoroughly consecrated missionary physicians and nurses, both men and women.

In the face of overwhelming evidence from the various fields the Prudential Committee took a great step forward in 1897 when they decided that henceforth medical personnel in the service of the Board should have the status of "missionary," not "assistant missionary," as had been the case for eighty-seven years. This meant that physicians and nurses were entitled to voting privileges in each mission, subject to the usual rules regarding residence and language proficiency. This was in reality a very belated action by the Board.

Nationals as Physicians and Nurses

Another great step forward was taken when the Board decided to put the stamp of its approval upon the policy of training nationals as physicians and nurses. This step was not registered in a sudden decision but came as the result of cumulative evidence as to its importance and wisdom.

In Ceylon, as has been noted, Dr. Samuel F. Green in 1847 began training Tamil young men as physians in order to "raise the whole standard of medical practice among the Tamils, substituting science for superstition and honorable practice for quackery."[1] Dr. Green and his assistants translated many medical textbooks into Tamil. During his period of service Dr. Green trained sixty young men for medical work in villages.

Dr. Edward Chester had an uphill struggle in the Madura District in India to counteract the maltreatment by Hindu medical men. At first he trained midwives, dressers and hospital assistants (1865) for work in local dispensaries. Later (1875) the Madura Local Fund Board which he helped to found, opened a medical school in Dindigul. Of nine candidates from this school presented in 1882 seven passed the examinations of Madras University.

Dr. Azariah Smith had blazed this trail at Aintab, Turkey in the eighteen-fifties. His classmates at Yale (1838) gave the funds for the first hospital building, erected at Aintab in 1879. The medical department of Central Turkey College, responsible for the Azariah Smith Memorial Hospital, trained twenty-one young men between 1874 and 1888. These physicians were pioneers of modern medicine and Christian standards in a wide area in Asia Minor.

Dr. John C. Berry and Miss Linda Richards responded to Joseph Neesima's dream for a medical school and a nurses' training school under Christian auspices in Japan. The nurses' training school was opened in 1887 in Kyoto but it was thought wise not to attempt a medical school. This was the first school of its kind in Japan. Miss Richards, America's first fully trained

[1] Helen I. Root, compiler, *A Century in Ceylon,* (Jaffna, The American Ceylon Mission, 1916), pp. 43, 44.

nurse, spent five years in Japan, giving a lead to the organization of many schools for training nurses.[1]

The physicians sent with the missionaries to North China had to start from scratch in training their assistants. From 1880 onward hospitals and dispensaries proved their value in multiplying friendly contacts with the people. Patients came, for instance, from 1031 villages to the dispensary at Pangchuang during the first decade of its operation. Drs. Porter (1872), Peck (1880), Atwood, Murdock (1881), Holbrook (1882), Perkins (1886), Ingram (1887), Wagner (1890), Waples (1894) demonstrated the value of the medical arm of missionary service and the training of nationals.

The report of the Board's Deputation to India and Ceylon in 1901 set up another milestone on the medical service highway. After most painstaking travel and observation Messrs. Whittemore, Loba and Barton made this statement: "The missionary physicians are to the people the best illustration possible of the life of Jesus Christ. This work is a perpetual sermon that the masses can grasp."[2]

After surveying the development of medical missions, one begins to wonder what forces were hindering a wider recognition of their value and importance. Two historic causes can be discerned. First, the religious objective of the Board was traditionally conceived by many supporters in narrow terms. Second, it has always been difficult to recruit properly qualified, Christ-motivated medical personnel. President S. B. L. Penrose of Whitman College, Walla Walla, Washington, was not of the narrower-minded group. He said to the Board in 1904 as chairman of a committee reviewing the reports from several fields:

> We question whether the Board has yet appreciated the full importance of the medical missionary. To him, to her, doors open which are shut to the evangelist and the teach-

[1] *Reminiscences of Linda Richards*, (Boston, M. Barrows and Co., Fourth Printing, 1929). Japanese sentiment as to the importance of modern medical training was rapidly developing and plans for well-equipped Government hospitals and medical schools were under way. The American Board had neither adequate funds nor personnel to undertake a high-standard medical school and hospital, even had it seemed desirable to enter that field. Nurses' training schools were a different matter.
[2] Deputation Report, 1901, pp. 30, 31 (with AR, 1901).

er. Still as of old the multitudes throng to be healed. In Oriental countries the Great Physician draws where the divine Savior is unknown. We feel that our medical work ought to be strengthened and extended. Our hospitals should be equipped with the best appliances, our doctors indued with the best modern training, more doctors and nurses should be sent . . . and the medical department of our work put upon a recognized level with the evangelistic and educational.[1]

Dr. J. H. DeForest, one of the first American Board missionaries to go to Japan (1874), in a reminiscent mood once paid this tribute to the medical personnel of his mission:

It is like a dream in these days of absolute freedom of travel and work to look back only thirty years and see how medical men were in the vanguard of the missionaries, going before them, allaying the apprehensions, and changing the prejudices of the people, and thus preparing the way for the wide proclamation of the Gospel. They were the ones who made it possible to hire houses and open preaching places, where otherwise it would not have been done for long years.[2]

Medical Missions Domesticated in the Board's Policy and Administration

Credit should be given to the Western Turkey Mission for setting in motion a plan of far-reaching importance to the medical work of the Board. At its annual meeting in 1921 that Mission asked the Board to appoint a medical secretary who should coordinate the Board's medical enterprises, find new sources of support and help select new medical personnel.

Unfortunately the financial condition of the Board led the Prudential Committee to postpone action. But the need could not be ignored nor the proposal forgotten. In 1923 Dr. George L. Richards told the Committee after a visit to Board missions in the Near and Far East: "As one-fourth of our work is medical

[1] AR, 1904, p. xviii.
[2] Quoted by Dr. J. C. Berry, M.D., in his "History of the Medical Work of the Japan Mission," 1919 (In manuscript form in American Board archives, Japan 12, Z9).

and is the least expensive and in my opinion the most efficient, this branch certainly merits having its own executive officer in the Home Office. . . . Such a secretary should have personal knowledge of field conditions and be somewhat in touch with medical affairs at home. He should have charge of candidates for the medical work and should see and care for the health of all those returning from the field. . . . "[1]

Dr. Mark H. Ward who had served as a medical missionary in Harpoot, Turkey was at home on furlough when Dr. Richards gave his report. The Prudential Committee seized the opportunity to elect him "Acting Candidate Secretary" May 1, 1923, and at the same time asked Dr. Joel E. Goldthwait, a distinguished Boston physician who had recently been elected a member of the Committee, to prepare a statement regarding the health problems of missionary personnel and to make recommendations as to how the Board should deal with them. Dr. Goldthwait's paper is a historic document. Its recommendations are comprehensive and practical. They formed the basis of what may be called a new medical policy for the Board. He urged that there be a medical officer at Board headquarters, charged with the responsibility to carry out the plans suggested and to serve as a natural medium of communication between medical personnel abroad and the best sources of medical and health knowledge in America. He recommended that Dr. Ward who had just been elected Acting Candidate Secretary serve as medical supervisor.

Medical Missions 1925-1952

Dr. Goldthwait's paper was acted on two years later, in the annual meeting of 1925. The recommendation was made that the medical office be established and that Dr. Ward be elected Medical Secretary beginning January 1, 1926. It was so voted.

Dr. Ward submitted his first report as medical secretary in 1926. This report served mainly as a forecast of the duties of his office throughout the years of his service, 1926-1952.

[1] Prudential Committee Minutes. Vol. XXXI, March 13, 1923.

The statistical report for the year 1925-1926 revealed the basic facts for that year. It shows what proportions the medical work had assumed: thirty hospitals, sixty-three dispensaries, thirty-three American men physicians, fourteen American women physicians, ten other associate physicians (men and women), twenty-six nurses, hospital patients 18,220 (new cases), total treatments 433,864. Each year a statistical summary of the medical department was prepared.

Dr. Ward set up new standards with a view to improved health for all missionaries and missionary candidates. He established a service as adviser and counsellor of physicians and nurses related to the medical institutions sustained in whole or in part by the Board. New buildings were sometimes projected, up-to-date equipment provided, new personnel secured, locally or from abroad; new policies within budgetary limits were developed. And at the same time, the Medical Secretary in the Home Office was a constant reminder that the whole ministry of health and healing is conceived of as Christian witness to a God of truth and love as revealed by Jesus Christ.

A third important function of the Medical Secretary related to the securing of greater financial support for medical missions. Dr. Ward did not overlook the progress of medical institutions toward self-support, but hoped to supplement and help where expansion of services and facilities were urgently needed. He said: "A large endowment fund similar to that of the Higher Educational Fund would be of great assistance in making more efficient the work of our medical missionaries on the field."[1]

Dr. Ward was very careful to seek to maintain the unity of the overseas program. The medical work took its recognized place as an integral part of a mission just as the evangelistic or educational, but the unity of it all was a constant concern of the corresponding secretaries, including Dr. Ward. He held steadily in mind the indigenous development of medical work. He closed his first report with these words: "What nobler gift

[1] AR, 1926, p. 49.

could we leave behind us in China, India, or Africa than a self-supporting institution of healing, founded and established in the name of our Lord and Master, Jesus Christ."[1]

The Board greeted this new development with great enthusiasm. Dr. Ward was given time to organize his work, develop his policies and get acquainted with the medical personnel on the various fields. He became a very useful member of the staff. There were 787 missionaries of the Board in 1926, every one of whom was an individual in Dr. Ward's sight, to be greeted on arrival on furlough or checked up on medically abroad, counselled with or warned as might be necessary. Throughout the twenty-seven years of service at headquarters Dr. Ward was known as a great personal friend who cared sincerely for the welfare of all missionaries and stood ready to do what he could in every emergency.

The Medical Department had barely gotten under way when the fateful events of October 1929 on the economic scene began to smother hopes and compel readjustments. During the thirties the annual income of the Board from all sources decreased by fifty percent. Hopes for the proper development of the medical work as well as of other branches dimmed. Then came the Second World War, 1939 to 1945, which threw many fields into confusion and uncertainty, especially affecting their institutions, both educational and medical. It was not a question of opportunity but of resources. When the armistice came, the immense task of rehabilitation began. The Board was one of many cooperating agencies for relief and rehabilitation, especially in the Near East. There was even greater demand for medical personnel and it took years to reach what could be called full resumption of medical work as an integral part of the Board's regular program.

At its meeting October 4, 1948 Dr. Ward presented to the Medical Committee a statistical summary which showed a greatly depleted personnel situation. With twenty-three hospitals and thirty-four dispensaries in operation, only twelve

[1] AR, 1926, p. 49.

American physicians and twenty-two American nurses were on duty. He called for eighteen additional physicians and fourteen additional nurses — all Americans — to bring the staff up to what he considered minimum requirements. The Candidate Secretary reported that he was authorized by the Prudential Committee to find twelve physicians and fourteen nurses.

Dr. Ward served as Assistant Clerk (1925-1933) of the Prudential Committee and from 1933 to 1952 as Clerk in addition to his duties as Medical Secretary. This took no small part of his time. In December 1948 he addressed the Personnel Committee requesting that "the Board . . . make a fresh study of the duties of the Medical Secretary and his relationships with other departments. . . . " This request led to a restudy and in the meantime Dr. Ward was relieved in part of his duties as Clerk of the Prudential Committee. During the course of this restudy the Medical Committee under Dr. Ward's leadership tackled the major problem of relief and rehabilitation in addition to many postwar administrative questions and the regular duties of supervision of the health of the missionary staff. Unfortunately Dr. Ward's own health was threatened. His vigor was much impaired and his friends far and wide were shocked to hear of his sudden death from a heart attack December 22, 1952.

During the difficult years of the Great Depression and of the Second World War the American Board shared with many other boards a stepped-up program of cooperation in many fields and functions. In the area of medical work great advance was made during the thirties and forties.

In 1933 the Associated Medical Mission Office was organized with headquarers in New York. Five foreign mission boards (Baptist, Congregational, Episcopal, Methodist, Presbyterian) participated at the outset. The AMMO office undertook to examine for health purposes all missionary candidates and missionary personnel coming on furlough or returning to their fields. Their work included laboratory tests and examination for tropical parasites. The budget was pro-rated among the participating boards but services of the office were available to all missionary agencies, irrespective of membership, at charges according to the service rendered.

Says an AMMO report: "Of the estimated three thousand missionaries examined in a year only one-third go through this office. The others are seen by physicians throughout the country. But papers for all of them are sent to and surveyed by AMMO and evaluated for medical clearance. . . . " The American Board from the beginning in 1933 has borne its share in the support of this office and continues to value its work most highly. Cooperation in this department means economy and greater efficiency.

Another need in the field of medical missions was so deeply felt that on June 3, 1938 delegates from twelve North American Mission boards met to establish the Christian Medical Council for Overseas Work. The chief functions of this Council which has continued to commend itself most highly to all those interested in medical missions are (1) to aid boards in the selection and training of medical personnel; (2) to encourage cooperative planning in the professional problems of medical missions; (3) to aid in the promotion of a better understanding in North America of the world significance of medical missions; (4) to promote the continued restudy of medical missionary institutions and personnel; (5) to serve medical missionary personnel on furlough as they seek refresher professional study; (6) to advise and guide, so far as is desired, the non-American medical personnel from missionary institutions who come to America for graduate study; (7) to serve as a clearing house among mission boards for discussion and assistance in the development of their medical work. The American Board, one of the original twelve boards which set up the Council, has greatly profited in this cooperative venture. At many points the Council has been of great help to missionaries.

Since the death of Dr. Ward, December 22, 1952, the medical work of the Board has faced something of a dilemma. The core of the difficulty seems to be the matter of long range policy, both at the home office and on the fields. A number of factors have conspired to delay vigorous and definite action.

On the one hand, the interdenominational, cooperative bodies (AMMO and CMCOW) have greatly influenced opinion as to whether the American Board should maintain a full-time medical secretary. These bodies perform, in large part, at least two of the three main functions which since 1925 have been considered the responsibility of a full-time medical secretary, namely, (1) care of the health of missionary personnel; (2) counselling service regarding (a) development of medical work in field after field, (b) guidance of medical personnel and candidates as to study and refresher courses, (c) choice of candidates for medical work. The third main function which cannot well be performed by an interdenominational body for any board is the financial undergirding of medical missions year after year.

On the other hand, the wisdom of securing a full-time medical secretary has been questioned. It is contended that the work in every mission should be under the care of secretaries at headquarters on a regional, not on a functional basis. Medical work is an integral part of the program of nearly every mission and as such falls under the supervision of the area secretary and his area committee within the Prudential Committee.

The Present Situation

The upshot of the matter is a temporary arrangement that may become permanent. In place of a full-time medical secretary, a part-time medical consultant has been available in Boston with a junior secretary on duty to care for all routine matters under the supervision of the area secretaries and the medical sub-committee of the Prudential Committee.[1]

It remains to be said that there is no doubt whatever but that medical missions will and should continue to be a major

[1] Dr. Hale Cook now at Vadala, India, served as part-time medical consultant from September, 1954 to May, 1955, Dr. William L. Nute, Jr., now at Ankara, Turkey, from September, 1955 to July, 1956. At present Dr. Carl E. Taylor (Presbyterian), formerly of Ludhiana, India, now teaching at Harvard School of Public Health, is the Board's medical consultant.

concern of the American Board. Under changing conditions, both at home and abroad, both within the pattern of inter-denominational cooperation and within the varying demands of developed and under-developed areas of service, the fundamental Christian witness of skilled physicians, surgeons and nurses will continue to be needed and respected as a mighty force for righteousness.

The present chairman of the Medical Committee, Elmer L. Severinghaus, M.D., has given an indication of his idea of the future of medical missions in these words: "Probably the new emphasis in the work of many medical missionaries will be in the application of modern scientific medicine to large numbers of people rather than to individual patients alone." He adds: "The actual practice of public health needs to be infused with the concern for human beings which is one of the fundamentals of Christianity."[1]

[1] *Advance*, December 28, 1955, p. 20.

7

ENLARGING THE CONCEPT OF
MISSIONARY SERVICE – SOCIAL ACTION

Broadly speaking, missionary work that is not primarily evangelistic, educational or medical may rightfully be classified as Christian Social Action. It is even reasonable to include under this term specialized education in the mechanical, industrial and agricultural arts. Christian Social Action has the broadest possible reference to human welfare. In American Board history its line runs from accounts of spectacular service in famine relief to the humdrum routines of caring for thousands of orphans. It takes account of such episodes in international relations as Dr. Arthur H. Smith's pleading with President Theodore Roosevelt to use the Boxer indemnity funds for the education of Chinese youth. It points with satisfaction to the creative work of Dr. Ray Phillips at the Bantu Social Center in Johannesburg in the realm of race relations in the Union of South Africa. It records with amazement Corinna Shattuck's linen industry for thousands of orphans and widows in Asia Minor.

There has been a great deal of humanitarian service by missionaries in every American Board field, prompted by spontaneous sympathy for suffering humanity, without any laborious elaboration of theories of social ethics as justification. The impulse to give a cup of cold water to a thirsty person in the Master's name is second nature in a missionary. This has always been so even though at the outset the concept of missionary work was sharply limited to evangelism, even to what today is regarded as a very narrow conception of evangelism.

One may distinguish at least three stages historically in the official attitude of the American Board toward Social Action.

First, the negative phase prevailed for about fifty years, until pressure from the missionaries re-enforced the growing conviction in America that deeds of mercy on an increasing scale, well-planned and well-directed, should be an inevitable accompaniment of the preaching of the Gospel. Missionaries faced grim facts of poverty, disease, famine and natural catastrophes and were moved to do what they could to help. Second, the Board accepted the idea that medical missions, industrial and agricultural reforms might well serve the evangelistic purpose. Many argued that normal human contacts at points of severe physical need were open doors to evangelism and conversion to the Christian faith.

The third stage has been marked by emphasis upon deeds of mercy and upon all efforts for human rehabilitation and education which though incomplete are acts of Christian witness not requiring any further justification. Christian Social Action should be accompanied by the interpretative preaching of the Word of God but it is valid as Christian witness even when preaching, public or private, is impossible.

The biblical basis for all Christian Social Action is that faith and works are parts of one stream of witness. An individual or a society cannot be saved by works alone. Service is not an approved substitute for faith. On the other hand, "Faith by itself, if it has no works, is dead" (James 2:17 RSV). Genuine service has spiritual roots of some kind. The broader vision of the Church and its witness as leaven in the lump of human society everywhere has become an essential part of missionary thinking and action. Incidentally, one curious aspect of medical missions in Muslim lands is suggested by a question occasionally asked: "Of what great sin has the Doctor been guilty in his earlier life that he should have to atone for it in this sacrificial way?"

The Board has sponsored few if any missionaries who have failed to put faith first, but many missionaries have realized that many kinds of Social Action are necessary to provide the kind of spiritual climate and soil in which the seed of the

Gospel can sprout and grow. A starving person doesn't want to listen to "talk." He wants physical food at once. The victims of plague or cholera are not concerned with the faith of the American physician but they respond at once to his loving care. In all walks of life help at points of deeply felt need takes precedence and prepares the way for better things.

One topic around which debate surged in the early decades of American Board history was whether, as it was then stated, Christianity should precede or follow civilization. This subject was particularly relevant to Board undertakings among people who were classed in the eighteen hundreds as uncivilized: American Indians, Hawaiians, Zulus. Many thoughtful missionaries found themselves in a dilemma. On the one hand, they knew that they were sent to preach the Gospel. On the other, they instinctively felt that it was absurd not to undertake the task of trying to lift the people around them above savage, bestial habits of life, above the whole complex of primitive existence. In the face of this dilemma there was hesitation, even failure in those early decades to make provision for serious undertakings in Social Action.

The Larger View

As late as 1893 an official spokesman of the Board insisted that industrial education, for instance, was an "unsolved problem." He presented the problem to an annual meeting so:

> This experiment [industrial education] in one form or another, has been attempted in many mission fields by different boards, but with little success. More important than any result achieved in the lines proposed has been the lesson that civilization in any form does not precede, but follows the Gospel. . . . The best work yet done by any native pastors or preachers has been done by men who were trained to industrial habits.[1]

Yet before 1900 Board officers pointed with satisfaction to several projects which had demonstrated the value of

[1] AR, 1893, p. xxi.

agricultural and industrial training: Samokov, Bulgaria (carpentry, shoeshop, farm work), Bardezag and Marsovan (now Merzifon) in Turkey (carpentry, shoeshop, weaving), Ahmednagar, Sirur, and Pasumalai in India (animal husbandry, farm work, mechanical arts), Tillipally in Ceylon (printing press, crafts), Amanzimtote, Zululand in Africa (well developed agricultural and industrial courses), Dondi, Angola in Africa (printing press, agricultural work, animal husbandry, industrial arts). In many girls' schools domestic science courses were given. All these names connoted remarkable achievements in human rehabilitation. Of these and other projects, reflecting an enlarging conception of missionary service Secretary N. G. Clark said: "Such education is only to be introduced in subordination to the mission purpose to raise up self-reliant, self-respecting men and women who shall introduce the acts of civilized life and prepare the way for self-supporting Christian communities."[1]

Thus it is clear that Board thinking went through three familiar stages in regard to agricultural and industrial education: First, it was thought of mainly as self-help for students who had nothing but labor to give in partial return for school privileges. Second, it was thought of as equipping a student with better means to earn a living later for himself and his family. Third, it was considered to have a broad vital relation to the economic strength of a Christian community on its march toward self-reliance and self-support.

The Madras Assembly of the International Missionary Council in 1938 included in mission policy generally the point of view that the welfare and even the continuing existence of churches on mission fields is conditioned upon a reasonably adequate economic base. In great measure, this step forward was the result of the careful field work of J. Merle Davis, who for several years pioneered in the economics of the Younger Churches. Mr. Davis explored this field and developed his ideas and recommendations when serving as the

[1] AR, 1893, p. xxii.

Director of the Department of Social and Economic Research and Counsel of the International Missionary Council. This Department was organized as one result of the 1928 Jerusalem Meeting of the Council. For a decade, 1928 to 1938, Mr. Davis focused attention on what has been called the "Fourth Dimension in Christian Missions."[1] By his numerous reports of field work[2] with analyses and syntheses of their results he established beyond any question the validity of Christian Social Action in relation to the problems of the Younger Churches.

It would be enlightening to review in some detail many projects undertaken by American Board missionaries which have won well-deserved recognition as valuable agencies contributing to human welfare along social and economic lines. This would require a volume or more. Interested readers are referred to a selected bibliography in an appendix of this volume. But special mention must be made here of the greatest Christian effort in the cause of human relief and rehabilitation ever undertaken by foreign mission boards — Near East Relief. Early in the First World War Secretary Barton who was following developments in the Near East very closely became involved in interdenominational relief work for Armenian and Syrian refugees. The operation became so vast and complicated that for several years he gave it a large proportion of his time.

---

[1] Evangelism, Education, Medical Missions of course being the first three traditional dimensions of missionary service.

[2] Davis, J. M. *Modern Industry and the African,* (London, Macmillan, 1933).

Economic and Social Environment of the Younger Churches, (New York and London, International Missionary Council, 1938.)

Finance Policies of the Missionary Societies, (New York and London, International Missionary Council, 1938).

The Batak Church, (New York and London, International Missionary Council, 1938).

The Economic Basis of the Church, Vol. V, The Madras Series, (New York and London, International Missionary Council, 1939).

The Economic Basis of the Evangelical Church in Mexico, (New York and London, International Missionary Council, 1940).

The Cuban Church in a Sugar Economy, (New York and London, International Missionary Council, 1942).

The Church in the New Jamaica, (New York and London, International Missionary Council, 1942).

The Church in Puerto Rico's Dilemma, (New York and London, International Missionary Council, 1942).

The Evangelical Church in the River Plate Republics, (New York and London, International Missionary Council, 1943).

How the Church Grows in Brazil, (New York and London, International Missionary Council, 1943).

New Buildings on Old Foundations, A Handbook on Stabilizing the Younger Churches in Their Environment, (New York and London, International Missionary Council, 1945).

Mr. Davis, son of Dr. and Mrs. J. D. Davis, early American Board missionaries in Japan, served with distinction for fifteen years as a Y.M.C.A. secretary in Japan prior to his epoch-making service with the International Missionary Council.

He initiated extensive plans for raising funds in America and for supervising personnel and expenditures abroad. He has told the exciting story in a book.[1]

In American parlance today the term Christian Social Action covers methods and projects which seek primarily to stir Christian folk to intelligent action on a variety of social issues. Since the Congregational Christian Council for Social Action was formed in 1934, church folk have been steadily challenged to take an active interest in all the live issues that face American society.[2] On the international front there has been a quiet but deep understanding between the American Board and the Council for Social Action to the effect that the Council for Social Action concerns itself with social problems that affect international society as a whole, while the American Board representatives in this or that field deal mainly with local or national issues.

Missionaries of the American Board have been alert to social issues of many kinds in the areas where they have lived and worked. Many of them have been deeply disturbed by economic conditions and social horizons within which multitudes have lived and had their being. With such issues as slavery, polygamy and intemperance some have agonized and wrestled. But a moment's reflection will summon the thought that it is one thing for a citizen of a country to cry out against this or that social evil and quite another thing for a foreigner (missionary) who has chosen to live indefinitely in a country to take up the gauntlet for this or that social reform. It has been done in some cases with the result that the troublesome missionary has been expelled from the country by the Government.

---

[1] James L. Barton, *Story of the Near East Relief, an Interpretation, 1915-1930,* (New York, The Macmillan Company, 1930).

[2] The Council for Social Action was formed by the General Council of Congregational Christian Churches at Oberlin, Ohio, June 25, 1934. Its purpose was stated thus: "The purpose of this Council for Social Action shall be to help the churches to make the Christian Gospel more effective in society, national and world-wide, through research, education and action in cooperation with the Home and Foreign Boards, Conferences, Associations, and local churches." The Minutes of the meeting include these sentences: "Stirred by the deep need of humanity for justice, security and spiritual freedom and growth, aware of the urgent demand within our churches for action to match our Gospel, and clearly persuaded that the Gospel of Jesus can be the solvent of social as well as of all other problems, we hereby vote . . . Believing that the Church will find itself as it loses itself in the struggle to achieve a warless, just, and brotherly world, we launch this venture." From General Council Minutes, 1934, pp. 887, 888.

Today the working relation between Christian social action enthusiasts in America and American Board missionaries abroad can be characterized by four points: First, recognition of the importance of social education and well-considered action. The Christian Gospel demands righteous living. It is at once as simple and as profound as that. Second, recognition of the fact that New Testament principles for society are revolutionary in all cultures. Third, willingness on the part of the missionary patiently and wisely to plant the good seed which, when and as it ripens, will bear fruit in a social as well as in an individual context. Fourth, recognition of the importance of the work of the Council for Social Action in America as a lens to focus attention on social injustices, and in international circles to do what can be done, independently and through such organizations as the United Nations and its agencies, to create a brotherly world civilization.

There is unity of purpose and effort between the proponents of social action and the missionaries of the American Board. Social education and action abroad are understood to be quite different from the programs of the Council for Social Action in America and in its international relations, yet all aspects of the enterprise are regarded as valid parts of the Christian mission in a troubled world.

An Interlude: II
THE AMERICAN BOARD CONFRONTS SOCIAL ISSUES

During the eighteenth and nineteenth centuries American merchants, explorers, scholars, diplomats and missionaries knew relatively little about the folkways and life generally of the non-European, non-Anglo-Saxon nations. The American Board missionaries who went before 1865 to India and Ceylon, to the Sandwich Islands and other islands of the South Pacific, to the American Indian territories, to Zululand in South Africa, to the various countries of the Middle East, to Southeast Asia and to China — hardly surmised what they were facing as they sought to deal directly with the people of those vast areas.

Ignorance of and indifference to social and political conditions on the part of Americans were not the result of ill-will or even of willful negligence but of inadequate preparation. Few but pioneers ever dreamed of the nature of the social, economic and political issues which would confront missionaries. These issues sooner or later forced themselves upon the attention of missionaries more insistently than upon any other class of people who left Western shores, for the reason that the purpose of the missionary went much further and deeper than the purpose of the trader or diplomat or explorer. The missionary wished to communicate a message and he soon found that he faced major obstacles in his attempts to deliver that message. Some of these obstacles inhered in the background and social structure of the peoples concerned, some of them lay in the fact that the missionary based his work on presuppositions which were alien to the thought and life of the people.

Be that as it may, missionaries of the American Board were amazed by the variety and complexity of cultural life and were appalled though not routed by the actual facts of human degradation, misery and superstition which they encountered.

There is certainly a deeper aspect to this whole matter. It may be asked: What justification was there for American Christians or even a small minority of them to turn their attention to the affairs of the non-American world? The founders and missionaries of the American Board had a ready answer. They did not overlook the spiritual needs of the new American nation or of the unevangelized Indian tribes. But they had a world horizon. Most of the nations of the world were sitting in darkness and did not know the truth as it is in Jesus, they said. But beyond their convictions which furnished them with compelling motives for action, there lies the question whether human welfare in any area of the world is served by an attempt to deliver a "message" to people of an alien culture — primitive or advanced — when the bearers of that message know so little of the nature of the cultural background and presumably therefore lack the wisdom to communicate their message without running roughshod over many human values.

Some American historians[1] ably express the view and write most interestingly of the missionary movement in early America as an integral part of the thrust of American life, so full of energy and of the spirit of adventure. Frontiers invited explorers. Possibilities of trade beckoned merchants and sea captains. Not colonialism but commercialism and curiosity lured alert Americans into all corners of the world. In some cases the missionary preceded the flag. In other cases, the missionary, part and parcel of American culture, carried on his mission.

As an essential part of the process of appraisal and interpretation of the ways in which missionaries dealt with a wide variety of non-theological issues, one must examine the records and discover the actual facts. What major social issues did the early American missionaries face and how did they deal with them? What patterns of action emerged?

[1] For example, C. J. Phillips, *The American Board 1810-1860*, (Thesis presented to Harvard College in partial fulfillment of requirements for the Ph.D. degree 1953); Paul A. Varg, *Missionaries, Chinese, and Diplomats*, (Princeton, N. J., Princeton University Press, 1958).

Ignorance loomed as a great dark cloud. There is a sense in which primitive peoples are not ignorant even though illiterate, and a sense in which people who have a rich cultural inheritance like the peoples of India and of the Near East are wise even though largely ignorant of their backgrounds. But the missionary of the nineteenth century felt that slavery to gross superstitions, ignorance of the three R's and of the simplest rules of personal and social hygiene placed a people under such handicaps that the need for spiritual enlightenment was seldom realized. Schools were not considered the most likely means of salvation but without elementary education, at least so the first missionaries thought, little or no success would attend the proclamation of the Christian faith. So primary education was deemed an essential aid to evangelization. Across the decades the degree to which missionaries should engage in educational activities grew to be a moot question, but no one doubted that ignorance is the mother of many evils.

Poverty and disease are children of ignorance. No wonder that compassionate missionaries, sometimes in silent opposition to the prevailing missonary policy, did all they could to improve living standards and to alleviate suffering caused by disease.

The low status of womanhood all over the non-Christian world seemed an appalling fact to the Christian conscience and as such was the basis of many an appeal to the home constituency. The harems of the Muslim world, the life of women living in purdah (veiled seclusion) in India, what seemed to be the slave status of most women in primitive societies like Hawaii and Zululand, the neglect and abuse of little children, the utter neglect of education even of the simplest sort for girls in the lands where non-Christian religions had long been dominant — these and related facts posed problems, and dictated a policy for Christian missionaries.

Human slavery in one form or another has been a characteristic of human society all over the world from the beginning of history. The Christian protest against this evil stems from

Jesus' estimate of the eternal value of each individual person in the eyes of God, a Heavenly Father. The protest received compelling emphasis in apostolic times. The brief letter of Paul to Philemon is one poignant witness to this. Slavery and the institution of polygamy so often associated with slavery were held by most Christians in the eighteenth and nineteenth centuries, both theologically and practically, to be utterly incompatible with the ideals and the maintenance of a Christian society. Though exceptions occurred, to be sure, in some areas among Christians, the missionaries of the American Board met these issues boldly whenever and wherever they appeared.

Closely linked with the roots of the system of human slavery and polygamy are the attitudes of race prejudice and racial superiority. It can be taken for granted that no person would presume to go as a Christian missionary who disliked people. But it is otherwise when it comes to a question of a superiority complex. The rising tide of nationalism during the nineteenth century in revolt against the onerous colonialism of the modern era has magnified the difficulties of interracial cooperation.

When we consider the clash of political facts and ideas, we realize that the American missionary has always trod on very delicate ground. His very presence constitutes a challenge to some regimes while it cannot be denied that the American Revolution has been and still is looked upon by some rulers as the seedbed of impractical and noisome ideas of democracy.

In a word, all issues which involve human welfare are inescapable problems for those who would plant and nourish a Christian community. Social education and social action are inevitably a part of the Christian mission in all parts of the world. No Christian movement that neglects, evades or fails to wrestle with the day-to-day concerns of human living and welfare can hope to become truly indigenous.

An example of an area of social concern with which missionaries were forced to deal is the caste practices of Ceylon and India. Caste has been a major curse in these lands, condemned by thoughtful nationals as well as by sensitized outsiders. This is not the place to rehearse the history of the struggle of missionaries and their national colleagues against the caste system — a struggle which dates from the early years of the Christian movement in India and Ceylon. But two points may be emphasized and illustrated to make clear how the Board has confronted this stubborn issue.

The experience in Ceylon is particularly instructive. Prior to the visit of the Deputation from the Board in 1854-55, missionaries in Ceylon had recognized the nature of the evil of the caste system and had taken the position that there could be no approval of caste — high or low or outcast — within the Christian community and church. Rev. M. D. Sanders, one of the members of the Ceylon Mission, made a special study of the caste system. He gave a succinct report to the Deputation at one of the sessions when social issues were on the agenda. He referred for details to an article from his pen published in the *American Bibliotheca Sacra* of July 1834, pages 470ff. But he was particularly concerned to point out to the Deputation what the missionaries and the churches of the Mission were doing to combat what they called "this giant evil." It could not be denied, he said, that the subtle influence of the caste system was still felt in the Christian community. At Christian wedding feasts and at other social gatherings, incidents occurred which betrayed the presence of the caste spirit, dictating conduct and even conversation. The most difficult situations arose when Christians dealt with non-Christian relatives who were easily offended by non-observance of caste customs.

Neither the Mission nor the churches have thought it wise "to use compulsory measures, believing that light from the Word of God, love, sympathy and the whole round of Gospel discipline are the appropriate weapons to be used in this warfare." Persons desiring to unite with the church, younger or older, are fully informed of the church's attitude in this matter and are asked to state their willingness to abide by the standard of brotherhood proclaimed by the church. What may be described as the crux of the test of discipleship comes in the distribution of the cup at the Lord's Supper. No caste distinctions can be tolerated there. Native preachers and catechists act as deacons and are particularly careful to serve all without reference to prior caste distinctions.

Even so, the leaders of the native churches are aware of the strain and stress to which church members are put in all matters of daily intercourse. With this in mind, at one of the yearly convocations, the subject was again discussed with a view to still more loyal observance of the Christian standard of intercourse. Ninety leading men, delegates from the churches, prepared and signed a declaration which rejoiced the hearts of the missionaries. "We, the undersigned, do solemnly pledge ourselves and affirm, that we will wholly renounce in ourselves, and discountenance in others, all caste and other distinctions and usages in society, which tend to foster pride, impair the affections, and hinder the kindly offices of Christian love, and that we will not object to eating any kind of food, on account of the caste of the person or persons by whom it is cooked, or offered to us."[1]

It takes only a moment's reflection in the West as well as in the East to realize that "the caste spirit" is like an infection which may annoy and even destroy the reality of Christian fellowship. The caste system of Hinduism has to some extent its counterparts in other regions of the world. There are undoubtedly castes based upon wealth, prestige, race, ancestry and the like which are often among the unrecognized social sins of Christian as well as non-Christian communities in all parts of the world, including the United States of America. It is widely recognized that the caste spirit whenever it appears is un-Christian. It is un-Christian because pride in anything human is un-Christlike. Some able theologians insist that pride in any form is the soul's most heinous sin. Be this as it may, it is one of the evils to be met and conquered only by the vigilance and loyalty of regenerated souls in an alert society.

For another illustration of the problems which the caste

[1] Minutes of special Meeting of the Ceylon Mission, April, 1855, p. 41.

system and spirit created one may look in on the Madura Mission in South India.

The question of caste inevitably became a burning issue in the Madura Mission at the very beginning. Secretary Anderson anticipated that this would be the case and warned the missionaries as he wrote in November 1835: "We are not to require the manners of eastern natives to be of course conformed to our occidental notions; but . . . can you not make a distinction between caste and customs, and aim to abolish the one, while you attempt no needless innovations on the other?"[1]

The most numerous castes in Madura city, the center of six million Tamils in South India, were the Saurashtras from Gujerat, Vellalas and Naidus from the Telegu country and Shanas from the South. Brahmans though few were prominent and influential. There were also large communities of the depressed classes. The Pallans were practically agricultural slaves. All told, there were at least eighty Tamil castes. John S. Chandler gives a vivid account of the occasional, often violent, inter-caste disturbances. When the missionaries opened schools in 1835, they welcomed youth from both sexes and from all classes of society. For instance, in 1839 in the schools there were boys from nineteen castes and girls from five.[2] Of the "first hundred workers," that is, teachers and catechists as analyzed in 1851, forty were from the Vellala caste and twenty-eight from the Paraia caste. The remaining third came from a dozen castes. Each worker was a door of entrance into the caste from which he came. As the workers came from many castes, so did those who joined the Christian community.[3]

The missionaries were quite prepared to take and to hold a very positive stand. Caste could not be tolerated. It was doubtful whether, in accordance with Secretary Anderson's advice "caste and customs" could be entirely separated but the disposition of the Mission was to try. In this effort they had both colleagues and critics. The Anglican Bishop of Calcutta

[1] John S. Chandler, *Seventy-five years in the Madura Mission*, (1909), pp. 22-26.
[2] *Ibid*, p. 56.
[3] *Ibid*.

tried to banish caste from his congregations. On the other hand, the Director of Evangelical Lutheran Missions of Peipsic stated that the American missionaries could not gain much influence since their mission rule brought them into a false position in regard to caste. His theory was one of non-interference.

After initial successes in establishing many schools, including boarding schools, the missionaries were impressed by the depth of the caste system and spirit in Hindu society. It obtruded itself to such an extent in the boarding schools and in gatherings of mission workers, that in 1847 the Mission decided to take stern measures. The quarterly meeting of the Mission on July 6, 1847 in Dindigul tackled the problem anew. There was some division as to the wisest procedure but there was no question as to the objective. After prolonged discussion these four resolutions were adopted and made the basis of operations:

> Resolved, That the mission regard that giving up caste implies at least a readiness to eat under proper circumstances with any Christians of any caste, and to treat them in respect to hospitality and other acts of kindness as if there had never been any distinction of caste
>
> Resolved, That we consider it to be the duty of all those who are members of our Churches, after receiving proper instructions, to give some satisfactory test of their having forsaken the evil before we can thereafter administer the Sacrament to them.
>
> Resolved, That we will not hereafter receive into our service as catechist any one who does not give satisfactory evidence of having renounced caste.
>
> Resolved, That the brethren in charge of the boarding schools be allowed to employ for their schools Paraia cooks, whenever they think it expedient.

The observance of these resolutions proved to be costly in terms of harmony among native assistants and in school attendance. Chandler calls the results "disastrous" but he hardly means what that word implies. There was confusion and resistance for a time even among communicants and attendance

at the boarding schools fell off markedly. Seventy-two catechists and teachers were suspended on account of non-compli-
ance. All the churches lost membership. But it was felt that in
the end the Christian cause gained great strength.

The Mission's stand against caste was especially obnoxious
to the Vannias in Dindigul, for instance. Rev. Edward Webb
(in missionary service 1846-1864) feared that his work there
would prove a failure because he had insisted on the abolition
of caste in the Christian community.

> He made every effort to enlighten them, telling them that
> as long as they remained catechumens the renunciation of
> caste would not be made compulsory, but that by contin-
> uing to cleave to such heathen distinctions they would
> exclude themselves from the privileges of the church.
> Finally two influential families in 1853 cheerfully re-
> nounced the distinctions of caste and were received into
> the church, themselves and their children receiving Chris-
> tian baptism. In token of their sincerity they took food in
> the house of a Christian brother whom they had previously
> regarded as excluded by his birth from all social inter-
> course with them.[1]

The most difficult hurdle in the effort to abolish caste in the
Christian community was the reform of marriage customs.
These customs had very deep roots in Hindu society with im-
plications which violated the Christian conscience.

The visit of the Deputation from Board headquarters in
March 1855 was the occasion for a brief review of the position
of the Mission with regard to caste. Rev. J. T. Noyes was chairman of the committee asked to report on the issues of caste and
polygamy within the church. He closed his report with these
sentences:

> This Mission took a step in 1847 in advance of all other
> missions in Southern India. In religious observances caste
> had surrendered, and it now was to be attacked in a
> stronger point, viz., in social life. Here the struggle was a

[1] Chandler, op. cit., p. 271.

severe one. Some valuable men were lost, and it threatened the disbanding of our dearest institutions. But the victory was gained. Many, who at first left us, came back willing to renounce their caste; and now, our catechists, teachers and church members seldom excuse themselves when invited, from attending the love feast; and the influence of these social gatherings on the members of the church has been found very beneficial.[1]

It would be a joy to be able to say that the caste spirit and system had been completely banished from the Christian communities in India. Sometimes the impression is given that Mahatma Gandhi's campaign against untouchability has resulted in the overthrow of the caste system. That is far from the truth, although some progress toward the ideal of brotherhood has undoubtedly been made. The Indian Constitution does not recognize caste distinctions. That is a great gain. That the Christian communities are in the forefront of this long, long struggle is certainly true but that they are models of brotherhood is not true. In insidious ways related, for instance, to the giving of scholarship aid to students or to attitudes toward candidates in church elections or to the appointment of personnel to important posts in Church or Government, the question of caste origin often receives consideration. The last stronghold of the caste spirit is marriage. Even in Christian communities today one does not expect caste lines to be crossed in marriage though exceptions do occur. People whose caste origins differ, differ also in clothes, to some extent also in manners. There is little or no segregation in seating arrangements in the churches. But the caste spirit continues to be a problem which varies according to time and circumstances. American missionaries tend to be inconoclastic in this matter. Would that America itself were free from the caste spirit!

[1] Report of American Board Deputation, pp. 94, 95.

8

MISSION AND CHURCH — RELATIONSHIPS

In the long and somewhat involved negotiations which took place before the first missionaries sailed from America in February, 1812, two concerns stand out clearly. "The great object of your Mission is to impart to those who sit in darkness, and in the region and shadow of death, the saving knowledge of Christ."[1] This was sometimes referred to as "the great design" of the Board.[2] This was the first major concern — the Mission.

The second major concern was the Church. "No time should be lost in forming yourselves into a church, according to the order divinely prescribed, that you may attend in due form upon the worship and ordinances of Christ's house. This will be of great importance, both to yourselves, and to the people among whom you dwell."[3]

Not many years passed before both Prudential Committee and the missionaries in the first fields — Bombay (1813), Ceylon (1816), American Indians (1817), Sandwich Islands (1819) — were led to ponder the relation of the Church to the Mission. The stage was soon set for a prolonged effort to clarify the distinction between the Mission and the Church.

The term "Mission" came to be used somewhat indiscriminately in at least two senses. Originally it was used to describe the motivating force which led to the practical effort "to spread the Gospel of salvation" throughout the world.[4] Very soon it came to be used to designate the group of missionaries sent to a particular area or country through whose efforts it was hoped to evangelize the people of that area or country.

[1] AR, 1812, p. 14.
[2] AR, 1810, p. 14.
[3] AR, 1812, p. 13.
[4] AR, 1811, p. 23.

The term Church was not subject to the same kind of indiscriminating use but the hazards of the development and relationships of the Church were possibly greater. The missionaries assigned to a single area actually formed themselves, as advised, into a Church. The Church in the Ceylon Mission was organized shortly after the arrival at Colombo of the first company of nine missionaries in 1816. The Church in the Sandwich Islands was formed in Boston at Park Street Church October 12, 1819 just before the party of nineteen missionaries sailed for the Islands. The intention and the practice for a considerable period was to add to this "Church" not only new missionaries as they arrived, but also converts from the native people.

Many questions of orderly procedure as the Church grew were either not foreseen or were left unsolved in the early years. There was general agreement at first that a missionary should be chosen as the pastor of the Church with the usual responsibilities.

It was a great day when the first native convert in any field was baptized and received into the Church. In the annals of the Ceylon Mission the conversion and service of the first convert, Gabriel Tissera, led the editor of the Annual Report for 1823 to include thirty pages of Tissera's journal, so full was it of human interest![1]

But as time passed and additions to the Church from the native populations multiplied, questions arose. Should not a church be led by a native pastor? Should the missionary members of the Church withdraw and allow the Church to begin its own life and service without too much shepherding by missionaries? Was not one great object of the Mission to train leaders for the churches and steadily place major responsibility upon them for the development of church life and service? Should the ordained members of the Mission exercise any ecclesiastical control over the native churches? Should there be an effort by the missionaries to determine the doctrinal

[1] AR, 1823, pp. 147-177.

standards of the native churches? Should the missionaries form their own church among themselves or be more or less silent members of one or the other of the native churches? What control — ecclesiastical or doctrinal — should the Prudential Committee exercise over the missionaries and the churches that grew up as the result of their labors?

Such questions began to emerge in every field. They were answered practically in various ways in different fields. The Prudential Committee was inclined to take certain positions which shed light on the problems presented by the growing churches. In the course of time the missionaries came to understand these principles as laid down by the Board:

First, the American Board is not an ecclesiastical body. It will not exercise any ecclesiastical functions. It refuses to ordain men to the Christian ministry in the United States; so its missionaries when organized as a Mission, that is, a functional unit of the American Board, will not ordain men to the Christian ministry on any field. Native pastors, when ordained, must be ordained in the first instance by ordained missionaries acting as an ecclesiastical body of some kind, that is, a church, an association, or a presbytery. Later on it is to be expected that native pastors and their churches will — with little or no assistance from the missionaries — ordain their own pastors and direct their own affairs as churches in various types of fellowship.[1]

Second, except in very special cases or for brief periods of time a missionary should not serve as the pastor of a church in a mission field. This position was regarded as a corollary of the essential principle of the autonomy of the churches of the fields. In the freedom of free church polity there is no essential reason why a congregation on the mission field or elsewhere should not choose whomever it deems worthy to serve as its pastor, missionary or native. But as a practical measure calculated to develop indigenous strength on the part of the churches, the

[1] In establishing this position the officers of the American Board were following what they were sure was the established practice and desire of their interdenominational constituency. Both ecclesiastically and doctrinally the Board sought to reflect the life and thought of those who made it their agent in spreading the Gospel.

Board insisted that native churches should be led by native pastors.

Third, the Board early took the position that the main business of the missionary is to preach the Gospel. One cannot escape the impression, as he reads the voluminous records of the first fifty years of the Board's history, that all the developing operations of a Mission — educational, literary, medical, industrial, social, even ecclesiastical — should be focused so far as possible on the object of the oral proclamation of the Gospel, if the mandate of the Board were to be fulfilled. The missionary was expected to preach effectively in the vernacular. He should be able to expound the Bible in the native tongue. He should be able to set native helpers and the native ministers a good example as a preacher. It did not take many decades of experience, however, to persuade both the Board and the missionaries that as soon as a native ministry came into existence, the function of the missionary as preacher dropped to second rank. A competent native pastor, well-trained and spiritually dedicated, it was found, could surpass the most competent missionary in the proclamation of the Gospel. This leads to a fourth position which in the course of time was well established.

Fourth, as native churches grew in their ability to govern themselves, to support their pastors and other servants, and to evangelize their environing multitudes, the main function of the missionary, indeed the main function of the Mission as a whole, was to train young men and young women for leadership in one or another aspect of the Christian movement at the heart of which stands the Church.

These points and other related ones are well summed up in a document of 1848, a special report on "the control . . . to be exercised over Missions and Mission Churches." The document was prepared by three Secretaries of the Board, Messrs. Anderson, Greene and Treat. As printed in the Annual Report for 1848 it covers eighteen pages of fine print (pp. 62-80). Its preamble reads as follows:

It will be seen that this call upon the Prudential Committee involves a discussion of the whole working of the system of Foreign Missions. We must determine the ecclesiastical standing and liberty of missionaries, and of the churches they gather among the heathen; inquire whether ecclesiastical liberty be not as safe for missionaries abroad, as for pastors at home, and whether missionaries and pastors are not in fact controlled by similar means and influences; show in what manner missionaries are obtained, what are the nature and force of their voluntary engagements, what are the powers and responsibilities of the Board, and what is the actual extent of the claims of missionaries upon the Board, and upon the churches. . . . In respect to the native mission churches, the inquiry will arise, how far they ought to be independent of the jurisdiction of all bodies of men in this country; how they are to be trained to self-support and self-government; what expectations it is reasonable to cherish concerning them; and what are the responsibilies of the Board for the teaching of the missionaries, and for the character of the mission churches.[1]

The report itself is divided into two sections. Section I deals with The Missionaries (The Ecclesiastical Liberty Belonging to Missionaries, and How the Responsibility of Missionaries is Secured). Section II treats The Mission Churches (The Liberty Belonging to Mission Churches, and How Far the Board is Responsible for the Teaching of the Missionaries and for the Character of the Mission Churches).

As indicated in the preamble, the Prudential Committee and the secretaries were agreed that the report should involve a discussion of the working of the system of foreign missions as policies and practice had developed since 1810. The document was to be a statement of tested practice. It is therefore somewhat surprising to read in the annual report of the Board for 1849 that the Special Report was "received as a record of [the Prudential Committee's] experience in the long

[1] AR, 1848, pp. 62, 63.

period of their official duty," but not adopted. It was not adopted formally because as the secretaries said "it is not to be supposed that the measure of our experience is yet full, in any one of the great departments or modes of operating in the work of missions. Doubtless we have much yet to learn, both through our failures and successes, connected with a prayerful contemplation of the word and providence of God."[1]

Nevertheless, this Special Report on a matter of such vital importance to the whole enterprise of foreign missions deserves to be studied as an historic statement of great significance. It laid the ground-work for the future policy and practice of the Board. It was of creative significance in its influence upon the practice of many other foreign mission boards. It has not been superseded by later statements of American Board policy. The founders of the Japan Mission, begun in 1869, greatly profited by the principles enunciated in this statement in their relations with the Kumiai churches and with the Church of Christ of Japan of which those churches became a part in 1940. It had a vital bearing upon the attitude of the missionaries of the American Board and their Indian colleagues as they shared in the conferences over thirty years which preceded the formation of the Church of South India in 1947.

The first section of the document concludes with a vigorous defense of the Constitution of the Board as a voluntary, democratic agency of the churches (and denominations) which support it. "Our fathers were providentially led to adopt the existing form of organization for conducting foreign missions as best adapted to their day; and when the existing form is found not to answer the purpose, their children will doubtless change it."[2]

The second section of the document on "The Mission Churches" systematically takes up and reviews questions on which the Prudential Committee was ready to take a clear and firm stand. In the most emphatic and explicit manner they asserted the autonomy of mission churches in foreign lands.

[1] AR, 1849, p. 71.
[2] AR, 1848, p. 73.

"We can claim no jurisdiction over them because we planted them." Great responsibility rests upon the missionaries, however, when the time comes in any field for the organizing of native converts into churches. They must act "in behalf of these children in knowledge, and in the power of self-organization and government," according to what *they*, the missionaries, not the Board, "regard as the apostolical usage in similar cases." "Experience has clearly shown that it is not well to attempt the transfer of the religious denominations of Christendom, full-grown and with all their peculiarities, into heathen lands. . . . The experience acquired in lands long Christian partially fails us . . . we need to gain a new experience, and to revise many of our principles and usages." (p. 75)

The basis of this position with respect to the liberty of mission churches is nothing less than the concept of Christian liberty, the birthright of all Christian disciples. The missionary will train mission churches for complete independence. He will aim to provide a native pastor for each church "that the spiritual machinery may be homogeneous and complete in all its parts and may the sooner be made to work without foreign aid. In no other way can he secure *the grand result* for which he labors — the development of the self-sustaining, self-governing power in the native Christian community." (pp. 75, 76)

To the abiding credit of the officers of the Board in those days one reads their assertion that "We ought cheerfully to abide the consequences of the full assertion of our principles." (p. 76). They support this assertion by quoting from the Cambridge Platform, XII:3, and by citing the experience of Paul and John of New Testament times with the churches which they gathered and shepherded. Irregularities and disorders, even scandals, are to be expected. Missionaries must face with patience the ignorance, weakness and sin in churches that are gathered in Africa, India, the Sandwich Islands, and among Indian tribes, just as Paul faced similar situations in the churches at Ephesus, Corinth, Colossae, and the cities of Galatia in order to secure "the grand result." (p. 78)

At this point the Special Report was amended by inserting a long paragraph intended to show that while "the Board is responsible for the *teaching* of the missionaries, . . . this responsibility does not interfere with that of Ecclesiastical Bodies in respect to the same thing." Among 275 ordained missionaries, but one case can be cited where, after the Board dismissed a missionary the ecclesiastical body to which he was responsible deposed him from the ministry. "The Board does not assume to decide upon the fitness of an individual to be a minister of the Gospel; but it is their duty to decide on his original and continued fitness to be sustained, by the funds committed to their disposal, as a missionary."[1]

It should be noted that the Board records its expectation that a mission when fully organized, may on occasion constitute itself an ecclesiastical body. The report does not go into the conditions under which the "mission" might cease to be an ecclesiastical body when the native churches have become responsible for ecclesiastical functions in the area.

The limits of the responsibility of the Prudential Committee for the teaching of the missionaries and the character of the mission churches evidently gave the constituency of the Board grave concern. The issue of slavery was becoming acute in the States. There were some slave-holding Indians among the membership of churches gathered among the Cherokees and Choctaws. How far was the Board responsible for the character of its mission churches? The answer given in this Special Report is not explicit. The Board is responsible directly for the teaching of the missionaries but it cannot and does not wish to enforce entire uniformity in their teaching. The Report very specifically defines the Board's responsibility in these words:

> Its responsibility is limited to the proper selection of fields to be cultivated; to the judicious appointment and designation of missionaries; to the constitution and laws by which the several missions are formed into self-governing communities; to the equitable distribution of funds placed at

[1] AR, 1849, pp. 68-71.

its disposal; to the just and proper instruction of the missionaries in matters within the province of the Board; to timely and needful suggestions, admonitions, exhortations, and appeals, fraternally addressed; and finally, to a faithful superintendence of the missions, and a decisive intervention when there are manifest departures from duty in the missionaries.[1]

But having said this the Board faces the question: "How long should we bear with mission churches that do not come up to our standard of duty?" This is what the Committee were not able to decide. A most commendable hesitation and humility characterizes the closing sentences of the Report. "We need an abounding charity. . . . We should remember that none of us are principals in this work of missions. The work is Christ's, not ours. . . . If we look into our own churches, and consider their manifold imperfections, we shall find abundant cause for charity and forbearance. . . . If we study the intellectual and moral condition of the pagan world, we shall only wonder that the first generation of converts from heathenism can be so far raised in the scale of Christian morals and general excellence of character."[2]

It should be recalled that at this time (1848-1849) the Board and its missionaries were rapidly gaining firsthand experience with paganism in its multiple forms. Churches were being gathered and shepherded among primitive peoples in the Sandwich Islands, in Zululand, among North American Indian tribes, and among the peoples of ancient non-Christian civilizations in India and in Ceylon. Churches were developing among the peoples of the Ottoman Empire and in Persia in the Near East. No wonder that the Prudential Committee urged the Board as a whole to study conditions surrounding the great task of planting and nurturing churches in all these fields and to recognize humbly the fact that "the measure of our experience is not yet full." It is not even full today after nearly one hundred and fifty years!

[1] AR, 1848, p. 78.
[2] Ibid., p. 80.

In years to come the matters treated in the Special Report demanded study again and again. They were live issues, and kept reappearing. In 1856 following the report of the Anderson-Thompson Deputation (see pages 53 and 54 of this volume), a resolution on the relation of missions and churches in the mission fields was voted, reaffirming "the principle of the Board is that of entire non-intervention" with missionary-founded churches. Later, in his book, *Foreign Missions, Their Relations and Claims*,[1] Rufus Anderson summed up thirty-four years of experience as a secretary of the Board by stating the right of mission-founded churches to be "complete in [themselves] . . . left to determine their ecclesiastical relations for themselves, with the aid of judicious advice from their missionary fathers."[2] Secretary Anderson felt that native churches could achieve self-support and self-government more rapidly than missionaries liked to admit.[3] And though he did not live to see the day when some native churches would be so fully established that they were taking over all mission functions, one senses that he would have rejoiced in it.

In 1869 Secretary Wood reported for the Prudential Committee at annual meeting in Pittsburgh, Pennsylvania, on "The Relations of Foreign Missionaries and Native Churches and Ministers." Missionaries are counsellors only, and missionaries and native ministers are equal in their office as ministers, he said. The missionaries are evangelists and are temporary, but they have responsibility for the funds sent out by the Board.[4] The report longs for "the removal of all difficulties in the relation of the foreign missionary and the native element in our mission fields [which] can be accomplished only . . . in the assumption by the native Christian communities, of the support of their own institutions and the evangelization of the waste places around them by their own means."

The basic policy of the 1848 statement was reaffirmed in a report by Secretary Clark to the National Council Meeting at

[1] New York, Charles Scribner and Co., 1869.
[2] *Ibid.*, p. 114.
[3] *Ibid.*, p. 101.
[4] AR, 1869, xviii.

New Haven in 1874. The subject was "Our Foreign Missionary Churches: Their Internal Organization, Mutual Relations, and Relations to the Churches at Home." The report stated that churches have been left to act for themselves with only suggestions from the missionaries. The relation of the mission churches to the churches at home is rather like that of children who have left home to make their own way, yet bearing with them the ripened wisdom and experience of the homestead. The relation is not one of authority and dependence, but of love and gratitude, of Christian fellowship "unto the Kingdom of God."

Through the years, no matter what new conditions have come because of the development of indigenous churches overseas, Board policy has not changed basically beyond that point. Nor, indeed, has it been defined better. In this age of the ecumenical mission, it is clear that our fathers planned well in seeking to give fledgling churches the right to test and use their wings.

9

THE AMERICAN BOARD CONFRONTS
DOCTRINAL ISSUES

The American Board has been called upon very rarely to deal with controversial doctrinal issues.

The major exception in this enviable record, the so-called Andover Controversy of the eighteen-eighties, acquires greater significance as the decades roll on, significance that underscores the wisdom of the founders of the Board and their immediate successors. Before we examine that controversy, let us look at the Board in its relation to its theological heritage and environment.

The American Board came into being about the middle of the century which was dominated by the New England Theology, 1750-1850. The men who gathered at Bradford in 1810 at the meeting of the General Association of Massachusetts Congregational Ministers were part and parcel of the theological trend of the times. They were very much aware of the rising tide of thought in Eastern Massachusetts which later led to the Unitarian Schism and wished to base the new student movement for missions on a sound evangelical foundation. There was no doubt in their minds that the New England Theology afforded the valid theological base. At the same time, paradoxically enough, they insisted upon intellectual freedom and they were willing to accept for the missionaries of the American Board the same standards and privileges as were in force for ministers at home. They did not wish the American Board to set itself up as a judge of the orthodoxy of its missionaries. As a consequence, the Board declined to become an ecclesiastical body. The churches which ordained ministers for American churches should also ordain missionaries for work overseas. The principle of freedom of thought applied to the work of both ministers and missionaries, provided the freedom was exercised within the framework of the theology generally accepted by the sustaining churches and individuals.

Consequently, American Board officers normally refused to pass upon the theology of a candidate for missionary appointment, provided he appeared as a young man who had been ordained in proper form by an approved ecclesiastical body. From 1810 to 1880 such theological discussion as arose was confined largely to Prudential Committee meetings.

The Andover Controversy

The Andover Controversy was a delayed explosion. Explosive materials accumulated as some theologians began to see the weakness or inadequacy of the New England Theology which had for decades dominated the thinking of the major theological seminaries, except Harvard, and of American Board officers, members and friends. Thought patterns which have been cut deep in human thinking are not readily changed. The Andover Controversy is essentially an illustration of the pressure which the rethinking of evangelical theology puts upon those who see no reason to modify long-cherished opinions.

The most sensitive center of American Board operations was the appointment of missionaries. The Home Secretary was primarily responsible for bringing to the attention of the Committee young men whom he thought worthy of consideration. Imagine the consternation, then, which arose at Board headquarters and elsewhere when it was said that a young missionary who had served one term in India and had returned for a furlough in the homeland, was understood to take the position theologically that a Hindu or other non-Christian who had not heard of Christ in this life might have, as it were, a second chance for salvation after death. This young man, Rev. Robert A. Hume of Ahmednagar, Bombay Presidency in India, became a storm center. How had he slipped through the home office of the Board and received his appointment? Where had he received his theological training? Who among his teachers were primarily responsible for his heretical leanings? Added to these questions were questions concerning the appointment of other applicants, among them William Noyes and D. T. Torrey. When it was found that the main source of these so-called irregularities was Andover Theological Seminary, from which Robert A. Hume had graduated in 1873 and where William Noyes was a student after having graduated from Amherst College in 1884, the storm broke. The principals of the controversy were thus the American Board and Andover Theological Seminary. Some Andover professors were said to be forsaking the main tenets of the New England Theology to which the officers, members and friends of the American Board had for so long been committed.[1]

The nub of the Andover Controversy was a question which, unlike many theological problems, could be very simply stated and instantly understood by reasonably careful readers of the New Testament: Does a person who in this mortal life has never heard of Jesus and of salvation through him, have another opportunity after death to respond to God's plan of redemption through Jesus?

The stage was set to debate this question at the annual meeting of the Board in Des Moines, Iowa, October 7, 1886. The Opera House where the session was held was packed. Great excitement reigned. Never before had such a galaxy of notables appeared in Iowa. President Mark Hopkins of Williams College who had been president of the American Board for twenty-nine years was in the chair. The debate began with the report on the Home Department of the Board submitted by President Samuel C. Bartlett of Dartmouth College.

The Home Secretary of the American Board, Dr. E. K. Alden, became the storm center of the debate which followed a resolution presented by President Bartlett at the close of his report on the Home Department. This resolution was designed

---

[1] Interestingly enough, Dr. Enoch Fry Bell, for thirty-four years a secretary of the Board, made the story of the Andover Controversy the subject of the Hyde Lecture at Andover Theological Seminary in 1943, fifty-seven years after the climax of that controversy! His lecture has not been published.

to protect Dr. Alden from excessive criticism, the point of which was that he was unwisely, if not unjustly, denying missionary appointment to candidates who disagreed with the New England Theology.

The debate surged with excitement for several hours. Prof. Egbert E. Smyth, professor of Ecclesiastical History at Andover, was the champion of Andover's "Progressive Orthodoxy" which, he asserted, "stands squarely without any hesitation or wavering upon the common platform of evangelical belief." He implied that the American Board was rejecting candidates who were judged on points that are "inferior and of secondary importance." He made a special point of commending young Robert A. Hume. "If you only knew Brother Hume, I know what your answer would be. If you knew his boyhood, his filial love, his toil to provide a home for his mother, his consecration to the service, the work he has done in India, the importance of that work; if you knew it all, and had communed with him as I have done in the love of Christ, would you personally take the responsibility of holding such a man back from his work? . . . I have spoken freely and frankly out of a full heart. I have spoken in love, I trust. I have spoken simply from the love of Christ and a belief that He is the Savior of mankind."

Dr. Alden himself followed Prof. Egbert Smyth. He was given a tremendous ovation. He stood by the statement in the American Board Manual, produced in large part under his direction, "that the only divinely appointed period of human probation is the present earthly life; that for those who remain impenitent until death, neglecting the light which God gives in some measure to every man, the day of grace then ceases; and that the issues of the final judgment are determined for all men according to the deeds done in the body." He admitted declining to recommend for missionary appointment several young men who entertained "serious doubts as to the present life being the only decisive period of human probation." He insisted that widespread contrary belief at this point would cut "the nerve of missions." He said his position was supported by the majority of the Prudential Committee as well as by many ministers and missionaries who had written to the Board to protest against Hume's position.

Bartlett's resolution prevailed at the close of the day. Secretary Alden was sustained. But this was not the end of the story.

In appraising the effects of the Andover Controversy on the American Board, one is constrained to remark that this episode was as near a heresy trial as the Congregationalists have ever come. It was but an incident compared with the prolonged crisis which ended with the Unitarian schism in 1825, yet even that schism was not marked by a heresy trial. The reason is not far to seek: American Congregationalists believe heart and soul in intellectual freedom. Historically, since the deplorable witch-hunting days in early Massachusetts, they have refused to deny to any individual the right and privilege of private judgment and belief.

The Andover Controversy from one point of view ought never to have arisen. It was contrary to Congregational traditions and accepted usage. It was a tempest in a teapot, albeit a very large teapot. The American Board suffered considerable loss of prestige as a result of it. It took at least two decades to achieve again the full confidence and support of its constituency. The immediate effect was the discrediting, albeit courteously, of its Home Secretary and of one or two members of the Prudential Committee. They misjudged the deeper trend of the times theologically. Before his death Dr. Alden, the Home Secretary, realized his mistake.

At the same time it is logical to think that at some point in the life and thought of the churches the transition from so rigid a system as the New England Theology to a position more consistent with intellectual freedom was sure to be marked by dramatic events. Men like Horace Bushnell, Theodore S. Munger, Newman Smyth and Washington Gladden were powerful leaven in the Congregational lump. Young Rev. Robert A. Hume and the American Board were, shall we say, the unwilling or unfortunate tools of a painful operation by which the fellowship of the churches stood to gain new vigor in the long run and to become the fertile matrix of theological leaders and movements extending to the present day.

Dr. Enoch F. Bell is inclined to think that the effects of the Andover Controversy on the American Board were mainly in the realm of the nature of the ecclesiastical or organic relationship of the Board to the churches.[1] He and Dr. Patton were of the opinion that many churchmen out of a mood of impatience with the Board for getting involved in the Andover Controversy, worked toward a relationship which should make the secretaries and Prudential Committee members more responsive to denominational trends of thought and work. Undoubtedly there is ground for this emphasis but they admit that the process of making closer the Board-National Council relationship had begun at least as early as 1865. Furthermore, all the boards or societies in which Congregationalists had a major part were involved in the developing organizational process that culminated in 1913. The Andover Controversy undoubtedly drew special attention to the nature of the prevailing structure and thereby strengthened the advocates of change but it seems clear that had the Andover Controversy not occurred, the structural changes would have come about.

The Prudential Committee made serious efforts to adjust the Board to the rising tide of denominational consciousness as expressed in the Controversy and related events. For instance, they proposed that the corporate membership of the Board be approximately doubled so as to include more members from church bodies west of the Hudson River and in the Far West. They also increased the number of persons to serve on the Prudential Committee, thereby making it more representative, and at the same time set a limit to their term of office. Henceforth it could not occur that a person could serve as did Charles Stoddard for forty-one years as a member of the Committee (1832-1875) or as did Alpheus Hardy for twenty-nine years (1857-1886).

[1] See E. F. Bell, Andover Hyde Lecture, 1943.

By the centennial year of 1910 the unfavorable effects of the Andover Controversy had disappeared. Restored prestige was largely due to the effort of new members of the American Board secretariat, notably Dr. James L. Barton, Dr. Cornelius H. Patton, and Dr. William E. Strong, and to an extraordinarily able, active layman, Dr. Samuel B. Capen, President of the Board. Fresh impetus had been given to the cause of foreign missions by the rise of the Student Volunteer Movement in 1886 and the centennial celebration of the Williams College "Haystack Meeting" in 1906 at Williamstown. In the opinion of the writer, no more remarkable meeting of the American Board has ever been held than the Haystack Centennial in 1906. College presidents including King of Oberlin, Tucker of Dartmouth, Gates of Pomona, Hyde of Bowdoin, Hopkins of Williams, Eaton of Beloit, Seelye of Smith,[1] Woolley of Mt. Holyoke, vied with leading Congregational laymen and clergymen from Congregational and other churches in proclaiming the wisdom and devotion of the founders and their followers and the solemn obligation of the churches of America to make Christ known and loved around the world.

"Rethinking Missions"

It may seem a far cry from the stirring Andover Controversy of the eighteen-eighties to the mild theological discussion provoked by the Laymen's Foreign Mission Inquiry of the nineteen-thirties.

Rethinking Missions was the designation of an ambitious appraisal project undertaken by the Laymen's Foreign Missions Inquiry, elaborately planned by the Institute of Religious and Social Research in New York and adequately financed by Mr. John D. Rockefeller, Jr. who became interested in a proposal that Christian laymen in America should evaluate the foreign missionary movement. He hoped that as a result they would commend it more effectively to American church folk of all denominations.

---

[1] L. Clark Seelye, first president of Smith College (1873-1910) — not to be confused with Julius H. Seelye, president of Amherst 1876-1890, who is quoted in chapter 5.

This is not the place to recount the history of the effort even in summary. That has been well done already.[1] Here we wish to focus on the theological aspect of the Inquiry which in the end came, unfortunately perhaps, to assume undue importance and to generate unnecessary heat. It was light that was wanted but heat developed in some circles, and befogged the light.

The Prudential Committee of the American Board, in company with many other American foreign mission boards, gave its blessing to the Inquiry and instructed its missionaries on various fields to cooperate heartily with researchers and appraisers as best they might in view of their absorbing tasks. This was done with varying success and in many cases with great delight and profit.

Professor William Ernest Hocking, the Chairman of the Appraisers, became the center of controversy when he presented his report entitled "Rethinking Missions."[2] Many of the thousand or more foreign mission enthusiasts and board officers who were present at the famous assembly in Hotel Roosevelt, New York, the evening of November 18, 1932 will not soon forget the dramatic features of that unique occasion. The first four chapters of the fascinating report dealt with the basic theological issues and attitudes in presenting the Christian Gospel to non-Christians, especially to the adherents of the major non-Christian religions.

"Rethinking Missions" surveyed the whole enterprise. In a sense the introductory chapters dealing with theological and philosophical issues were the threshold only of the edifice. It was here on this threshold that many friends and supporters of missions stumbled or took offense. The theological aspects of the enterprise were not meant to be as provocative of discussion and disagreements as they became.

The American Board acknowledged a special debt of appreciation to two members of its staff as the report came before the Prudential Committee and the entire constituency of the

---

[1] *Rethinking Missions with the American Board,* (Boston, American Board, 1932), p. 63.
[2] *Rethinking Missions, A Laymen's Inquiry After One Hundred Years,* (New York, Harpers, 1932).

Board for consideration and action. The one, Dr. Hugh Vernon White, a philosopher and theologian in his own right, was one of the secretaries of missionary education. The other, Dr. Alden Hyde Clark, an experienced missionary from India and board administrator with theological background and training, was one of the foreign department secretaries. These two men in consultation with their colleagues guided the discussion of the Report in Board circles. The chief preliminary result was the printed "Statement of the American Board's Attitude to the Laymen's Report" presented, discussed and officially adopted by the Prudential Committee at its meeting in Evanston, Illinois, January 18, 1933. The first two sections of that Statement are as follows:

I. The Spirit of Report

We welcome the Report of the Laymen's Inquiry on Foreign Missions. Its attitude is friendly, it faces its problems fairly, and it presents its conclusions fearlessly. The Commission, using every agency for scientific evaluation, came unanimously and enthusiastically to the conclusion that Foreign Missions should go on: that they are an essential expression of the Christian spirit and, if rightly conducted, have abiding value. We are at one with the Commission in their emphasis on the necessity of adjusting the missionary enterprise to the present-day world. That is a necessity which rests upon every living enterprise and we pledge ourselves anew not only to a careful reconsideration of the principles and practices of our present missionary enterprise, but to a flexibility of attitude which shall always seek to make necessary adjustments to changing conditions.

II. The Motive of Missions

The conception of the motive and aim of foreign missions set forth by the Commission seem to us stimulating and compelling. We realize that in order to become an all-pervading and dominant influence in the world the religion of Jesus must express itself everywhere in truly indigenous ways. We believe that the best experience of the Orient has much to teach us. We should be on the alert to find and assimilate everything good in the culture and faith of the people to whom we go. We should be eager to cooperate with every promising effort for the betterment of their life. But we would state with greater emphasis than the Report has done our conviction of the uniqueness of the revelation of God in Christ. The experience of the Christian movement the world around confirms our faith that Jesus, both by what he taught and by what he did, has a necessary gift for every race and condition of men. That gift is applicable to the complex conditions of the modern world no less than it was to the simple life of Galilee and to the Orient no less than to the Occident. He is the hope of our sinful, broken, suffering world. He is the Savior of men. By word and by deed to express His spirit and lead men to His discipleship is the supreme task and privilege of the Christian missionary.

In the perspective of many decades it is clear that the Board in dealing with this Report had learned well the major lesson of the Andover Controversy. Intellectual freedom is the right of every person — missionary, secretary, pastor, layman — of the Congregational churches. There was not the slightest effort on the part of the Prudential Committee or the Staff to coerce dissidents at home or abroad. The Board was concerned to state its "Attitude" and with positive but irenic statements to throw the whole matter open for untrammeled discussion, confident that the cause of the growth of the World Christian Community would best be served in that way.

Positive steps were promptly taken to enable church folk at home and abroad to study the Report and make known their conclusions for the guidance of responsible Board committees. A sixty-four page booklet entitled *Rethinking Foreign Missions with the American Board* was published and widely distributed in December 1932. The foreign secretaries addressed a letter November 1, 1932 to all "Missions of the Board and Associated National Bodies" inviting comments and conclusions after careful study of *Rethinking Missions*. This was followed up by a second letter February 20, 1933, in which fourteen specific questions were asked. Later on a summary of the many replies received was presented to the Prudential Committee and was also available to those desiring a copy.

Paralleling the approach just described Dr. White and other members of the staff sent letters to thousands of pastors and laymen in Congregational Christian churches. The last paragraph of Dr. White's letter of December 17, 1932 was this: "We want your opinion on the issues discussed in this Report and in our booklet. . . . The American Board wants the wisest and frankest counsel of leaders in the churches as to the future of our work abroad. This booklet is our word to you; what is the Church's word to us?"

The Board's archives contain many unpublished letters from pastors and others sent in reply to Dr. White.

It was expected that replies to Board inquiries and statements from ministers, missionaries and other friends at home and abroad would reflect a great variety of opinions. No single comprehensive and careful study has been made of the mass of correspondence evoked by the Laymen's Inquiry. Generalities without such study are of little value. It can be truthfully said, however, that as far as the American Board was concerned, the care with which the secretaries and Prudential Committee members treated this correspondence extending over many months led to the conclusion that the great majority of its friends and supporters at home and abroad agreed substantially with the printed Statement approved by the Prudential Committee in January 1933. There was also wide approval, for instance, of Dr. Clark's position and attitude made clear in one paragraph of his statement in his review of the volume *Rethinking Missions* in the *Missionary Herald*, December 1932. Dr. Clark wrote:

> In these chapters [first four] the Commissioners have frankly acknowledged marked doctrinal differences among themselves and in the churches that support missions, and have sought to base their position on "underlying agree-

ments belonging to the essence of Christianity as a historic religion." In spite of this, from the point of view of many leaders of missions the liberalism of these chapters is so pronounced that it has already caused grave concern. For myself, I have become increasingly convinced that our great task is to present Christ by life and word in the sure faith that He will draw men unto Himself. As this faith has deepened through observation of His power over men, anxiety as to the exact ways of this expression has grown less. To combine the liberal approach of these four chapters with deep Christian experience and devotion as some of the greatest missionaries are now doing, seems to me the most effective form of Christian evangelism and the one most likely to result in a strong Church as well as a pervasive influence!

All in all, the American Board felt deeply its obligation to the Laymen's Inquiry and its Report for the impetus given to more incisive thinking about the obligation of Christians everywhere to witness to their faith in Christ and in the relevance of that faith to individuals and society in today's world. The American Board was not unaware of the unfavorable reception which the Report received on both its major points — theology and administration — by many foreign mission boards in America. It is not a part of our present task to study these unfavorable reactions, valuable as such a comprehensive study would be. It is pertinent, however, to quote Mr. Rockefeller. He wrote under date of December 27, 1932 to the Executive Vice-President:

> Thank you for your letter of December 20th. The booklet on the Laymen's Report which you enclosed I shall read with much pleasure. . . . Your comments on the Report . . . are most gratifying, and the position which your Board has taken indicates an open-mindedness and a vision that is inspiring and encouraging in the highest degree. . . . That a new day has dawned for the churches as well as the missions is undoubtedly true, in spite of the fact that there are many people who are unwilling to recognize its arrival.

Stimulated by the Inquiry and as a part of the Board's continuing obligation to serve churches at home and abroad in their effort to understand and interpret the relevance of the Christian faith, the Board asked Dr. Hugh Vernon White to give special time and thought to seminars, conferences and to other occasions where a competent theological representative of the Board might make a welcome contribution. His response was generous and effective. His thought was enriched by a year's observation and study as he visited missions in many parts of the world in 1935-1936. He wrote three books in quick succession in his desire to share with all interested persons his convictions on the deeper issues of Rethinking Missions: *A Theology for Christian Missions*, (Chicago, Willett Clark, 1937); *A Working Faith for the World*, (New York, Harpers, 1938); *One Gospel for Mankind*, (New York, Friendship Press, 1939).

It is pertinent to add that the major reply to the general theological position of the first four chapters of *Rethinking Missions* was made by the Dutch missionary and theologian, Dr. Hendrik Kraemer, in his volume prepared for study in preparation for the Madras (India) meeting of the International Missionary Council in December 1938, entitled *The Christian Message for the Non-Christian World*. The secretaries of missionary education of the American Board made wide use of Dr. Kraemer's book and of Dr. White's books as well as of many other books and booklets in the effort to stimulate thinking and encourage appropriate action as widely as possible in America. The fact that there were mild as well as vigorous opponents of the general attitude taken by the American Board was regarded as a help, not a hindrance, in the task of world evangelization.

There have been theological issues of interest in the years since the Andover Controversy and the Rethinking Missions discussion. One of them, related to the Rethinking Missions study, concerns the relation of Christian and non-Christian religions.[1] Another is concerned with the nature of the Christian

---

[1] See Appendix III.

Church. But the discussion of these issues has remained rather more private than public, and it cannot be said that doctrinal matters were controversial. Generally it may be stated that the Board's witness has continued to allow for wide divergency in theological point of view, with mutual respect among those who differ. The principle of freedom of thought within the generally accepted framework of the theological thinking of the churches and persons supporting the Board has prevailed from earliest times. And it continues to the present day.

10

THE ECUMENICAL SPIRIT OF THE AMERICAN BOARD

In at least three ways the American Board has served the ecumenical ideal throughout its history.

First, the purpose of the Board has been consistently stated in terms which few if any Christian churches would refuse to approve. Article 2 of the Constitution adopted in 1810 stated that "the object of this Board is to devise, adopt and prosecute ways and means for propagating the Gospel among those who are destitute of the knowledge of Christianity."[1] Neither in this article nor in any other of the fourteen articles of the Constitution is any reference made to the ecclesiastical or creedal concerns of any Christian denomination. The nearest approach to such a reference is in Article 12 which states that "a report of the transactions of this Board shall annually be made, in writing, to the respective bodies by which the commissioners are appointed." This provision left ample leeway for unrestricted cooperation on the basis of a faith which sees God in Christ reconciling the world to Himself.

No doubt some denominational bodies desire statements of purpose much more specific and theological than Article 2 just quoted. A careful study of all modifications since 1810 of the original statement of purpose reveals no effort to exclude the participation of any church or group or individual who desires to make Jesus Christ and the Bible known throughout the world. The Board has consistently regarded itself "as an institution for diffusing a knowledge of the Gospel among the unevangelized nations of the earth."[2] More than this, wide cooperation on the evangelical basis has earnestly been sought by

[1] AR, 1810, p. 11.
[2] AR, 1833, p. 136.

the Prudential Committee and by most missionaries of the Board. It has been recognized that fine-spun theological statements of purpose tend to divide rather than to unite Christians in the effort to evangelize unevangelized millions at home and abroad. Theological freedom within the evangelical framework has been felt as an essential condition of ecumenical life and work.

Second, the missionary personnel of the Board has been recruited from many evangelical denominations. The Prudential Committee has never refused to appoint any applicant as a missionary on account of his denominational affiliation. Allowance is made for differences of ecclesiastical convictions and for theological opinions within the framework of the wide fellowship of evangelical churches. Questions are asked concerning health, training, Christian experience, attitude toward people of other races and religions, desire to communicate the Christian Gospel by life and word, and personal traits such as the disposition to cooperate with one's colleagues. The Board has never required that an accepted non-Congregational candidate transfer membership to a local Congregational Church.

Third, freedom from arrogance has characterized the policy of the Prudential Committee in regard to cooperation with the foreign mission boards of other denominations. Aside from the facts of intimate cooperation with Presbyterian, Dutch Reformed and German Reformed Churches which will shortly be discussed, the American Board, broadly speaking, has adhered strictly to these principles which go far in loyalty to the ecumenical ideal: (1) The churches and individuals which make possible the work of missionaries appointed by the American Board are members of the Body of Christ. His Body embraces all of his sincere disciples. (2) In locating a mission in any country thought has been given to Christian work already under way by other bodies, and fields have been chosen which were either totally unoccupied or, if occupied, were subject to agreements which when loyally carried out prevent all "overlapping" or unseemly competition. (3) In cases where missionaries from other boards desire to enter a field already occupied by American Board missionaries, agreements are sought which will allow ample scope for the new arrivals and will aim to secure the maximum results of effort and a united Christian witness.

You can not be much more ecumenical than that.

Presbyterians and Congregationalists

The General Association of Congregational Ministers in Massachusetts, after listening to the ardent young men from Andover Theological Seminary who appeared before them at Bradford in June 1810, apparently did not at the outset anticipate that support for the proposed foreign missionary enterprise would come from other than Congregational churches and individuals. They did assume that the Congregational churches of Connecticut, as well as of Massachusetts, would be interested and made immediate provision for their participation.

However, the men at Bradford were not jealous denominationalists. In choosing the name of the new body, in arranging for representation on its executive group and its corporate body and in many other ways, they sought to develop the interest and enlist the support of Christian people regardless of denominational affiliation. Interestingly enough it was found that there was unexpected response not only from Congregational folk in Connecticut but from Presbyterians thereabouts and in New York State and elsewhere.

In 1811 the Board therefore suggested to the General Assembly of the Presbyterian Church (organized in 1789) that that body form "an institution similar to theirs, between which and them may be such a cooperation as shall promote the great object of missions." The General Assembly, deep in denominational disagreement but most cordial in its attitudes toward Edwardean Congregationalists, declined to do this and proceeded to commend the American Board to Presbyterians as an appropriate agency for foreign missions. And so it came about that in 1812 Presbyterian Churches were reckoned an important part of the constituency of the American Board and given representation in its official bodies.

That year six Presbyterian men were elected as corporate members. The Board was now composed of twenty-four members: six Presbyterians, one Episcopalian, one Dutch Reformed, and sixteen Congregationalists.[1]

There were differences of opinion among Presbyterians as to the advisability of this policy of cooperation with the Congregationalists in foreign missons. In the first place, there were various missionary societies in which Presbyterians were already cooperating. To be sure, most of those were home mission enterprises, although the American Indians beyond the boundaries of the States at that time were included in their purview. In 1802 the General Assembly had constituted a Standing Committee on Missions. This Standing Committee served for a number of years with such success that in 1816 they recommended to the General Assembly that it create a more permanent organization to be known as "the Board of Missions acting under the authorization of the General Assembly of the Presbyterian Church in the U.S." This was done but the next year (1817) the General Assembly joined the Dutch Reformed and Associate Reformed Churches in forming the United Foreign Missionary Society. This society operated for nearly ten years but on July 3, 1826 voted "that the missionary stations, papers, books and property of the United Foreign Missionary Society be forthwith transferred to the American Board of Commissioners for Foreign Missions." The historian of the Presbyterian Board explains this action in these words:

---

[1] The list included:
John Jay, Episcopalian, former Chief Justice of the Supreme Court of the United States; Egbert Benson, Dutch Reformed, Presiding Judge of the Circuit Court of the U.S., New York; Elias Boudinot, Presbyterian, former President of the Congress of the U.S.; Rev. Ashbel Green, Presbyterian, President of Princeton College, New Jersey; Rev. Samuel Miller, Presbyterian, Professor in Theological Seminary, Princeton, New Jersey; Rev. Eliphalet Nott, Presbyterian, President of Union College, Schenectady, New York; Robert Ralston, Presbyterian, of Philadelphia; Rev. James Richards, Presbyterian, Professor in Auburn Theological Seminary. The sixteen Congregationalists were: *Ministers:* Calvin Chapin and Timothy Dwight (President of Yale College) of Connecticut; Seth Payson of New Hampshire; Joseph Lyman, Jedidiah Morse, Samuel Spring, Samuel Worcester of Massachusetts; Henry Davis (President of Middlebury College) of Vermont. *Laymen:* General Huntington, John Treadwell (former Governor) of Connecticut; John Langdon (former Governor) of New Hampshire; John Hooker, William Phillips (former Lieutenant Governor), William Bartlett, Jeremiah Evarts, of Massachusetts; William Jones (former Governor) of Rhode Island. See AR, 1812, p. 37.

> In view of the enlarging operations and popularity of the American Board of Commissioners for Foreign Missions, the opinion began to be expressed that it was unwise to perpetuate two societies which were appealing to the same constituency and that the cause which both had at heart would be strengthened by a merger.[1]

But some Presbyterians felt that an important principle was at stake. The American Board was a non-ecclesiastical, self-perpetuating, incorporated body of individuals interested in foreign missions. No recognition of the evangelistic passion, breadth of vision and irenic spirit of the body could conceal the fact that the American Board was not an integral and official part of any branch of the Christian Church. Some Presbyterians insisted that foreign missions be conducted by the Church through a regularly established and officially recognized and controlled agency. Repeated efforts on their part to secure the formation of a church board of foreign missions failed.

In 1826 when the United Foreign Missionary Society transferred all its work and responsibilities to the American Board, it was proposed that the General Assembly recognize the American Board as a "national institution." The General Assembly chose not to do this but to commend the American "Board to the favorable notice and Christian support of the Church and people under their care." In 1831 Presbyterian supporters of the American Board through a lengthy committee report "recommended that the General Assembly commit itself to official cooperation with the American Board and refrain from appointing a board of its own." Again the General Assembly contented itself with the statement "that while the Assembly would express no opinion in relation to the principles contained in the report, they cordially recommend the ABCFM to the affection and patronage of their churches."[2]

The advocates of the church board principle turned immediately to the Presbyterian Synod of Pittsburgh. This Synod

[1] A. J. Brown, *One Hundred Years*, (New York, Revell, 1936), p. 16.
[2] Brown, *op. cit.*, p. 21.

responded by constituting on October 3, 1831 the Western Foreign Missionary Society. The circular letter which was sent by the Society to all Presbyterian churches began with this sentence: "The Society did not originate in any feeling of jealousy or dissatisfaction with the American Board . . . , or in any desire to diminish its resources or impair that measure of public confidence which it certainly and justly enjoys."

This Society represented a considerable body of Presbyterians who earnestly believed in the church board principle. An undenominational, autonomous foreign mission board simply did not satisfy them. They brought the issue before the General Assembly again in 1834 and again were disappointed. In 1835 the issue appeared on the agenda of the General Assembly in the form of a notable memorial called "An Act and Testimony." This memorial proposed that "the Western Foreign Missionary Society should receive the countenance, as it appears to merit the confidence of those who cherish an attachment to the doctrines and order of the Church to which we belong."[1] The Assembly was moved by this memorial and acted favorably by appointing a committee to carry forward negotiations on its behalf with the Synod of Pittsburgh. In 1836 the Committee reported on the terms of agreement which the Synod had accepted. Their report was referred to another committee of the Assembly which at a later session recommended ratification. One member, however, submitted a minority report which read as follows: "Whereas, the American Board of Commissioners for Foreign Missions has been connected with the Presbyterian Church from the year of its incorporation, by the very elements of its existence; and whereas, at the present time, the majority of the whole of that Board are Presbyterians; and whereas, as it is undesirable, in conducting the work of Foreign Missions, that there should be any collision at home or abroad; therefore, Resolved, That it is inexpedient that the Assembly should organize a separate foreign missionary institution."[2]

[1] Brown, *op. cit.*, p. 30.
[2] Brown, *op. cit.*, p. 31.

After prolonged, lively discussion the minority report was adopted by a very close vote — 110 to 106. The advocates of the church board principle were astounded, dismayed but not convinced. Their next move followed in a fortnight. They called a conference of their sympathizers and the directors of the Western Foreign Missionary Society in Philadelphia to consider a statement drafted by the Secretary of the Society, Rev. Elisha P. Swift. The 4,000 word statement took its stand on the duty of the Church as such. It disclaimed the charge that their attitude implied lack of confidence in the American Board. The statement was approved and widely distributed. It won powerful new support. The Society moved its headquarters from Pittsburgh to New York, as it were in anticipation of the vote (108 to 29) of the General Assembly on June 7, 1837, to "superintend and conduct, by its own proper authority, the work of Foreign Missions of the Presbyterian Church."

The immediate sequel of this action should be given in the words of the historian of the Presbyterian Board:

> Unfortunately, the Board, while having the full sanction of the General Assembly, did not have the support of a united church. Synods and presbyteries and many churches which had been affiliated with the American Board transferred their support to the Presbyterian Board; but some churches and individual Presbyterians continued to adhere to the American Board to which they had become attached by long association and from which they were unwilling to withdraw.
>
> Moreover, within less than a year after the organization of the Presbyterian Board, a theological controversy, which had long been brewing between conservative and liberal Presbyterians, rent the Church in twain, and in 1838 the schism resulted in which were henceforth known as Old School and New School Presbyterian Churches. The Old School Church retained the Board of Foreign Missions and the New School Church thereupon affiliated with the American Board.[1]

[1] Brown, *op. cit.*, p. 41.

The "New School Church" of the Presbyterians continued its affiliation with the American Board until 1870 when theological controversy had faded, denominational loyalties had grown much stronger, and the "official board principle" had prevailed.[1]

The union of the New School and Old School Presbyterian churches in 1870 quite naturally led to united support of the official Board of Foreign Missions sustained since 1839 by the Old School churches. The American Board immediately entered into negotiations for the transfer of certain missions to the Presbyterian Board. The Seneca and Ojibwa Indian Missions in the United States, the Gaboon Mission in Africa, and the Syria and Persia Missions in the Near East were added to the responsibilities of the Presbyterian Board. Terms of transfer were most amicably discussed and arranged. All Presbyterians serving as missionaries of the American Board were given the opportunity of continuing or of transferring to the administration of the Presbyterian Board. Not many outside the Gaboon, Syria and Persia Missions withdrew.

At the annual meeting of the American Board in 1870 at Brooklyn, N. Y., Secretary Treat on behalf of the Prudential Committee presented a paper entitled "The Undenominational Character of the Board." In this paper he briefly sketched the history of Congregational-Presbyterian cooperation in the foreign missionary enterprise. He stressed the fact that the Board remembered its predecessors and missionaries "as soldiers of Christ, with little thought of the banners under which they marched." "The Committee takes pleasure in saying," he continued, "that cooperation abroad has been as easy and as pleasant for them as cooperation at home. Avoiding all interference with questions purely ecclesiastical, asking only that the Gospel of Christ be preached zealously and faithfully, within the range of that liberty which is recognized by our constituency, and permitting missionaries to organize churches

[1] It should be noted that the debate between the advocates of the "church board" principle and the proponents of the "voluntary society" principle has an extensive background, especially in England, Scandinavia and other countries in northern Europe. The debate has not yet ceased to interest some member churches of the World Council of Churches.

according to their own convictions of duty in the circumstances, we have experienced in this line of things no embarrassment whatever. Questions purely missionary have, indeed, taxed our wisdom to the utmost; but other questions have seemed uniformly to admit of a ready solution."[1]

There followed in Secretary Treat's paper the nine specific resolutions submitted by the Prudential Committee to the Board for consideration regarding the withdrawal of the New School Presbyterians from the American Board. In approving these resolutions the Board added a series of six resolutions among which the following sentences are worthy of special note:

> Resolved, That notwithstanding the change now taking place, this Board, in its spirit, its appointments, and its administration, will adhere to its time-honored basis of undenominational catholicity; and will maintain, without discrimination, all the missionaries who shall continue in its service; according to the fundamental declaration of its charter, that the American Board of Commissioners for Foreign Missions exists "for the purpose of propagating the Gospel in heathen lands, by supporting missionaries and diffusing a knowledge of the Holy Scriptures."
>
> Resolved, That notwithstanding the determination of the Presbyterian Church, in its organic character, to prosecute the work of missions through a Board of its own creation, this Board, being founded upon the principle of voluntary cooperation in the work of Christ, still desires and hopes to retain in its membership the individual members of that church who do not find in their own circumstances, feelings, or preferences, a reason for withdrawing their personal cooperation.[2]

To this day the American Board has continued to appoint as missionaries qualified Presbyterians desiring to serve in American Board fields. In other respects, also, both formal and informal, personal and collective, cooperation has characterized the relations of the two boards since 1871.

[1] AR, 1870, pp. xxi, xxii.
[2] *Ibid*, p. xxvi.

The Reformed Church in America (Dutch Reformed) and Congregationalists

In 1817 the Dutch Reformed and Associate Reformed Churches united with New York Presbyterians in forming the United Foreign Missionary Society. In 1826 this Society, as has been related,[1] voted to merge with the American Board. Thus began a happy relationship between Congregationalists and members of the sturdy Dutch Reformed Churches.

This relationship assumed the form of a "compact" in 1832. Up to that time the Board had sustained precisely the same relationship to the Dutch Reformed Church as it sustained to Presbyterian and Congregational bodies. Nine members of that church were among the corporate members of the Board. A distinguished lay member, Hon. Stephen van Rensselaer, LL.D., Lieutenant Governor of New York State in 1801, served as Vice President of the Board, 1826-1839. At least two of the members of that church had for years been missionaries of the Board, one of whom, Rev. David Abeel, explored mission fields in Indonesia and later was a pioneer of the Amoy Mission in China (1842).

The compact between the Board and the Dutch Reformed Church was unique in one respect. It provided, contrary to American Board practice elsewhere before or since, that the missionaries appointed from the Dutch Reformed Church would be at liberty to form separate missions "with an ecclesiastical organization and public worship according to their own views and wishes." These missions were to be in every respect subject to the administration of the Prudential Committee just as other missions of the Board. This Compact in effect meant that the Dutch Reformed Church employed the American Board as its "almoners and agents," as the records express it, "in conducting missions among the heathen; and at the same time, have the satisfaction of supporting missionaries from their own Church."[2]

---

[1] See above, p. 127.
[2] AR, 1857, p. 23.

Four missionaries from the Dutch Reformed Church were sent to Netherlands-India in 1836. Five others joined them within a few years. Much to their disappointment the government of Netherlands-India restricted missionary effort to Western Borneo, a field which proved most difficult and inhospitable. Disease and disaster led to the closing of the mission in 1849. The surviving missionaries were transferred to Amoy on the Coast of China where a Dutch Reformed Mission continued for a century more. In the meantime the Arcot Mission in an area just west of Madras was manned exclusively by missionaries of the Dutch Reformed Church, five of them children of Dr. and Mrs. John Scudder, American Board missionaries first in Ceylon, then in Madras. This Mission also had remarkable success.

In 1857 the General Synod of the Dutch Reformed Church through its Stated Clerk transmitted to the Prudential Committee a series of five resolutions spelling out in detail their reasons and desires in asking the Board to dissolve the Compact of 1832. The Dutch Reformed Church considered it "the duty of the Church in her distinctive capacity as such to take charge of" its missions. "In dissolving the pleasant and useful connection we have maintained for the last twenty-five years we are not influenced by any dissatisfaction with their [ABCFM] modes of action, or any want of fidelity on their part to the terms of this connection."[1]

In a most amicable spirit the American Board responded to this request and immediately asked the Prudential Committee to carry out the transfer of the Amoy and Arcot Missions to the new Board of Foreign Missions of the Dutch Reformed Church. The American Board, in its careful regard for correct administrative procedure stipulated only that the missionaries in those missions should individually request release from their obligation as missionaries of the American Board. Mission property in those missions was also transferred.

The association in foreign missions between these two church bodies had not proceeded without disagreements, but on the

[1] AR, 1857, p. 21

whole a high level of fellowship was maintained.[1] It should be recalled that from 1841 to 1857, the year of the dissolution of the Compact, Hon. Theodore Frelinghuysen, LL.D., a Dutch Reformed layman, had been president of the American Board. William Lloyd Garrison said of him: "No American layman of his time was associated with so many national organizations of religion and charity." He had been successively U. S. Attorney General, U. S. Senator, Chancellor of the University of the City of New York, and President of Rutgers College.

Congregationalists and Dutch Reformed folk ever since 1857 have looked back upon the quarter century of intimate co-operation in foreign missions with deep satisfaction. No two boards since that year have been more eager to embody the true ecumenical spirit.

The Reformed Church in the United States (German Reformed) and the American Board[2]

In 1793 the Coetus, the first judicatory of the German Reformed Church, was resolved into the Synod of the German Reformed Church in the United States of North America. By this action the Church became independent of the European synods which had nurtured it since 1751.

With the rise of missionary interest in American churches in the early nineteenth century, the new Synod constituted a "Board of Missions" in 1827. For several years the Board functioned as a promotional agency, developing "missionary intelligence and interest among ministers and people," though it performed no actual missionary work abroad. In 1834 the Susquehanna Classis asked the Synod through an annual meeting resolution "Whether the time is not at hand when the Reformed Church, instead of giving its contributions as heretofore to other churches for the spread of the Gospel among the heathen, should think of establishing an institution of its own

---

[1] See *Memorial Volume of the First Fifty Years of the American Board*, (Boston, published by the Board, 1862), pp. 90 ff.

[2] Information in this section has been derived largely from (1) *Fifty Years of Foreign Missions*, (Philadelphia, Board of Foreign Missions, 1927); (2) James I. Good, *Life of Benjamin Schneider*, (Philadelphia, Board of Foreign Missions, 1897).

for the purpose?" Three years later the Synod's Board of Missions "respectfully" asked the Synod "to engage in the work of foreign missions." The result of that recommendation was the decision in 1838 to "unite in the foreign missionary enterprise with the American Board." A Committee was appointed "to make such plans of cooperation as will promote the interests of all concerned." After agreeable negotiations terms of cooperation were drawn up and adopted.[1]

The Board of Missions of the German Reformed Church discovered that a son of that Church, Rev. Benjamin Schneider, had been appointed a missionary of the American Board in 1833 and sent to the Near East. Mr. Schneider had been born of Pennsylvania-German ancestry at New Hanover, January 18, 1807. He had been reared in the Reformed Church but had united with the Presbyterian Church when a student at Norristown, Pa. He had graduated from Amherst College in 1830 and from Andover Theological Seminary in 1833. After ordination as a Presbyterian minister and appointment by the American Board he and his wife had sailed from Boston and arrived in Constantinople in February 1834. He was assigned to Brousa, the first capital of the Ottoman Empire.

Upon learning these facts regarding Mr. and Mrs. Schneider the Synod requested that Mr. Schneider become a minister of the Reformed Church with the understanding that the Church would assume the support of the Mission at Brousa. This arrangement continued until 1849. It was in effect also at Aintab where Mr. Schneider served until 1866. He was a versatile, devoted pioneer. Rev. James I. Good has written his "Life," published by the Board of Foreign Missions in 1897. The German Reformed Church undertook work abroad under their own direction in 1866. Mr. and Mrs. Schneider remained with the American Board, serving in Turkey until 1875.

[1] From 1840 to 1865 Professor John W. Nevin, a professor in the German Reformed Theological Seminary at Mercersburg, Pennsylvania, was the representative of the Church on the American Board as a corporate member. Dr. R. Pierce Beaver, a member of the Evangelical and Reformed Church and an eminent church historian now on the Federated Theological Faculty of the University of Chicago, says of Professor Nevin: He was "the great father of the Mercersburg movement (in the German Reformed Church) — the most important native American contribution to ecumenical thinking in the nineteenth century."

It is of interest to note that the German Reformed Church and the Evangelical Synod with headquarters in St. Louis united in 1934 to form the Evangelical and Reformed Church. It is this group whose ruling body was united with the Congregational Christian General Council in 1957, to form the United Church of Christ. The American Board is the foreign mission society for the United Church of Christ — continuing its ministry of ecumenical outreach in behalf of varying traditions.

Other Churches

It would be appropriate to refer here to two other churches for whom the American Board has served as agent in overseas missions. From about 1880 to 1925 the Congregational Churches of Canada contributed both personnel and funds to the work of the American Board. Two distinguished Canadian missionaries were Dr. Alexander MacLachlan and Dr. Frederick W. MacCallum of the Near East missions of the Board. This cooperation ceased when the Congregational Churches of Canada became part of the United Church of Canada.

The full story of the Schwenckfelder churches of Pennsylvania would include some account of their support of American Board missions in China from 1904 to 1950. Miss Flora Heebner was their special representative from 1904 to 1942, succeeded by Miss Mabel H. Reiff.

At Seattle, Washington in 1931 the General Convention of Christian Churches and the National Council of Congregational Churches united to form the General Council of Congregational and Christian Churches. Shortly thereafter the Christian Foreign Missionary Society and the American Board united, the American Board acting in accordance with a vote of June 4, 1929 approving the Plan of Union. Japan being the only field overseas where the Christian Society was at work, the two missions in Japan became one with relevant action at the home base. Thus the names of several highly esteemed missionaries were added to the list of American Board personnel.

11

THE AMERICAN BOARD AND THE CONGREGATIONAL CHURCHES OF THE UNITED STATES OF AMERICA

The ecumenical outlook of the American Board, by and large, may be regarded as one fruit of the spirit of Congregationalism. Be that as it may, the Board has always been closely related to the Congregational Christian Churches of the United States. The meeting in Bradford, Massachusetts where the Board was born was a meeting of Congregational ministers. The Board's first missionaries were ordained Congregationalists and commissioned for missionary service in a Congregational church. Through the years the Board has leaned heavily — and primarily — on Congregational church folk for support. Most of the leadership of the Board has come from Congregational sources. Most of the candidates for missionary service have been Congregational young people.[1]

The relationships of the Board with Congregationalists have changed somewhat in the course of time. Several distinct periods may be detected or differentiated in a careful reading of the Board's history. It is the intention of the present chapter to note the various stages in the relationships which have prevailed through the years.

The first stage runs roughly from 1810 to 1870. It may be called the "creative period" for both the Board and the Congregational churches. During this time there was no national Congregational organization whose function was to promote the fellowship and mutual support of the churches. The lack was not keenly felt at first. From its inception the American Board had provided a sort of meeting-house for fellowship among the churches as a by-product of its function as an organization charged with missionary responsibilities. Meetings of

[1] But see Appendix V.

the Home Mission Societies served a similar function, though to lesser degree. The annual meetings of the Board came to be regarded widely as the chief event of the church year so far as Congregational affairs were concerned. Careful records of the attendance of corporate, corresponding and honorary members of the Board were kept for annual meetings. Attendances of 600 were not unusual, and the lists of names of members who made up those attendance figures were also impressive.[1] The time was one of great assemblies, and those of the Board were featured by a fellowship and sense of Christian service which was not quite equalled elsewhere.

As in later years, the officers and members of the Prudential Committee were extremely sensitive to the thought and will of the people in the churches giving it their support. Repeatedly one finds in the records of correspondence and executive action reference to the principle that the Board was under obligation to act in accordance with the expressed or implied mind and will of its supporting constituency. In reply to correspondence from missionaries regarding doctrinal or polity questions, the secretaries of the Board held — as they have in other periods also — that nothing basically inconsistent with the principles and practices of its sustaining constituency should be permitted or approved.

As the Board was eager to stay close to its supporters, so were the Congregational churches eager to stay close to the Board. Denominational meetings carried allusions to the Board — even when the principal business of the meetings was quite distant from American Board and foreign mission concern. The General Convention of Congregational Ministers and Delegates in the United States, held in Albany, New York, October 5-8, 1852, is a case in point. The main business of the Convention was to abrogate the Plan of Union in which Congregational and Presbyterian denominations had shared in the development of churches west of the Hudson River, and to strengthen

---

[1] For instance, at the sixty-first Annual Meeting held in Brooklyn, New York, October 4-7, 1870, 102 corporate members were present, 463 male honorary members were present together with a large company of visitors, men and women. Eighteen states were represented.

the Congregational churches which had developed "at the west." Though the Board is not mentioned directly, even at that meeting there was a resolution stressing "the utmost importance" of systematic support of "the great enterprises of Christian beneficence . . . when there is so much to be done for the salvation of our country and the diffusion of the Gospel throughout the world."[1]

Similarly at the Congregational Council meeting at Boston in 1865, called to consider issues growing out of the Civil War and "to take stock of the situation and plan for the future,"[2] a committee report recommended that the Council "as representatives of the churches," should testify to their deep sense of the importance of foreign missions, and their unabated devotion to the prosecution of the enterprise. "We need it for ourselves," the Council explained. "The work will die at home if it languishes abroad. It is the sign of our fellowship with Christ. It is the condition of his blessing. We need it in every sense, and for every reason." The Council rejected the idea of any new organization for foreign missions and pleaded for a more systematized plan for benevolence giving to the boards by the churches. It proclaimed the value of the Congregational conception of the Church, asserting that it is as well fitted to all latitudes and longitudes as to New England.

While serving for many years as the foreign mission society of some Presbyterian and Reformed churches, the Board was most closely related to Congregational Churches. It was natural that the Prudential Committee should vote at its meeting October 31, 1871, that "one of the secretaries [be named] to attend the National Congregational Council to be held at Oberlin, Ohio, November 15, in case the executive officers shall deem it advisable that one be present." Secretary Clark was appointed to attend the meeting.

That 1871 gathering was to bring to a close the first period of the history of the American Board's relationship with the

[1] *Proceedings of the General Convention of Congregational Ministers and Delegates in the United States*, (New York, S. W. Benedict, 1852), p. 26.
[2] G. G. Atkins and F. L. Fagley, *History of American Congregationalism*, (Boston, Pilgrim Press, 1942), p. 199.

Congregational Churches. More than 275 delegates from twenty-five states and territories gathered for the establishment of the National Council of Congregational Churches. Henceforth there would be a national headquarters for the Congregational Churches. Henceforth other meetings than those conducted by the American Board were to become all-important in the life of the denomination. Henceforth Congregationalism was a national fellowship independent of its boards, among them the foreign mission society which had been born a long sixty-one years before.

The year 1869 marked the beginning of the end of another kind of relationship for the American Board also. Under the aegis of the General Assembly of the Presbyterian Church, as we have seen, the breach between the "Old School" and the "New School" churches was healed. The reunion brought to the support of the Presbyterian Board of Foreign Missions most of the New School churches which had helped sustain the work of the American Board.

There was, of course, a basic connection between these two events. The connection lies in the upsurge of denominational consciousness characteristic of many Protestant churches in America during the middle of the nineteenth century. The churches based upon a congregational order as well as those episcopally or semi-episcopally organized began to feel their need for intensified fellowship and cooperation within their own denominational circles.

A Period of Adjustment 1871-1876

The changes of 1871 did not come without warning. At the sixty-first annual meeting of the Board, held in Brooklyn, New York, October 4-7, 1870, Secretary Treat's paper, to which reference has been made (p. 131), showed that the Board was fully aware of what was to come. Treat reviewed the purpose of the Board as a non-sectarian, non-ecclesiastical agency with singleness of purpose and loyalty to an ever-widening constituency. He could not conceal the fact that the "sundering of the tenderest ties is hard to bear. . . . The thought that churches which have stood shoulder to shoulder during so many years are now to separate, though it be from no lack of affection or confidence, is exceedingly painful." But he closes his paper with emphasis on two points. First, "Our denominational co-operation has not ceased," and second, "New responsibilities devolve upon the Congregational Churches." The new responsibilities were in essence, of course, the old ones — that "all the resources of the disciples of Christ may be brought out to meet the promise of His providence in the fulfillment of his last command."[1]

It was inevitable that the withdrawal of the major support of the New School Presbyterians should have various repercussions. The financial effects will be referred to elsewhere. The organizational effects gave the officers of the Board considerable concern. In the years immediately following the withdrawal, such questions as these were often raised: Was the basis on which the Board was founded (on the voluntary support of individuals) valid? Did the founders make a mistake in not more closely identifying the Board with the Congregational Churches? Should the Board become an ecclesiastical body or subject to the denomination? The debate, within the Prudential Committee and elsewhere, went on for years.

Meanwhile, the National Council of the Congregational Churches was meeting every three years. At all meetings American Board representatives were present, though voting privileges were not given them until 1901. The Council assumed some sort of claim on the Board, however, for in 1871 it defined the word "Congregational" to be "in the broad sense . . . inclusive of societies whose constituency and control are substantially congregational." It also appointed a committee on Consolidation of Missionary Societies while recommending to the churches "systematic and regular contributions" to them. That committee, reporting in 1874, declined to advise overall consolidation but recommended that the American Board

[1] AR, 1870, p. xxvii.

transfer its American Indian Missions to the American Missionary Association and that the latter body in turn transfer its work in Africa to the American Board. The transfers were made in 1883. The Committee also recommended consolidation of the Congregational missionary magazines.

In addition, in 1871 the Council voted to recommend to the churches that they should divert to the American Board funds which they had been sending to the American and Foreign Christian Union. As a consequence the Union, a society interested primarily in missions in papal lands, was disbanded and its work and assets transferred to the American Board. Fagley in his *History of American Congregationalism,* says that this was the first vote of the National Council "directly affecting the affairs of a missionary agency."[1]

The annual meeting in Chicago in October 1875 heard a paper by Secretary Treat entitled "The Organization of the American Board." It was an important matter. Things were happening in Congregationalism: state organizations, called conferences, were being organized and were growing in influence and responsibility. The National Council was developing a structure and authority. It seemed as though the American Board might have to come to terms with these forces. That would mean that its character as a self-perpetuating corporation of individuals who were sincerely and sacrificially interested in missions might be at stake. Treat reaffirmed the Board's independence.

"It was not a Massachusetts society . . . it was not a New England society. It was an American Society. Though born in the midst of Puritan memories, it was not a Congregational society . . . it was made so catholic, so undenominational, that with no lack of fidelity to its earliest constituency it could open its arms to all of like faith and purpose and labor with them. . . ."[2] He reaffirmed the nature of the Board as made up of interested individuals, bound together by a commanding evangelical concern. But he assured Congregationalists that the

[1] Atkins and Fagley, *op. cit.,* p. 308.
[2] AR, 1875, p. xvi.

Board had been progressively aware of the need, if not the demand, for closer fellowship with the churches as such. He underscored the importance of the honorary members of the Board, now more than 19,500 in number (all of them listed in the 1870 annual report), whose presence in Board deliberations gave the lie to charges that the Board was "an irresponsible corporation."

Secretary Treat then suggested practical ways in which the churches might be brought into still closer fellowship with the Board. A Committee of Seventeen which was appointed to consider Secretary Treat's paper and make recommendations reported some of the suggestions favorably; the active membership of the Board should be increased to 200, with a special effort made to include proportional representation from the western states. Though not very radical, the changes indicated that the Board was eager to adjust to the new reality of a national Congregationalism which more and more it regarded as its principal base of operation and support.

A Period of Experience with
Expanding Congregationalism 1876-1913

Beginning in 1876 there was for some years a lull in the discussion of the relation of the Board to the National Council and the Congregational Churches. It may have been that the denomination was in too great a state of flux and development to give much attention to such matters. Certainly Congregationalism was in a period of great expansion and change. During the years 1876 to 1913 the number of Congregational Churches grew from less than 4,000 to 6,096 and membership grew from approximately 350,000 to more than 750,000. Gifts for benevolences (including home and foreign missions) doubled in those years, to approach $2,400,000 in 1913, while gifts for local church expense rose from less than $4,000,000 to more than $10,000,000. During the same period also the number of State Congregational Conferences, some of them avowedly home missionary societies, some of them begun under home missionary auspices, rose sharply. Conferences were organized rapidly in the early years of the twentieth century: Wisconsin and Northern California in 1907, Michigan and Southern California in 1908, Nebraska and South Dakota in 1909, Kansas, Missouri, Illinois and Iowa in 1910, Rhode Island in 1911, and Washington, North Dakota and Colorado in 1912.

The National Council continued to meet every three years and from time to time called for reports from the national boards at its sessions, providing also for the circulation of printed statements by the boards. Occasionally, too, there were discussions on relations of boards and churches – though now the discussions were initiated by other groups than the boards themselves. In 1889 the Connecticut General Conference memorialized the National Council: "Though related to the Congregational Churches in every point of fact [the mission boards] are nevertheless wholly independent of them in law and management. . . . These facts not only discredit our polity but [also] threaten our peace."[1] This was an important memorial, and it had consequences.

In 1892 the National Council appointed a committee to study the relationship of the boards to the churches and another committee to consider the relationships of the various boards one to another. The committees were charged to report in 1895, and they did. They decided that the time was not ripe for radical reorganization and reported that any measures taken should "originate in the societies themselves and be such as commend themselves to those who have had long experience in the management of our affairs."[2] As a result of this position, the Council awaited action initiated by the boards. The churches, particularly those in the western states, were disappointed by the delay, and pressed for action. The result was that in 1907 a new committee was appointed by the Council, which reported in 1910 as follows:

[1] Atkins and Fagley, *op cit.*, p. 309.
[2] Minutes of National Council, 1895, p. 211.

> Resolved, that this council is in favor of developing administrative relations between the Council and the National Societies, that it believes the next step in such development consists in constituting the delegates of the Council the voting membership of the several societies with the addition of such members-at-large as may prove to be necessary, and that it refers the practical working out of those new relations to the Commission of Fifteen on Polity, . . . report to be made at the next regular or special or adjourned session of this Council.[1]

The Commission of Fifteen became the Commission of Nineteen which at last brought decisive action at the historic Kansas City National Council meeting in 1913. The American Board, prior to the Commission's report, addressed the Council in these words:

> Your committee rejoices in this attention which is being given to the administration of our denominational missionary work, feeling that the more churches can concern themselves in what all must regard as their leading interest, the better will they be able to perform their part in establishing Christ's kingdom in the earth. As in the past, the Board on its own account has from time to time sought to bring itself into closer relations to the churches, so now that the matter has, in a measure, been taken out of our hands and thrown into the arena of general denominational debate, the members of the Prudential Committee and the officers of the Board, speaking for themselves, stand ready to favor such further changes as the churches may desire, in so far as these changes are found to be legal and practicable.[2]

The Council adopted two major recommendations of the Commission of Nineteen, both of which affected the boards and the churches through the National Council and directly. By one recommendation voting delegates to the meetings of the National Council were to become ipso facto voting mem-

[1] Atkins and Fagley, *op cit.*, p. 315.
[2] Minutes of the National Council, 1913, pp. 102, 103.

bers — that is, corporate members — of the boards. Thus a large proportion of the membership of the boards was chosen by the churches, not by the boards, and the memberships of the National Council and of the boards became in large measure identical. By the other recommendation the work of the boards was to be conducted under the "advisory supervision" of a Commission on Missions which the National Council would appoint. Thus the boards were to be brought into direct relation with the Council at the level of board activity as well as at the level of constitutional membership.

There was some feeling at the time that the word "Congregational" ought somehow to be inserted in the American Board's name. To this feeling there was understandable opposition. The opposition was based on the fact of the Board's ecumenical outlook and history and on the fact that to change the name of the Board at home would vastly complicate financial operations abroad. One would like to believe also that some prophetic souls foresaw the day when the intensity of denominational lines would soften and the earlier vision of a truly ecumenical world mission should again dominate the disciples of our One Lord.

A Period of Experimental Integration 1913-1936

A careful review of the discussions and actions regarding relationships between boards, churches and National Council during the period 1913-1936 should focus on the basic problem for which a solution was earnestly sought: HOW — by what cooperative agreements and arrangements can autonomous churches and autonomous national boards carry forward efficiently and harmoniously their common missionary obligations without denying essential Congregationalism for which both the independence of the local church and the fellowship of the churches are central principles?

The period 1913-1936 was a period of intensive, sometimes painful, experiments in attempting to find a satisfactory solution for this problem in cooperative democracy. Dr. Fagley devotes twenty pages to a detailed examination of these experiments during the first half of this period.[1] The primary sources for the study are, naturally, the voluminous records of the meetings, committees and commissions of the National Council and the equally voluminous records of the national boards and state conferences. In Congregational fashion the results of studies by committees and commissions were brought to the attention of the representative Congregational body — the National Council. That Council made its recommendations to the churches and state conferences and national boards, leaving the practical operation to the appropriate bodies.

There is one term which emerges in all these discussions of of the basic problem which has connoted the deepest desire of the churches — *unified* promotion.[2] It became apparent after 1913 that the churches and state conferences did not seriously propose to control the board's work administratively. The boards over their long history had won and were clearly enjoying the confidence of the churches as far as their mission field operations were concerned. What the churches really sought was the elimination of unseemly competition and the multiplicity of appeals for funds with which the field work could be successfully carried on. They wanted some systematic and realistic cooperation among the boards in presenting their needs to the churches.

The Commission on Missions was the first serious device which it was hoped would assure unified promotion — that is, the securing of income cooperatively. That Commission, set up as we have seen by the National Council in 1913, operated until 1936. Judged by the results of its efforts, it was only partially successful. The main flaw in the plan as it was tried out was that the secretary of the National Council as the secretary of the Commission became overburdened with its work and from the point of view of the autonomous boards carried an unwelcome semblance of centralized authority into

[1] Atkins and Fagley, *op. cit.*, pp. 320-339.

[2] A variant, though largely unacceptable variant of that term is *united* promotion — a distinction not without a difference in Congregational usage.

board administrative circles. A minor flaw was that the Commission on Missions tried to function both as judge and as advocate regarding the financial needs of the boards. As a result, in 1925 the Commission on Missions was made the organ of the boards rather than of the National Council and its functions limited strictly to missionary education and promotion. Even this readjustment was found unsatisfactory with the result that in 1936 the Commission on Missions gave way to the Missions Council, a body entirely subject to the boards in the work of unified missionary education and promotion.

Under the aegis of the Commission on Missions both during the period 1913-1925 when it was primarily an instrument of the National Council and during the period 1925-1936 when it was more specifically an instrument of the boards collectively, the record of giving to the national boards and state conferences does not show the results that were anticipated. The most that the Commission on Missions could say in 1927 was "the Commission records with gratification the fact that in these years of re-organization the treasuries of the societies have not suffered from decreases."[1] It was the dream of those who sponsored unified promotion that there would be greater enthusiasm and more sacrificial giving if the outreach of the churches beyond their own parishes could be systematically presented as one organically related enterprise, free from competitive enthusiasms and practices, wisely administered by a representative centralized "Commission." The comparative failure of plans during the first period of integration may be traced to two basic facts: First, no one of the boards, least of all perhaps the American Board, could quickly divest itself of its heritage as a body of people for whom missions in some very concrete form were a preferred interest. The theory that *all* the people in *all* the churches would take an interest in and generously support the work of *every* board remained a theory — beautiful in conception but disappointing in practice. Second, the essential genius of Congregationalism showed itself

[1] Minutes of the National Council, 1927, p. 45.

in church after church, state conference after state conference
during this period in the form of more or less unwillingness to
be coerced or regimented in the matter of benevolence giving.
There was evident a spirit of resistance, rising to revolt in
some cases, against the method of centralized control characteristic of the early stages of the unified promotion process.

However, great progress was made, it must be said, in this
period of intensive experiment, 1913-1936. There was now no
doubt whatsoever that the churches and the boards were
working toward a common end.

A Period of Intimate Cooperation 1936-1956

As the responsible administrative committees of the Home
Boards and the American Board "took stock" at the conclusion
of the Mt. Holyoke College meeting of the National Council in
1936, the lessons of the previous experimental period of integration, 1913-1936, were vividly in the minds of "the veterans"
on these committees. They knew more about how to proceed
than "the innovators" of 1913.

First, the dominant desire of the churches in pleading for a
closer relationship between national boards, churches and state
conferences stemmed more, in fact almost entirely, from resentment against multiple, even competitive, appeals for funds
rather than from dissatisfaction with the administration of the
field work, that is, the real work of these boards. The device
by which in 1913 the delegates to the National Council were
nominated as voting members of the home and foreign boards
apparently satisfied those who craved a voice in board administration. At any rate, across the years no crisis involving
recommendations for changes at this point arose. Compara-
tively few "delegate corporate members" of the American
Board attended the annual meetings of the Board in alternate
years. The corporate members-at-large, nominated and elected
by the Board, carried on as before.

Second, it was recognized by all informed members of the
administrative committees that unified promotion as a process

must be worked out by the boards themselves, not by the National Council. This fact of experience echoed the voice of historic Congregationalism. The boards actually though not formally resented legislation by the National Council. It was clear, however, that unified promotion must be a major concern of the boards. The churches had long felt the need for more sensible and effective cooperation by the national boards in presenting their needs to their common, growing constituency. The action of the home boards in devolving upon the state conferences a great deal of their work in states where the conferences had become self-supporting made state conference officials "promotion conscious," thereby underscoring the desire for thorough-going unified promotion.

Third, the General Secretary of the General (formerly National) Council, Dr. Charles Emerson Burton, whose experience with these matters was unexcelled, succinctly expressed in 1936 the thoughts of many who had doubted the wisdom of the set-up of the Commission on Missions in 1913. He said at Mt. Holyoke:

> The Commission on Missions is a creature of the General Council, which draws together the membership of the responsible Boards for the purpose of unifying promotion. The members of the Boards have constituted nearly ninety percent of the Commission on Missions membership. Its meetings are therefore practically joint meetings of the Boards, nevertheless the Commission on Missions is technically an outside agency, and the Secretary of the General Council is its General Secretary. This set up has dulled somewhat the sense of responsibility of the Boards for the Commission and their feeling of dependence upon it for promotional effectiveness.[1]

And so it came about that the Commission on Missions was replaced by the Missions Council, an unincorporated body made up of the Prudential Committee of the American Board, the Directors of the Board of Home Missions, and the Directors

[1] Atkins and Fagley, *op. cit.*, p. 336.

of the Council for Social Education and Action. This body directed the work of a large joint staff, employed to promote missionary education and support in Congregational Christian Churches in the United States.

With the organization of the Missions Council there was relatively little change in organization but a significant change in attitude. The Boards were now cooperatively responsible for all plans involving missionary education and promotion. They could proceed with their plans for unified promotion under their own impetus with their own Joint Staff. On one important point they were happy to have the continued co-operation of the Executive Committee of the General Council. It was remembered that the Commission on Missions had a two-fold function, first, annual survey and appraisal of the needs of the boards, and second, educational and promotional operations. The first of these functions was left by common consent with a sub-committee of the Executive Committee of the General Council.

One happy feature of the whole subject of the relationship of the boards and the churches during the period 1936 to 1956 has been the growing importance of "the Midwinter Meeting." This meeting has quite a history. It began with the state conference superintendents. As state conferences were organized and undertook heavier responsibilities year by year, their executives felt the need of common counsel. They found the month of January the most convenient time to assemble for unhurried conference. This meeting became a focal center for the Commission on Missions year by year. It steadily grew as related bodies planned to meet at the same time and place annually. Programs for the sessions were carefully coordinated. The core of the meeting was the membership of the Commission on Missions (after 1936, the Missions Council). The other related bodies that found it desirable to meet with the Midwinter Meeting were in addition to the state conference superintendents, the State Women Presidents' Fellowship, the Laymen's Fellowship, the Executive Committee of the General Council, and occasionally other bodies. The Midwinter Meeting assumed the character of a general staff meeting, planning not only operations for the coming year but also long range projects. In spite of a certain unwieldiness due to increased numbers, probably no single device has meant more than the annual Midwinter Meeting to lift morale, to deepen commitment to common tasks and to project wise plans for the entire Christian World Mission of the Congregational Christian Churches.

It would be foolish to imply that the relationships between the American Board and the Congregational Christian Churches will evolve no further. With the development of the United Church of Christ undoubtedly further changes will take place and newer schemes devised. But through the years one goal has been attained: the Churches and the American Board have found their way together, each recognizing the essential role of the other in carrying forward the cause of the Kingdom, and realizing that they must lend each other their mutual support.

12

THE WOMAN'S BOARDS — THEIR VISION
AND STRENGTH

By and large it can be said that the relation of the women of the churches to the World Mission of the Church passed through three phases from 1810 to the present. First, women were in the background, devoted but relatively silent, 1810-1868. Second, women demonstrated their ability, their devotion being unquestioned, 1868-1927. Third, women took their rightful place in the total fellowship of the churches, 1927 to date.

The interest of women in missions antedated the founding of the American Board by several years. In 1801 Congregational women had started "The Boston Female Society for Propagating the Diffusion of Christian Knowledge." In 1802 many "Female Cent Societies" were organized in churches for the purpose of giving one cent a week to missions. With the founding of the American Board the gifts of Congregational women helped to support the first missionary efforts of the new society. The first legacy assigned to the Board was found in the will of Mrs. Mary Norris of Salem, Mass., who died in 1811. The court confirmed the gift in 1815 when it amounted to $27,527.19 but provided that this sum should be put at interest until it amounted to $30,000, the figure mentioned in the will. Then it was sent to the American Board to be "kept as a permanent fund for promoting the objects of the Board."[1]

The second legacy to come to the Board was also from a woman — Miss Sally Thomas, a household servant at Cornish, New Hampshire. She had saved $500 which she gave for foreign missions. Her legacy was the first actually to be received by the Board.

[1] Joseph Tracey, *History of the ABCFM,* (New York, M. W. Dodd, 1842), p. 55.

Societies of women were associated with the American Board from the year 1813. Turn to the "pecuniary accounts of the Board" as reported, for instance, in the 1814 annual report. One finds there the names of scores of "Female Foreign Missions Societies" and "Female Cent Societies" which made contributions to the Board's treasury that year.[1]

By 1818 there were more than 250 local "missionary associations" in which women had a part, and by 1839 not fewer than 680 "ladies' associations" were at work with approximately 3,000 local agents collecting funds for foreign missions.

Though in the early days the American Board thought that single women should not be sent out as missionaries, there were some notable exceptions. Miss Judith Chase of Cornish, New Hampshire was appointed in 1818 to serve as a school mistress among the Cherokee Indians. She was the first unmarried woman to receive Board appointment, though not given missionary status.[2]

In 1823 Miss Betsy Stockton of Princeton, New Jersey, a colored woman qualified as a teacher, was sent with a group of missionaries to the Sandwich Islands. She had been a member of the household of President Ashbel Greene of Princeton College, an influential Presbyterian, a corporate member of the American Board. Her status in the Mission was that of a "domestic assistant" but she served so acceptably as a teacher that her domestic labors were secondary. She was the first unmarried woman sent overseas by the Board.

Miss Cynthia Farrar of Marlboro, New Hampshire, arrived at Bombay in December 1827, appointed by the Board to act as the "Superintendent of Female Schools." She served most helpfully until her death in 1862, having taken but one furlough in the United States during her thirty-five years on the field. In this case the Board had been encouraged to make this appointment when it learned of the success of English women missionaries in Bengal.[3]

---

[1] AR, 1814, pp. 46-49.
[2] But see below, p. 183.
[3] AR, 1827, pp. 28, 29.

By 1848 thirty-six single women were on the field, twenty-four of them in the American Indian Missions. In 1861 a compilation of names for the Board's Memorial Volume indicated that 140 single ladies had served the Board in one capacity or another since 1810. In 1868, the year of the founding of the Woman's Board of Missions, there were forty-three single women in mission service, seven in Western Turkey, four in Central Turkey, eight in Eastern Turkey, three in Syria, four in the Nestorian Mission (Persia), two in the Zulu Mission (South Africa), four in the Madura Mission (India), one in Foochow, South China, and three in North China, three in the Sandwich Islands and one among the American Indians. Eleven of the forty-three women were from the midwestern states.[1]

The growth in numbers of women missionaries reflected a development in Board thinking. Letters from the wives of missionaries in various parts of the world revealed the degradation and deprivations of native women and girls in non-Christian cultures. Even some letters from male missionaries described in fearful detail the low estate of non-Christian women. It became apparent that the missionary enterprise should initiate special activities among non-Christian women, and for that sort of effort women missionaries would be needed. Further, such work would enrich the missionary enterprise generally. Rev. David Abeel, a missionary in China, wrote in 1830 that the slow progress of mission endeavor in China was due in large part to the lack of Christian work among Chinese women.[2] In similar vein Mrs. Miron Winslow of Ceylon pointed out that "woman is the great hindrance to the conversion of men."[3]

When David Abeel returned to the United States because of ill health he came home by way of England, and spoke before women's groups in that country, telling them of his experiences

---

[1] Missionary Papers, (in American Board archives), December 3, 1868 — taken from an address by Dr. N. G. Clark, home secretary of the American Board. The same address reported that the American Board had more single women on its mission fields than the ten other mission societies in the United States and Great Britain combined.
[2] Grace T. Davis, *Neighbors in Christ*, (Chicago, James Watson & Co., 1926), p. 4.
[3] Kate G. Lamson, Manuscript in Board archives, p. 10.

and the civilization he had left behind. His efforts led to the formation among English women of the "Society for Promoting Female Education in the East" and of other kindred organizations. When Mr. Abeel reached America he made a similar appeal. As the result the "Woman's Union Missionary Society of New York" was organized in 1861 under the leadership of Mrs. Thomas C. Doremus.[1] This Society set some denominations thinking about woman's work for women, notably the Southern Baptist and the Congregational.[2] Seven years later that thinking — among Congregationalists at least — resulted in action, as we shall now see.

The Founding of the Woman's Boards

The secret of success in any cause is to be found in some individual who is on fire with an idea and a program. In the case of the Woman's Board of Missions of Boston that person was Mrs. Albert Bowker of Charlestown, Mass. Mrs. Bowker's parents and grandparents were God-fearing, mission-minded folk. She had been told that her grandmother used to rise in the night to pray for the salvation of the heathen. She knew also of what was going on under the leadership of women like Susan B. Anthony and Julia Ward Howe. She was aware that Mary Lyon at Ipswich, later at Mount Holyoke College, was demonstrating the ability of young women to climb the ladder of learning.

Mrs. Bowker came to Secretary Clark to plant her ideas and to urge that something be done to encourage women in missionary endeavor. Under date of April 19, 1867 he wrote her a letter suggesting a plan. She built on this plan and arranged for a meeting of women which was held January 2, 1868 in the

---

[1] The report of this society in 1868 stated: "The Woman's Union Missionary Society is a voluntary association of Christian ladies of all Evangelical denominations. . . . It was organized in view of the increasing demand for the labor which could only be performed on mission ground by single women. Its operations have been conducted entirely by ladies who freely give their services. The Society has employed twenty missionaries in eight stations; eighty Bible-women in all parts of the world; has established a Normal School for training native teachers; opened twenty-five schools for girls. . . . The new department of mission labor called zenana work, where women of high caste in India are taught in their own homes, has occupied the main efforts of the Society." (Missionary Papers, December 3, 1868, p. 2).

[2] Cox, Ethelene Boone, *Following in His Train*, (Nashville, Tenn., Boardman Press, 1938, 1948), pp. 41, 42.

chapel of Old South Church at Freeman Place in Boston. With imagination one can appreciate how carefully Mrs. Bowker had prepared for this gathering of women from as many communities in Eastern Massachusetts as she could reach.

Mrs. Homer Bartlett, wife of a Boston manufacturer, who later became treasurer, was asked to preside. She called on Mrs. Bowker for "detailed information" as to the purpose of the meeting. Then Mrs. Bartlett read several letters from missionary women, all emphasizing "the greatness of the opportunity that awaits Christian women in the foreign field." Two resolutions followed a period of discussion. Mrs. William Butler, a Methodist missionary from India, spoke. Two committees were appointed, one to consult with the officers of the American Board, the other to draft a constitution for a new woman's foreign missionary society. The wife of Secretary Rufus Anderson and the wife of Secretary N. G. Clark were members of the Committee on Constitution.

At the second meeting held a few days later, the report of the Committee on the Constitution was discussed and adopted, officers were elected, and far-reaching plans were made. Mrs. Bowker was elected president of the new society, Mrs. Miron Winslow and Mrs. H. M. Scudder, both of whom had seen service as missionaries, the one in Ceylon, the other in India, were elected corresponding secretaries. Thirteen women were chosen as "managers," and cleverly enough, ten men and one woman were elected as "Honorary Directors."

The new Board held its first meeting February 2, 1868 at the home of Mrs. Alpheus Hardy. Mr. Hardy was a prominent member of the Prudential Committee of the American Board. The most important administrative decision made at this first meeting was the eminently practical one to secure funds before voting appropriations. This item proved to be a widely heralded and much admired principle of action throughout the history of the W.B.M. Another important action at the first meeting was the "adoption" — the promise to give full financial support — of Mrs. Mary K. Edwards of the Zulu Mission. She was the heart and soul of what came to be Inanda Seminary, the first and one of the most successful boarding schools for girls in all Africa.

The second missionary to be adopted was Miss Mary Andrews of Tungchow, China and the third, Miss Olive L. Parmelee of Mardin, Turkey. These appointments were made March 9, 1868. Responsibilities undertaken abroad must be underwritten at home. A letter was addressed to the women of the churches of New England suggesting the organization in each church of a group to keep in touch with and send funds to the W.B.M. treasury. "Mission Bands" for children in the parishes were proposed. Suitable literature was projected. Frequent consultation with the officers of the American Board was taken for granted. It was noted that a sister organization had come into existence, the Women's Board of Missions of the Interior, with headquarters in Chicago. The "home base" of each board was defined. The W.B.M. was to operate in the states east of Ohio, the W.B.M.I. in the Midwestern States.

The W.B.M.I. had its beginnings in an even more stirring atmosphere than the W.B.M. A group of Congregational and Presbyterian women led by Mrs. Samuel C. Bartlett, wife of a professor at the recently organized Chicago Theological Seminary, took advantage of the presence of Secretary N. G. Clark on a visit in Chicago to call a meeting October 27, 1868 in the lecture room of the Second Presbyterian Church. Apparently Dr. Clark had been well conditioned by his dealings with the ladies of the W.B.M. In his address at the meeting he had nothing but encouragement for the ladies at Chicago but he did not fail to point out the aspects of the project of the Woman's Boards which gave rise to some questions as to the administration of their mission work.

The W.B.M.I., after appropriate organization, chose Miss Mary H. Porter as their first missionary. She was just about to sail for service at Peking in North China.

The Woman's Boards of Missions devised effective ways to win and hold the interest of thousands of women in the Congregational churches across America. It was the desire and practice of these Boards to appeal to the deepest Christian motives in their efforts to bring light and joy into the lives of their sisters overseas.

Notable and effective use was made of "The Covenant." The idea originated with the leaders of The Woman's Board of Missions of the Interior. It was the custom to hold regularly on Friday morning at W.B.M.I. headquarters a prayer meeting at which "The Hymn of the Covenant," composed by Mrs. G. B. Wilcox was sung. Following this "The Pledge of the Covenant," written by Mrs. Moses Smith, was recited. Groups of young women were organized in many churches as "Daughters of the Covenant." A beautiful, decorated scroll suitable for framing was prepared and distributed.

The words of "The Covenant" are these:

> Grateful that "I know that my Redeemer liveth" —
> Mindful that vast millions of women and girls can never hear the "tidings of great joy" unless a Christian woman can be sent to them —
> Remembering that Jesus made loving obedience the supreme test of discipleship, and that His last most solemn command was "Go teach all nations" —
> I glady enter into this covenant of obedience, that I will not cease to make offerings of Prayer, Time and Money to the end that the daughters of sorrow in Christless lands may know the love of Jesus.

The "great open spaces" in the western United States were obviously missionary territory during the second half of the nineteenth century. Pioneer work was the order of the day in the Pacific States. But devoted women in the few Congregational churches of California, most of them with the background of birth and experience in the eastern states, were moved by the same forces, including vision and courage, that had resulted in the organization of the two woman's boards based in Boston and in Chicago. In 1873 a small group of these women met in Santa Cruz and organized the Woman's

Board of Missions of the Pacific. They elected Mrs. Andrew Stone of San Francisco president, and assumed the support of Mrs. David Watkins who had recently gone with her husband, Rev. David Watkins, to Guadalajara, Mexico. Mr. Watkins was one of the three students of the first class graduated in 1872 from Pacific Theological Seminary in Oakland (now Pacific School of Religion, Berkeley, California). The W.B.M.P. planned also to share in the support of two schools for girls in the Orient.

Three women meriting special honor in connection with the organization and growth of the W.B.M.P. were Mrs. J. K. McLean, wife of the pastor of the First Congregational Church of Oakland, who served as the second president, Mrs. H. E. Jewett, who served as the fourth president for ten years and then for many years as secretary of the California Branch, and Mrs. R. E. Cole, who was the faithful treasurer for twenty years.

Principles of Administration

One cannot help being impressed with the systematic and thorough fashion in which the W.B.M. women launched their foreign missionary enterprise. They immediately set about securing funds from an informed constituency, forming "auxiliaries" wherever there were interested women — hopefully in each church. "Branches" were formed of a convenient number of auxiliaries in a designated area. The auxiliaries and branches as autonomous bodies were encouraged to exercise their ingenuity in all aspects of their work. It was not a matter simply of raising funds. The call for volunteers, single women, to go overseas after suitable training made the enterprise unusually exciting. The letters received from missionaries supported by various auxiliaries and branches personalized the whole effort and multiplied the gifts which poured through the local and general treasury. The prompt action of the new Boards in "adopting" missionaries and through them engaging local women in the various fields as workers among their fellow women infused reality and emphasized concreteness in the enterprise.

The principles upon which these women's boards based their work may be summarized in this fashion:

1. Our work is for our own sex.
2. Our missionaries are to be appointed by the American Board with which our work is to be closely associated, though separate to some extent in financial and administrative affairs.
3. We will send single women only as our missionaries.
4. We will employ competent native women as helpers under the supervision of our missionaries.
5. The funds for our work will be sought in such a way as not to diminish the current income of the American Board.
6. We will secure our funds each year before making appropriations.
7. We will consider the establishment and support of girls' boarding schools as of primary importance. Other lines of work for girls and women will be undertaken as opportunity offers and resources permit.
8. We will endeavor to keep our home constituency well-informed and to develop as close relations as possible between them and missionaries on the various fields. The method of "pledged work" in which local societies or groups underwrite specific enterprises will be encouraged.
9. We will do all in our power to keep administrative expense at the lowest figure possible, depending so far as feasible upon volunteer service.
10. Our treasury will be prompt in its correspondence, efficient in its accounting and reporting.

During the years of their activities the W.B.M. organized twenty-eight branches east of Ohio, the W.B.M.I. nineteen branches in the Midwest, and the W.B.M.P. eight in the Pacific area. As one peruses the annual reports of these Branches as well as their regular publications, the impression of concreteness in planning, efficiency in organization, faithfulness in accepted obligations is inescapable. For prolonged, faithful, ingenious service in the name of Christ, the women of those boards set standards which may never be surpassed.

It is quite understandable that in each case the Woman's Boards desired a certain geographical "spread" for both their personnel and their specific projects abroad. This provided a healthy diversity in many ways. Even though in some cases the personnel and projects of two or more boards were located in one country, the Woman's Boards were very careful not to give rise to confusing overlapping. It would be interesting to enumerate all the field projects for which these boards furnished the necessary personnel and funds but it must suffice in this connection to indicate the areas in which they carried on their "pledged work."

In Africa:	W.B.M.	W.B.M.I.	
Austria:	W.B.M.		
Bulgaria:		W.B.M.I.	
Ceylon:	W.B.M.	W.B.M.I.	
China:	W.B.M.	W.B.M.I.	W.B.M.P.
Dakota Indians:		W.B.M.I.	
India:	W.B.M.	W.B.M.I.	W.B.M.P.
Japan:	W.B.M.		W.B.M.P.
Mexico:	W.B.M.	W.B.M.I.	W.B.M.P.
Micronesia:	W.B.M.	W.B.M.I.	
Near East:	W.B.M.	W.B.M.I.	W.B.M.P.
Spain:	W.B.M.		

In 1877 the officers of the American Board became aware of some misunderstandings among the men and women of the Congregational churches across the country regarding "the relation which these most helpful and now indispensable auxiliaries bear to the American Board." In order to clarify this relationship the *Missionary Herald* in December, 1877, carried an editorial which emphasized these points:

1. The work sustained by the Woman's Boards in the foreign field, in its general scope and in all its details,

is under the direction of the Prudential Committee. Appropriations are made, missionaries appointed, sent out and located, and their labors supervised by the Committee, precisely as in other departments. Efforts made for the social and moral elevation of women in the mission fields, are thus made to harmonize with the general work, and to constitute an integral and most necessary part of it. There is everywhere the heartiest mutual cooperation.

2. The number of single ladies engaged in special labors for their own sex has been increased from ten to sixty since 1868. This is largely due to the *extra* efforts of the Woman's Boards.

3. The Woman's Boards have assumed the expense involved in the support of all single women on the fields and of the previously established boarding schools for girls.

4. The support of missionaries and evangelists, seminaries and schools, (except boarding schools for girls), the cost of Christian literature, and grants-in-aid to churches, etc. go on as before. Any falling off in contributions either to the Woman's Boards or to the American Board would result in curtailment.

5. The separate annual meetings of the Woman's Boards are worth all they cost in effort and money.

6. The Woman's Boards provide closer personal relations with their missionaries and they afford something more specific as the object of effort than could be attained in any other way.

7. The administrative expense incurred by the Woman's Boards is less than 2% of the receipts, due largely to so much "unpaid, freely given labor."

8. The Woman's Boards for foreign missions are "needed to keep up the balance of woman's work" between home and foreign missions.

This editorial followed up an extended statement issued by the officers of the W.B.M. under date of March 17, 1877, the key sentence of which is "One of the lessons that men and women have been learning in the latter days is, that concentrated effort is absolutely necessary . . . anything to be well done requires undivided attention."

In 1879 American Board officers made this comment: "By a well organized system of auxiliaries, by the communication of missionary intelligence through their monthly periodical *Life and Light*, through social and public meetings, and through a large correspondence and by varied and ingenious methods, their power is felt and acknowledged all over the land. During the past year their contributions to the Treasury of the American Board amounted to $73,957.04."[1] This was approximately 15% of the total income of the American Board in 1879.

Dr. A. N. Hitchcock, Secretary of the American Board in the Interior District in 1889, said of the W.B.M.I.: "No agency has been more fruitful in creating and supplying this call [for information] than the Woman's Board of Missions of the Interior. The value and efficiency of this work are seen in the constantly increasing receipts, and what is much, much more, in the growing numbers of those who, trained by intelligent and consecrated parents are offering themselves for personal service in the world-wide work." He reports that in 1889 the receipts from his district amounted to $93,164.38 of which $45,701.44 came through the W.B.M.I.[2]

In 1899 Rev. Walter Frear in his report for the Pacific Coast Agency of the American Board said that the Woman's Board of Missions of the Pacific had done its work with its usual efficiency. In the same year the treasurer of the American Board reported total receipts as $490,407.65 of which sum the W.B.M.P. contributed $4,467.58, the W.B.M.I. $66,541, and the W.B.M. $128,992.80, a total of $200,110.08. Slightly more than 40% of the total American Board income came from the Woman's Boards in 1899.[3]

Again in 1906 it seemed necessary to make an official, clarifying statement to the churches regarding the relation of the

[1] AR, 1879, p. 5.
[2] AR, 1889, pp. 11, 15.
[3] AR, 1899, pp. 19, 23.

Woman's Boards to the American Board. The officers of the Woman's Boards joined with the Prudential Committee of the American Board in making the following statement:

> The three Woman's Boards are corporate bodies, chartered under the statutes of Massachusetts, Illinois and California, respectively. Each cooperates with the American Board, and assumes the support of a part of the work under the care of the American Board.

> Unmarried women, after their adoption by the Woman's Boards, are commissioned by the American Board, and thus become members of its missions, always with a vote on questions pertaining to work for women, and in some missions with a vote upon all work of the American Board in that mission.

> It should be distinctly understood that, although the funds of the Woman's Boards are forwarded to the mission field through the treasurer of the American Board, all the money has been previously designated by the Woman's Boards, each of which has its specific work to be supported out of its own funds, without aid from the other Woman's Boards or from the American Board.

> The responsibility for providing funds for work supported by the Woman's Boards rests upon the women of the churches. Hence the absolute necessity that the proper constituency of the Woman's Boards among the women, girls and children in the churches should be preserved to these Boards, that they may be able to support the work and the workers to which they are pledged. The diversion directly to the treasurer of the American Board of gifts that are relied upon by the Woman's Boards is not only no gain, but it is sure to result in confusion and serious loss. On the other hand, it is clear that churches whose only offering to foreign missions is through the Woman's Boards are failing to support the larger work of the American Board, thus bringing inevitable loss to the whole work.

> The relation of the American Board and the Woman's Boards is that of harmonious co-operation to the same end, namely, the promotion of the work of foreign missions.

The Home Department of the Board in 1909, forecasting the plans and achievements of the centennial year 1910, voiced its reliance upon the three Woman's Boards in these words: "The three Woman's Boards have always been in the van of forward movements, often setting an example to the parent organization in the matter of enterprise and courageous planning. We are confident they will be quick to seize the special opportunity afforded by the Board's centennial, and undertake to secure a material increase in their gifts. During the past year the W.B.M. of Boston raised $150,056.56, the W.B.M.I. $94,453.25, and the W.B.M.P. $11,321.50, a total of $255,831.31."[1]

In 1919 the treasurer of the American Board reported that the total amount received that year from the three Woman's Boards reached the figure of $393,935.97. This sum was approximately 26% of the current total receipts of the American Board. For this help the treasurer recorded "profound appreciation."[2]

Speaking of receipts from the three Woman's Boards it is relevant to record the fact that during the first fifty years (1868-1918) of their activities total income reached these figures:

W.B.M.P.	$ 639,778.19
W.B.M.I.	3,342,105.27
W.B.M.	6,421,352.42
Grand Total	$10,403,235.88

This sum of approximately ten and one-half million dollars represents about 20% of the total receipts of the American Board from 1810 to 1918.[3]

It is to be noted also that the Woman's Boards conducted and paid for their own administrative and promotional expense through the years. The sums turned over to the American Board treasurer year by year were "net" figures.

[1] AR, 1909, pp. 15, 16.
[2] AR, 1919, pp. 41, 43.
[3] American Board receipts 1810-1918: $49,853,487.00.

Mission Accomplished!

The considerations which led ultimately to the merger of the three Woman's Boards with the American Board in 1927 were based primarily on three broad facts. First, the change in the status of women in America amounted to a revolution in public opinion and practice. This new status was not primarily a political fact embodied in the Twentieth Amendment (woman's suffrage), but a sociological fact which had emerged since the tide of opinion regarding woman's rights and abilities began to rise about the time of the Civil War. The rising tide affected the churches. Women were taking their places in the total life of the local church and refused to be limited to Ladies' Aid Societies and other purely female groups. Similar things were happening on the national level.

The second basic fact which formed the background of the merger might be described by the slogan "Nothing succeeds like success." The pioneering activities of the Woman's Boards for foreign missions gave rise to similar activities on the part of women especially interested in home missions. The Woman's Home Missionary Federation was a Congregational national body with representatives in many states. The question had arisen quite naturally "Why should there be multiple organizations of women working for a cause which is essentially one: the spread of the Christian Gospel?" There was a wholesome desire on the part of many pastors to see these two lines of effort combined in one.

The third basic fact relates to the major boards of the Congregational Churches. The nineteenth century, by and large, had been a century of beginnings in American church history. Not beginnings in theology or ecclesiastical relations but in the formation of societies ancillary to the churches for the accomplishment of tasks forced upon their attention by the great American frontier — and the vision of frontiers of human need and of Christian service abroad. The number of societies and boards that had come into existence and were actively appealing for personnel and funds to the same constituency forced the National Council of Congregational Churches to do something about an oft-injected question from the grass roots: "Why are we approached separately by so many boards, each with an urgent appeal?"

It is true to say that during the period of their separate existence (1868-1927) the Woman's Boards both in the field of foreign missions and in the field of home missions had served as pacemakers for the denomination as a whole as it more or less seriously faced its missionary obligations. But by 1927, it was fully apparent that the time had come when the Woman's Boards had accomplished their mission, had done so with remarkable success, and in the view of their wisest leaders and supporters the women of the churches were ready and willing and able to play their full part in the total Christian enterprise.

Mrs. Franklin Hynes Warner, president of the W.B.M. in the twenties, agreeing with the general argument in favor of the merger, boldly challenged the denomination to make for these highly trained, mission-minded, enthusiastic women in the churches a place as definite, as firmly fixed and as really useful as they had had in the old organizations. "They have heretofore chosen missions because they considered it to be the biggest task but the moment it ceases to be for them a real task, we have lost them."[1]

After prolonged consideration the Committee of Twelve, appointed by the National Council at Springfield in 1923, presented its proposals to the Council at Washington, D. C. in October, 1925. "Your Committee is aware that the desire of the churches for changes in organization often grows out of impatience with the multiplicity of appeal, which is a purely promotional problem." This statement of the Committee set the stage for their logical solution, rearrangement of all mission boards in such a way that there should be only two: one home and one foreign. The section of the report referring to the foreign work as adopted by the National Council called

[1] *Missionary Herald*, December 1925, p. 547.

for a complete unification of the Woman's Boards with the American Board, (a) in the conduct of the foreign mission work of the denomination overseas; (b) in the administration of the work in the departments at home; (c) in appeals to the denomination in behalf of foreign missions; (d) in foreign missionary education and promotion throughout the denomination.

The Committee recommended the reconstituting of the American Board with "a Prudential Committee of thirty-six, including at least one-third women," to "be elected by the American Board at its meeting in connection with the National Council, the total to be arranged so as to provide 'Constituent State' and regional representation . . . The women members in each case should be co-ordinate with the men in every respect as an integral part of the management, in order that the values of the Boards may be conserved."

The report urged that women should be considered eligible to become departmental secretaries as well.

The American Board met for its 116th annual meeting in connection with the National Council Assembly at Washington. On October 29, 1925 the Board heard a report from a Joint Committee representing the Woman's Boards, the Prudential Committee, and the Committee of Twelve. Among six resolutions which followed the report three are pertinent here: First, the American Board accepts and endorses the action of the National Council regarding the unification of the Foreign Boards. Second, the American Board invites the Woman's Boards to unite with them in consummating the unification. Third, we refer to the Prudential Committee, acting in conjunction with such committees as may be appointed by the Woman's Boards, the work of putting unification into effect.

The three Woman's Boards took approving action, the W.B.M.I. November 13, 1925, the W.B.M. November 12, 1925, and the W.B.M.P. September 15, 1926. Mrs. W. W. Ferrier, president of the W.B.M.P., wrote feelingly after the action of her Board in a spirit which was widely shared:

> There was a finality about it [our vote] similar to the feeling which possesses one upon handing in an examination paper. Any further effort was impossible: whatever lack there had been of earnestness and faith and endeavor could not be supplemented with an increased devotion later. This was the end of opportunity offered through the W.B.M.P. and the door was closed never to be reopened. . . . [But] a brighter vision soon dispelled this disheartening one, and brought strength and comfort with it. These fifty-three years marked not the extent of life of the W.B.M.P., but instead a time of sowing whose resultant harvests should continue through years never-ending. The joy had already been ours of seeing the tender blades in many a loved and prayer-watched field, and with hearts of faith we can leave the increase to God.

On December 31, 1926 the activities of the three Woman's Boards were formally ended. Unification with the American Board was complete, except for the continuance of necessary holding corporations responsible for invested funds. Thus closed a chapter in the life of the Congregational churches which saw more than ten million dollars contributed for work abroad; 3,000 local woman's societies and 1,800 young people's and children's groups active in foreign missions; the project method initiated and tested; extensive use made of three publications, *Life and Light* (W.B.M.), *Mission Studies* (W.B.M.I.), and *The Bulletin* (W.B.M.P.)

More than nine hundred missionaries had been supported in Africa, China, Ceylon, Japan, India, Mexico, Micronesia, the Near East, and Spain. Hundreds of day and boarding schools for girls, nine hospitals and dispensaries, and hundreds of teachers in rural areas had been maintained. Funds had been given for buildings and equipment in many institutions.

As the Woman's Boards closed their work there were two hundred and forty-six active missionaries on their rolls: the W.B.M. listed 128, the W.B.M.I. 104, the W.B.M.P. thirteen.

The total missionary personnel of the American Board, including these 248 was 769 on January 1, 1927.[1]

The relation of Christian women to the World Mission of the
Church has changed much in the last century. But there is no
reason to assume that changes have caused diminished loyalty.
Anyone inclined to assume so is invited to examine the rise and
record of the General Department of United Church Women
of the National Council of the Churches of Christ in the U.S.A.
This General Department is giving a demonstration of initiative
and ingenuity which is unmatched in consecrated, imaginative
Christian leadership. Women of the Congregational Christian
Churches have had their part in this development. The Department's president for the first two years was a former member of the Prudential Committee of the American Board, Miss
Amy Welcher of Hartford, Connecticut.

In contrast to the prevailing attitudes regarding women a
century ago, today church people seem to be taking seriously
Paul's injunction — that "there is neither Jew nor Greek, there
is neither slave nor free, there is neither male nor female, for
you are all one in Christ Jesus."[2]

We live indeed in an age which is a far cry from the days of
the first century (though the attitude of those days toward
women prevailed to some extent even into the twentieth century). Then Flavius Josephus could say, "In every respect

---

[1] Mrs. Mary Uline Dunlap, a woman with experience successively as a missionary in
Eastern Turkey, as a secretary of the W.B.M.I. in Chicago and as a secretary of the American Board after the merger in 1927, has made a careful study of the record of the 246
active missionaries and numerous institutions of the Woman's Boards whose support became
an American Board responsibility in 1927.

She points out that the former branches of the W.B.M. continued to support their 128
missionaries under the Project Plan adopted by the American Board. At the end of the two
decades, 1927-1947, twenty-five had died, twenty-six had retired, forty-six had withdrawn
for health or other reasons, thirty-one were in active service. In the meantime many unmarried women had been added to the roll of active American Board missionaries.

She does the same for the W.B.M.I. and the W.B.M.P. The branches in the Midwest
continued to support their 104 missionaries under the Project Plan. At the end of 1947,
twenty-one had died, twenty-two had retired, thirty-three had withdrawn, leaving twenty-
eight in active service.

Of the thirteen W.B.M.P. missionaries five had retired, six had withdrawn and two had
continued in active service.

Mrs. Dunlap further gives a spirited account of all the institutions in which the Woman's
Boards had been especially interested, commenting on the lights and shadows of greatest
interest during the twenty years 1927-1947. Her typescript of 107 pages is a very valuable
item in the archives of the American Board. She gives lists of all the 246 missionaries with
appropriate data. Her accounts of the many institutions related to these Boards in Africa,
Bulgaria, Ceylon, China, Greece, India, Japan, Micronesia, Mexico, Syria and Turkey are
impressive tributes to the vision and strength of the three Woman's Boards.

[2] Galatians 3:27, 28.

woman is inferior to man."[1] Then a wife was regarded as the property of her husband and ranked with children and slaves. Today, however, women are beckoned to take their full share as potentially equal partners with men in the fulfillment of the World Mission of the Church. "The Christian cause rests not on gender but on personality."[2]

The Christian Church is challenged today to marshal its *total* resources to witness to the truth as it is in Christ Jesus. There is so much to be done; the harvest is plenteous, but as in former days the laborers are few. The Church cannot afford to limit its ministry to men only or to think largely in terms of men only. Our mission demands the dedication of men and women, equally and together, in Christian witness to our interdependent world.

---

[1] Quoted in R. T. Stamm, *Interpreter's Bible,* (Nashville, Abingdon-Cokesbury Press, 1952), vol. 10, p. 519.
[2] O. F. Blockwelder, *Interpreter's Bible,* (Nashville, Abingdon-Cokesbury Press, 1952), vol. 10, p. 520.

An Interlude: III
THE SUSTAINED GLOW OF THE FIELD WORK
OF THE WOMAN'S BOARDS

"The fitful fires of enthusiasm, incident to every
new enterprise, had given place to a glow of steady,
intelligent purpose not to cease or falter in efforts to
evangelize the world, so long as our Lord's last commission stands."

Frances J. Dyer[1]

The officers of the Woman's Boards equally with the officers
of the American Board were continually conscious of the fact
that all that is done in Board offices and on field trips in America is done in the interests of what is going on "out there."
The raison d'etre of the boards and all their affairs is the
proclamation and communication of the Christian Gospel by
word and deed *overseas.* There can be no legitimate pride in
organization or accomplishment *"here,"* except as structure and
effort advance the welfare and effectiveness of those in contact
with the people, younger and older, *"out there"* with whom we
wish to share our spiritual treasures.

With this in mind, one realizes that while it is easy to dwell
on matters of secondary importance, what goes on "out there"
is of supreme interest. A real history of the three Woman's
Boards would necessarily give most attention to accounts of
the growth of the Kingdom of God in the lives of women and
girls and the communities of which they are a part overseas
in the actual settings in which they live and move and have
their being. It would also analyze the problems and interpret
the significance of the work in each field.

[1] In *Life and Light*, October 1917, p. 439.

Here are a few "glimpses" of what the Christian Gospel can mean to women and girls of many lands who have not known it or who have not benefitted by the transformations it creates in human hearts and lives. A reader of the voluminous correspondence cannot fail to feel the warmth of the sustained glow of devotion and achievement.

The following "glimpses" are selected in the confident hope that the reader will use the divine gift of imagination in order to evaluate at its true worth the service to humanity in the name of Christ of the missionaries of the Woman's Boards.

About 1890 Miss S. D. Riggs (later Mrs. Dana Getchell) of Marsovan, Turkey, described pioneer work among women in her area:

> Bible readers among the women, partly or wholly supported by the Woman's Board, have made a great impression upon social life in Turkey. The young married women, as a rule, in the early days had never learned to read. The effort of the Bible woman was to teach them to read until they could freely read their Bibles.
>
> In many of our stations there were especially set apart, touring missionaries, and Woman's Board missionaries were among the number. Their work was to teach. We all did more or less of touring work, but where there were many villages and towns to be visited, the appointed missionaries gave all their time to it. It was no easy job! Riding over mountains, on mule back, edging fearful precipices, crossing swollen rivers, sometimes amid robber regions, where there was real danger, — riding, riding, until you did not know whether you had any limbs or not, they were so stiff! And at night sleeping — or trying to — sometimes in stables, with the horses divided off by a single row of boards; sometimes in sheepfolds, whose sheep were turned out expressly to make room for you, and always with plenty of disagreeable company of minute form, against whom a line of battle must be formed at once. But the results justified the price. Jewels and friends were discovered in these same villages who made worthwhile material for schools and afterwards for churches.

The effect of schools and Bible teaching was felt in all the cities, towns and villages where there were Armenians and Greeks, throughout Turkey. The Moslem women were also touched. Individual cases occurred of conversion among Moslems, and individual women had their own Testaments which they read and loved and were fiercely persecuted for following. No doubt these would have numbered tens and hundreds, and even thousands, if religious liberty had come.[1]

Miss Virginia C. Murdock, M.D., the first medical missionary of the Woman's Board of Missions, wrote May 5, 1891 from North China:

Dear Young Ladies:

The medical work is a very important department of missions. It brings us into contact with many people and takes us often into their houses where we would not otherwise have been invited. It is the custom of the women in China to remain closely at home, but thousands come to the dispensary for medicines. On clinic days the patients sit in the dispensary waiting room sometimes for hours listening to the preaching of the missionary or the native Bible-woman. In the hospital the patients remain some days or weeks and can receive systematic instruction, attend morning prayers, church services and prayer meetings. A lady doctor has many calls to visit sick women in their homes.

Medical tours are another feature of the dispensary work. Starting early in the morning in our large Chinese springless carts, we jolt over the mountain roads to villages. A great crowd gathers. . . . The native women accompanying us talk all day with the people referring to our Savior and his love for us all and to the false gods men worship. The sick in China do not receive very kind care. They get but little attention from members of their families. Little night-watching is done. They hold all sorts of vagaries and believe in queer forms of superstition. The Chinese have high appreciation of the dispensary and hospital and

[1] Quoted by Kate Lamson, "History of the Woman's Board of Missions," (Manuscript ABCFM Archives, AB 16 L 21 H), pp. 21 ff.

can understand that we are doing a humane work, when medicines are given free of charge. . . . Their books say that the liver is on the left side of the body, that the heart has seven eyes, if a person has great talent. To diagnose the diseases of a woman, the left pulse must be felt; to find out the diseases of a man the pulse on his right wrist must be felt. If a man is not strong, what more potent dose of medicine can be given than tiger's bones — are not tigers strong?

About 1900 Mrs. Amy Cowles of Umzumbe, the daughter of missionaries and a missionary herself, writes of her life and work among the Zulus in Natal, South Africa:

Haven't I seen this Woman's Board of Missions work from the earliest stage up to the present? My earliest recollections date back to Umzumbe, and looming large in all those childhood bush experiences are the exciting, even dangerous, times which my father and mother had with the angry owners of runaway girls. Times when father warned us children not to wander far from our yard, for there were angry parents lurking near. I remember in those days father (H. M. Bridgman) had one of his cows stabbed out of spite by an angry father. After the Government made a rule that no girl should be forced in marriage it was much easier for the missionaries. As soon as a girl appeared at our back door, like a wild hunted thing, sometimes with welts all over her back, sometimes having slept out in the bushes for two or three nights as she dodged her way toward the Mission Station, when at last she reached our house she was welcomed, given food and a room to hide in, and told to lie low until her owner should appear. This always happened after one, two or three days. We children always knew them, these groups of angry relatives who refused to greet anybody as they sullenly made their way into our yard. Sticks and clubs and a huge hippo whip were always in evidence and, as father stepped out to meet them, angry looks and "give me my child" were his usual introduction to the wild beasts of Umzumbe. But father always kept calm and

smiling and at once the girl was called. Hardly daring to
look at her people, frightened and ready to run, the poor
girl would sit on the floor beside father's chair, or stand
huddled in the farthest corner. The parents were always
told that they could talk with the daughter as long as
they desired. If she chose to go home she could do so,
but if she chose to stay, she was not to be beaten or
molested in any way, and she could not by law be married
to any man whom she did not want. Upon giving this
ultimatum, father would plant his chair near the girl, take
up his book or paper, and proceed to sit for hours, while
the girl was threatened, scolded, yelled at, sworn at, etc.
The father would sometime lose control of himself and
in a burst of anger leap onto the verandah and start to
drag the girl off, as she screamed for help. Prompt action
on father's part, with threats of the law, usually brought
release to the girl.[1]

A building for the girls was finally provided and Mrs. Cowles
says of it, — "That school influenced not only the whole region
round about Umzumbe but also the region beyond. . . . The
results were Christian wives, mothers and homes, a multitude
of children going to school every day, clean, patched and well
dressed in clothes made for them by the Woman's Board
mothers."

Miss Louise Wilson of Sonoma, California was sent as a
representative of the Woman's Board of Missions for the
Pacific to Micronesia in 1893. Her letter of October 1913[2] gives
a glimpse of the down-to-earth nature of mission work among
the people of the islands.

Twenty years! A long time it may seem to some of you,
but not to me. I find it very interesting to look back and
see how when I first took up this unknown work, I did it
almost with "fear and trembling." Many things which
then looked like mountains seem very small now.

I thank God for the experiences of the past twenty
years, for the light that has shined out amidst the dark-

---

[1] Quoted by Lamson, *op. cit.* pp. 53-57.
[2] *Life and Light,* October 1913, pp. 440-442.

ness; for the lives of the children, the young men and young women, who have both tried and gladdened the missionary's heart. We soon forget that the skins of our island people are dark and love them as much as if they were white. It fills our hearts with joy as we watch the progress in their spiritual lives.

One of the girls in our Kusaie Girls' School speaking in prayer meeting once said "What did we know about forgiveness before coming here? We knew how to fight and quarrel, and if we had anything against another, we were always thinking of how we could get revenge. Did we ever think of forgiving them? Did we think of how we had hurt them? No, we only thought of how we were praised by others for coming off victorious in the fight. We were proud of it. You know we were all alike, we did not know what it meant to forgive one another."

The annual report of the W.B.M.P. for 1905 includes this statement about their interests in Foochow — Southern China:

In Foochow, Southern China, we have a kindergarten and a kindergarten training school. Just now an extra effort is being made by this Board to raise money to build a house for our kindergarten. We have some interest in the medical work and the station classes, while at Pagoda Anchorage there are eight station classes supported by W.B.M.P. These schools are under the general care of Mrs. Hubbard, and are taught mostly by native Christian women, who are faithful and efficient. There are eight Bible women, who work in connection with these schools, two of whom are supported by our Board. This work among the women is most important, and is vital to the evangelization of 500,000 women. Mrs. Hubbard says: "It is impossible to measure the full amount of work done, and the results accomplished, but it is a comfort to know that 'He knows.'" Present opportunities call more loudly than ever for workers both native and foreign. Is there even one who will come across the waters to help train the workers?

Miss Jean Brown, the teacher of this kindergarten, says:

"The kindergarten is more flourishing than ever before. Nearly eighty children on the roll. The class of four which graduated last year from the training school was the first in all the great Chinese Empire to finish a course of instruction in kindergarten work. And they are so enthusastic and so much in earnest. They are such a comfort. One of them is able to take my music class, besides giving twenty-five lessons a week at Ponasang. She does thorough, careful work, too. The transition class, with twenty-five children, is taught by two of the girl teachers. A mission class for heathen children in a district where there had not been much success, is in charge of two of the kindergarten girls, and they have really had wonderful success; an attendance of seventy children, besides several women."[1]

The W.B.M.I. took a deep interest in the education of girls in the Madura Mission in South India. Under the direction of Mrs. William B. Capron, a W.B.M. missionary whom the W.B.M.I. had adopted, girls were trained not only for home and church life, but especially as teachers for village schools and for reading the Bible to adult women in village homes. Mrs. Capron, who served from 1856 to 1889, writes in her early years on the field:

It was a ride of eight miles, at the slow pace of bullocks. I must be there early, to see the people in their houses before the sun is hot; so the stars were bright in the sky when we left home. If mamma goes, of course the children must go; and the two little girls sat in the end of the cart, delighted at the quiet beauty of the sky, upon which the dawn was just entering. Why did these words again and again come into my mind. "Tell his disciples and Peter, that He goeth before you into Galilee!" What a visit it will be, if the dear Lord goes before!

We were not expected so early and had halted before the modest mud schoolhouse, before our presence in the

[1] Quotations from Annual Report of Woman's Board of Missions of the Pacific, 1905, pp. 19, 20.

village was known. But how soon a crowd gathered! It was a pleasant look-out from the end of my cart. Close up were the Christian men of the village, and the gray-haired mother of two of them. Crowding between these were the children. A little farther back were the smiling faces of the Christian women, whom I greeted with — "Oh, you well know how much I like a straight parting in your hair!"

While sitting on the shady side of one of the houses, I had a deputation from the village school, with its heathen schoolmaster at the head. The boys were dressed up in style, with red jackets and marvelously large turbans. Each boy — and there were fourteen — had a slender bamboo wound with bright colored threads, which looked more like a very long slender Chinese pagoda than anything else I can think of. One of the boys chanted in honor of some heathen deity; to which his companions added a chorus of "Siva, Siva," rattling at the same time these showy wands, which had little stones concealed in the folds of the palmyra leaves with which they were ornamented. I had intended to have a children's meeting in the course of the day, and quickly resolved to have it then and there. The boys were bright, and followed me closely while I described the journey to my distant home, left so long ago. It was an easy transition to the home on high and its great King —. "The water boils!" said one of the nice women who had been looking after my teakettle, and running in and out of a side door to catch what she could of my talk with the children. The strip of friendly shade had grown narrow so I dismissed my audience, and went to the schoolhouse for my breakfast.[1]

[1] Quoted by Grace T. Davis, *Neighbors in Christ*, (Chicago, James Watson and Company, 1926), pp. 31-33.

13

THE ENLISTMENT AND TRAINING OF MISSIONARIES

Three things were taken for granted by its leaders when the American Board began operations in 1810. These assumptions were voiced again and again in early statements, particularly by Samuel Worcester, the Board's first corresponding secretary.[1]

First, it was assumed that the missionary enterprise was in accordance with God's will and loving purpose for mankind, and that therefore it ought to be undertaken by those who chose to do God's will. Because it was his will, it could not fail.

Second, only properly qualified men should be chosen to be missionaries. The primary qualification was felt to be two-fold: deep personal faith in God as revealed by Jesus Christ, and thorough education, the crown of which was, of course, theological training. Only ordained men would be given missionary status. Other men — and women, including wives — were to be known as "assistant missionaries."

The third assumption was that missionaries needed no special preparation for their task. If men were on fire to share the Gospel with "the heathen," and if they were qualified in other ways noted above, then they should be sent abroad and given the chance to share their message. Every part of the world needed the Gospel, no matter what might be the prevailing local religion or religions, regardless of local cultural or economic or social conditions. No need to study the missionary field before launching a mission! The early commissioners and American Board secretaries, in common with other Americans

---

[1] See, for example, *Address to the Christian Public*, November 1811 in AR, 1811, pp. 25-30; also *Instructions to the Missionaries to the East*, February 7, 1812, in AR, 1812, pp. 11-15.

of the time, knew very little about the conditions which their appointees would encounter, and could not have provided "adequate preparation" for their candidates even if they had desired to do so.

The records of the weekly meetings of the Prudential Committee are replete with references to the matter of choosing missionary candidates. The Committee, apparently from the very beginning, felt deeply its responsibility for appointing only the best available men. The procedure went something like this: the secretary of the Board, later to be known as the Home Secretary, would discover likely men in the seminaries or in the ministry, would ascertain their interest and then present their names to the Committee for consideration. Once a candidate was discovered, if the Committee approved, he was invited to appear in person before the Committee to be questioned as to his faith and Christian experience. He was examined as to his disposition and his ability to preach the Gospel and, together with others, to develop Christian communities among "the heathen."

The pattern of examination apparently was not fixed in every detail. But there were auxiliary requirements, information about which was collected early. The candidate's health, marriage or prospects of marriage, willingness to live abroad possibly without return to the United States, common sense, thrift and his knowledge of simple medical practice — these came under scrutiny. While no definite age limit was set, it was assumed that only "young" men would be appointed.

Such procedure and policy prevailed during the early years, but gradually evolved along various lines. The first change came in the matter of the sex of missionary personnel. An "unmarried female," Eliza Agnew, was given missionary status in 1839, and by the time of the Civil War there were other exceptions.[1] With the rise of the Woman's Boards in the late 1860s the importance of the service which women could render on the mission field became more and more obvious and

[1] But see above, pp. 155, 156.

women were actually sought for certain missionary tasks, especially teaching in girls' schools and nursing in mission hospitals and dispensaries. Yet, despite exceptions here and there, it was not until about 1900 that women were given full missionary status.

Candidate policy changed in other ways, too. The Andover Controversy in 1885 caused a shakeup in American Board offices, one upshot of which was a more tolerant doctrinal treatment of candidates. Candidates were less closely examined on their theology and their religious experience, though of course examination continued on these lines. Another consequence was increasing use of candidates who had other than theological training. From time to time as the concept of missionary service broadened, more persons were sought for missionary service who were trained in medicine or education or in arts and crafts, and it was expected that they would be as well trained for such work overseas as if they were seeking similar responsibilities in America. From 1893 onward men who had not been ordained but who had been chosen for particular mission tasks were occasionally called "missionaries" — a title previously reserved for ministers and other ordained and theologically trained persons.

A New Policy

At the turn of the century, with America discovering more and more about the world beyond its shores, it was becoming reasonable to assume that missionary candidates should learn something of the lands to which they were being sent. The Edinburgh World Missionary Conference in 1910 gave such assumptions firm status. At the Conference it became apparent that the new missionary procedures would require that candidates should study before departure the nation and culture in which they were to serve, and should be trained for their actual day-to-day work. Partly as a consequence of the Edinburgh meeting, "schools of missions" were opened in various parts of the United States, and in other countries, the first American school being Hartford's (Connecticut) School of Missions, later named the Kennedy School of Missions. In general the curricula of such schools were divided into two parts: general studies of anthropology, linguistics, Bible, "the missionary and his task," and area studies of the culture and history and local religions of particular countries. Missionary candidates were encouraged to study at these schools, sometimes at Board expense, in preparation for their overseas tasks.

Since 1890 the American Board has relied to some extent on the Student Volunteer Movement and on the theological seminaries themselves for aid in recruiting prospective missionaries. Great help from these sources came in the late nineteenth and early twentieth centuries. It is fitting to spend a moment or two reviewing their contributions.

The Student Volunteer Movement and the Seminaries

The Student Volunteer Movement for Foreign Missions traces its beginnings to student conferences held at Northfield, Massachusetts under the inspired guidance of Dwight L. Moody in the eighteen-eighties. Moody mobilized the spiritual resources and focused the imagination of young men like John R. Mott, Robert E. Speer and Robert P. Wilder upon the evangelization of the world. This is not the context in which even to sketch the history of that remarkable movement (for it was indeed a movement that moved!). But one of its outstanding effects felt by mission boards and theological seminaries was the demand for greater scope and higher standards in the training of young men and women expecting to go abroad as missionaries. They were stabbed awake by the new demand! They responded with a variety of plans and measures.

Theological seminaries during the greater part of the nineteenth century paid real though scant attention to foreign missions. For instance, Hartford Theological Seminary in Connecticut, organized in 1834, claims that up to 1901 "one-tenth of its graduates had found their work in foreign lands."[1]

---

[1] *The Study of Foreign Missions in Hartford Theological Seminary*, (Hartford, Hartford Seminary Press, 1902), p. 3.

As early as 1884 a permanent lectureship was held by Rev. Augustus C. Thompson, D.D., who served from 1849 to 1893 as a member of the Prudential Committee of the American Board. On his death in 1901 he was followed by Rev. Judson Smith, D.D., at that time the senior secretary of the American Board. That same year the Charles M. Lamson Missionary Fund of $50,000. was completed. The income of this Fund was used to finance a greatly enlarged program of special instruction for missionary candidates in all phases of missiology.

The records of Andover Theological Seminary show that during the first century of its existence, 1808 to 1908, out of 2,170 graduates 248, one in nine, entered upon missionary service, of whom 222 were connected with the American Board.[1] This record underscores two facts: first, the American Board chose its missionaries very largely from seminaries where training was of a high standard though not specifically for missionary candidates; and second, it was taken for granted that in almost every case a missionary must be an ordained minister (male). In time Andover Seminary felt the pressure to provide specialized training but its part in this development came much later in its history. The noteworthy Hyde Lectureship on Missions established in 1866, was a harbinger of greater things.

The story of the part played by Yale Divinity School in the study of missions and the training of missionaries differs sharply from those of Andover and Hartford. Professor Roland H. Bainton in his book *Yale and the Ministry*[2] gives the main facts. Yale's earliest missionary interest was in the American Indians, largely because of David Brainerd who was converted through the Great Awakening in 1742 while at Yale College. He dedicated himself to the winning of the Indians, and though his service was cut down by his death after four years, "he had never been forgotten at Yale."

Yale's delay in providing specific training for missionaries, avers Bainton, does not indicate a lack of interest in missions or

---

[1] *General Catalog, Andover Seminary 1808-1908,* (Boston, Thomas Todd, 1908), pp. 512-514.
[2] (New York, Harper, 1957).

a failure to supply recruits. It was pointed out at the semi-centennial of the Divinity School in 1872 that thirty-one of the 850 graduates had become foreign missionaries. This was one in twenty-eight as compared with one in nine at Andover and one in ten at Hartford.

Training for prospective missionaries really got under way at Yale when Harlan P. Beach was called to the chair of Missions in 1906. He had been an American Board missionary in China (1883-1890) and a secretary of the Student Volunteer Movement (1895-1906). For fifteen years he was a great teacher. Another of his greatest achievements was the building up of the George E. Day Missions Library reported to contain 20,742 volumes in 1921, now (1957) 70,000. His major contribution to scholarship was his statistical studies of foreign missions. Beach was followed by two scholars, John Clark Archer and Kenneth Scott Latourette. It seems reasonable to remark that Yale Divinity School's chief contribution to the training of missionaries has been along the line of inspiring personalities as professors rather than of broad, systematic courses of study of missiology as, for instance, at the Kennedy School of Missions at Hartford. This observation will undoubtedly raise a question in the minds, for instance, of the students of Professor Duncan B. MacDonald, the great Islamic scholar at Hartford.

These remarks about Andover, Hartford and Yale theological seminaries serve to illustrate the attitude and action of the theological seminaries generally regarding the training of prospective missionaries prior to 1910. Unfortunately space permits only cursory reference to several other seminaries to which the American Board has been indebted for recruits. Cooperation has become increasingly intimate. The list (with founding date) of seminaries from which recruits have come includes Princeton 1812, Harvard 1815, Bangor 1816, Auburn 1818, General 1819, Oberlin 1835, Union (in New York) 1836, Chicago 1855, Pacific 1866, as well as Andover, Yale, and Hartford.

The Board and Non-Anglo-Saxon Candidates

Quite naturally the American Board during the early years assumed that prospective missionaries would be recruited from among the young people in the churches of New England and of the Middle Atlantic area. These churches were largely Anglo-Saxon in background and membership. It was not long, however, before the question arose as to whether missionaries might not be appointed from among non-Anglo Saxon church groups.

The records show that the question first arose when persons of Armenian descent, some of whom had become American citizens, applied or were considered as potential missionaries among people of their own race in the Near East.[1] The first case seems to have been Mr. Christopher Seropyan in 1854, a member of the senior class in the Theological Department of Yale College.[2] The Prudential Committee was willing to assist him in returning to Turkey in case he planned to go thither, with assurance that he would work under the direction of the Mission in that area, but the Committee did not appoint him a missionary.

This decision was based to some extent on the experience with young men of non-American, non-Anglo-Saxon origin whom the Committee or missionaries of the Board in various fields had regarded as unusually promising for service as preachers or teachers among their own people.

It was recalled that, on the whole, the experiment of the Cornwall School[3] which operated from 1816 to 1826 proved

---

[1] American Board missionaries first came into contact with Armenians at Izmir (Smyrna) in 1820, but it was not until 1844 that Board records speak of the "Mission to the Armenians." Dr. William Goodell was sent to Constantinople (now Istanbul) in 1831 with major responsibility for work among the Armenians, all of whom were related to the Gregorian Armenian Church. Events in connection with the Mission to the Armenians led to the establishment of a Protestant-Armenian Community in 1847. A few Armenians of Gregorian Church connection had migrated to the United States and had allied themselves with Protestant Churches. They were interested to some extent in the religious experiences and ecclesiastical relationships of their people in "the old country."

[2] Prudential Committee Minutes, vol. IX, p. 330, Oct. 3, 1854.

[3] The Cornwall School was established by the Board at Cornwall, Connecticut in 1816 for the purpose of training "youths collected from heathen nations" with a view to their return as Christian workers among their own people. Young men from the tribes of American Indians, from the Sandwich Islands and from some other areas attended the school. In 1826 the Board accepted the report of a committee which recommended that the school be closed for the reason that "these natives can now be better educated for the purposes of the mission, at the schools" in their own countries. See AR, 1825, p. 22.

that it was unwise to bring immature young men from their native environments abroad to the United States for study and training as Christian workers. The Hawaiians and the American Indians who studied at the Cornwall School with few exceptions had disappointed their benefactors.

As a result, the Committee had advised all its missions not to send any young men to America for education at the expense of the Board unless the consent of the Committee had been secured in advance.[1] The Committee also had determined not to appoint national Christians, or Christians of overseas background, as missionaries in their own lands, though, as in the case of Mr. Seropyan, they should be encouraged to work as national Christian leaders. With few exceptions that policy has continued through the years.

In some missions there has been an understandable desire to give competent national Christian leaders the status of "missionary." This has been the practice in at least one mission — Marathi. But in general the Board has not favored the policy, believing that the Church rather than the Mission, a temporary body, should take appropriate action.

The American Board has occasionally appointed as missionaries nationals of other lands than America, provided they themselves are "sending" and not "receiving" lands. Australia, Switzerland, England, Germany and Canada have been thus represented in the personnel of the American Board. From 1882 to 1925 the American Board served as the foreign agency of the Congregational Churches of Canada, thus holding in its fellowship a number of Canadian missionaries. The United Church of Canada took over in 1925.

The Board and Negro Candidates

While the Board has discouraged overseas nationals of mission lands from seeking appointment as missionaries, it has from time to time encouraged Americans of Negro background. During the first hundred years of its history, the Board appoint-

[1] Prudential Committee Minutes, vol. IV, p. 117, July 18, 1835.

ed as full-fledged missionaries five Negroes of American citizenship:[1] two single men for work in West Africa, one couple and one single woman for work in East Africa. Their records briefly stated are as follows:

Benjamin V. James, b. Elizabethtown, N. Y., a printer; appointed and sailed 1836; worked in Fair Hope, Cape Palmas, later in Gaboon; released in 1846; joined colony at Liberia.

Samuel T. Miller, b. Burkeville, Va.; Hampton Institute; appointed and sailed (with Mr. Bagster, an Englishman, and Mr. Sanders, born in Ceylon) in 1880, for West Central Africa; returned December 1884, released 1885.

Rev. Benjamin F. Ousley, b. Warren, Miss.; Fisk University; Oberlin Theological Seminary; with his wife, *Mrs. Henrietta Bailey Ousley,* b. Washington Co., Miss.; Fisk University; appointed and sailed 1884, for Durban. In November of that year they were among the first missionaries to enter East Central Africa. Several locations around Inhambane Bay were occupied; but the region was too unhealthy for permanent location. Mr. Ousley reduced the Sheetswa language to writing so far as to translate into it some of the New Testament. The Ousleys were very fine people; "much liked by the Africans" — "pleasant to work with and highly respected." They returned to the U. S. in 1893; and because of health reasons were released from service. He later served as Professor in Alcorn College, Mississippi.

Nancy Jones, b. Hopkinsville, Ky.; Lemoyne Institute and Fisk University; appointed and sailed 1888, for Durban. She was one of a party who set out to establish a mission in East Africa. In the party also were Mr. and Mrs. Fred R. Bunker. Miss Jones is spoken of as somewhat "temperamental"; but she was "an effective, earnest worker," "well-liked by native people and missionaries." She, like the Ousleys, suffered ill-health, and was released from service in 1897.

---

[1] For information about a Negro teacher, though not a missionary, see p. 155.

From 1897 to 1915, the American Board was without the service of Negro missionaries. From 1915 to the present, however, several Negro missionaries have served with distinction.

Rev. and Mrs. Daniel Hastings were appointed missionaries to the West Africa Mission (Angola) and sailed in 1915. They were Jamaicans of African descent, British subjects. Mr. Hastings received his Master's and his Bachelor of Divinity degrees from the University of Chicago. Later he earned his Ph.D. from Hartford Theological Seminary. Mrs. Hastings was trained in the Bethlehem Normal School in Santa Cruz, Jamaica. In Angola they were assigned to Bailundo, the oldest and largest station, where they worked in close association with white colleagues until 1938. They proved themselves to be capable workers, much beloved by the Ovimbundu people with whom they came into very close contact. Ill health compelled them to withdraw in 1938. He died in Edinburgh in 1941.

Rev. and Mrs. Henry Curtis McDowell, both graduates of Talladega College in 1915, were appointed to Angola in 1919. He received his B.D. at Talladega and was honored by a D.D. in 1937. Mrs. McDowell received her M.A. at the Kennedy School of Missions in 1931. For three years the McDowells served with white colleagues at Chilesso and Dondi stations commending themselves as missionaries of the highest character and ability. They then pioneered in opening a new station at Galangue where they served until compelled by Mrs. McDowell's ill health to take leave of absence in America for ten years, 1937-1947. After Mrs. McDowell's death in 1942 and Dr. McDowell's remarriage in 1944 and a pastorate in New Haven, Connecticut, Dr. McDowell returned to Angola where he served until 1958 at Elende. The second Mrs. McDowell is a highly trained and experienced teacher, a graduate (1940) of the Teachers' College in Winston-Salem, North Carolina. The McDowells are now (1959) on pre-retirement furlough.[1]

Dr. McDowell's record and influence as a missionary has been outstanding. He has shown imaginative leadership, has

[1] See An Interlude: I (page 45).

proved to be an inspiring colleague, much beloved by nationals and missionaries.

The Negro Congregational Churches of the United States with headquarters in the South[1] responded to a challenge from the American Board to undertake a missionary project of their own, manned by missionaries from their own communities. The result was that in 1922 the McDowells were asked to open the Galangue Station of the Angola Mission, much to the satisfaction of their Negro friends in America. Mr. and Mrs. Samuel B. Coles in 1922 and Dr. and Mrs. Aaron M. McMillan (M.D.) in 1929, both highly qualified Negro families, were sent to join the McDowells in developing pioneer work in the vast, unoccupied Galangue region. Agricultural and medical work as well as evangelistic and educational were stressed. The field showed great promise, though the Mission was beginning to doubt the wisdom of a plan which looked like a segregated station. Largely for personal reasons the McMillans withdrew in 1948 and the Coles in 1951. Galangue Station was administered like any other station in the Mission, racially speaking. With the return of the McDowells in 1947 they were assigned to Elende Station and the experiment of a station manned by Negroes but definitely not a segregated unit of work, the project of the Negro Congregational churches of the United States, was terminated. The Negro Congregational Churches in America were asked to share in the work of the Board in Africa and elsewhere on the same basis as other Congregational Churches.

Rev. and Mrs. Walter C. Wynn, Negro members of the Pond Street Baptist Church of Providence, Rhode Island, were appointed missionaries of the Board in 1941 and designated to Angola for general and agricultural work. Unfortunately war restrictions and travel difficulties resulting in a long delay compelled the Wynns to seek an opportunity for Christian service in America.

The experience of the Angola mission in Portuguese West Africa is a vivid reminder that the non-Anglo Saxon Christians

---

[1] Organized in 1950 as the Convention of the South, Box 957, Greensboro, N. C.

of the United States are a worthy source of missionary candidates. Consequently, in recent years there have been more and more appointments of American Negroes and, in the immediate past, of Americans of Oriental background in mission service overseas.[1]

While there is still a long distance to go before it can be said that the American Board sustains a wholly interracial mission force around the world, since 1940 the foreign policy committee of the Board has affirmed that it "recognizes no racial restrictions in the appointment of missionaries, each case being considered on its merits."

Missionary Appointments By Areas 1810-1957

Until 1893, as has been indicated, the Board classified as "missionaries" only those men who had been ordained. All others, including the wives of ordained men, were "assistant missionaries." Increasingly since 1900 the Board has found it useful and wise to appoint young college graduates for limited terms of service, usually three years, mainly as tutors or junior staff in high schools and colleges associated in one way or another with the Board. The following lists include all categories of personnel from 1810 to 1957, divided only by terms of service:

	Career	Associates	Total
Indians (American)	558	65	623
South Africa (Zululand)	165	75	240
East Africa (Southern Rhodesia)	81	19	100
West Africa (Angola)	136	13	149
Cape Palmas (Africa)	11		11
Gaboon (Africa)	29		29
North China	368	64	432
Foochow (China)	138	9	147
Shaowu (China)	20	3	23
Canton (China)	37	2	39

[1] Rev. Thomas Okuma at the time of writing is a missionary in Angola. He is an American Hawaiian of Japanese background. Robert King served, 1945 to 1948, as a teacher at the American College at Tarsus in the Near East; he was an American Negro. Likewise, Dr. Yoshio Fukuyama, now Research Secretary of the Congregational Christian Board of Home Missions, served a three-year term as a teacher at Talas in the Near East.

Hongkong	6		6
Singapore	12		12
Siam	16		16
Borneo	10		10
Amoy (China)	6		6
Java-Sumatra	14		14
Marathi (India)	247	45	292
Madura	222	37	259
Ceylon	136	24	160
Arcot (India)	5		5
Near East	843	510	1353
(Turkey, Syria, Lebanon, Albania, Greece, Bulgaria)			
Persia	48		48
Cyprus	3		3
Malta	2		2
Austria (Czechoslovakia)	10		10
Italy	4		4
Spain	13	10	23
Mexico	77	21	98
Japan	240	106	346
Philippine Islands	50		50
Micronesia	82	16	98
Sandwich Islands (Hawaii)	180	6	186
Europe (France)	2	2	4
Patagonia (South America)	2		2
Totals	3773	1027	[1] 4800

Contemporary Candidate Policy and Procedure

Today the recruiting of missionaries is shared within the Congregational Christian denomination by the American Board and the National Office of Recruitment, located at 14 Beacon Street, Boston. The Board employs a full-time Candidate Sec-

[1] Note the graphs in Appendix V. First graph showing number of American Board missionaries, 1810-1955; second graph showing increase of indigenous workers related to the American Board Missions 1830-1956.

retary, who occasionally has been given a full-time associate. It is the responsibility of the Candidate Secretary to search for and enlist promising young people, advise them of Board requirements and desirable further preparation, and to assist in any way possible the development and growth of the missionary prospect.

The sort of missionary candidate who is sought today is described well in a statement from the International Missionary Council at Madras, India in 1938:[1]

> He must be physically fit to adjust himself to live in a new land. He must be intellectually qualified by thorough and broad education, have the capacity to learn a language, have a thorough knowledge of the Bible and possess the appropriate professional skills. He must be marked for his Christian character; that is, have a growing Christian experience, a sure grasp of the Christian faith, a sense of mission, the gift of interpreting and communicating his faith, the capacity to appreciate and cooperate with and the ability to identify himself with the best interests of other peoples.

Once a candidate is discovered, he is subjected to a series of tests and interviews. The tests are standard psychological indices of behavior patterns and attitudes concerning submissiveness, outgoingness-introspectiveness, other personality factors. In addition, the candidate is asked to state briefly his Christian faith and experience, something of his motivation in seeking appointment as a missionary, his cultural interests, his family background. A full questionnaire regarding the candidate is sent to persons suggested by the candidate, and to the candidate's pastor and college and seminary teachers and others known to be well acquainted with him.

Candidates rarely come in person before the Prudential Committee today. Instead the Committee reviews and studies papers prepared by the Candidate Secretary, papers which

---

[1] *The World Mission of the Church*, (New York, International Missionary Council, 1939), p. 84. It happened that the writer was chairman of the Seminar on the Preparation and Function of the Missionary.

summarize the findings of tests, the statements of the candidate and the evaluations of the references.

Candidates may be either men or women, and, as in years past, they are required to be members of "an evangelical church body," not necessarily a Congregational Christian Church. They are expected to have certain skills, and to be graduates of reputable colleges and graduate schools.

The Board's Candidate Secretary wrote in 1957:

> Most missionaries in this period of revolutionary change need to become specialists before they go overseas, and should, therefore, have postgraduate training. Ministers should have a B.D. degree, educators an M.A. or Ph.D., social workers an M.A. in a recognized graduate school of social work, agriculturalists a B.S. degree in agriculture or education with major in agriculture, nurses a B.S. and R.N., physicians an M.D. with rotating internships and sometimes with a specialty, business administrators, an M.A. from a school of business administration with one or two years' experience in their fields.

But more than academic capacity is required. "Advance degrees and specialization cannot be substituted for a sincere love of people and a concern for their welfare. Higher education is only a tool for more effective leadership and service in the cause of Christian missions." Board spokesmen often point out that also needed are an aptitude for language, a vital faith, an ability often to make do with very little, practical skills, resiliency, and a sense of humor. The standards for missionary service are high and exacting. Is it any wonder the laborers are few?

14

THE HOME OFFICE, ORGANIZATION AND RELATIONSHIPS

A Fellowship Center

Fourteen Beacon Street, Boston, has not always been the headquarters of the American Board. Several other addresses in the inner city of Boston from time to time were the pulsating center of the far-flung, thin line of missionaries around the world.[1] But since 1899, 14 Beacon Street has been so familiar and beloved a spot that one missionary burst into song:

> From every stormy wind that blows,
> From every swelling tide of woes,
> There is a calm and sure retreat;
> It is at fourteen Beacon Street.

There is more than appears on the surface in these lines. The visitor to the seventh floor of 14 Beacon Street at noontime is always invited to share in the brief service of worship held every office day at twelve fifteen. This service has become symbolic as well as traditional. No one knows precisely when it was started but it has become and is today the family hearthstone, as it were, of the world-wide fellowship of the American Board, including friends in America as well as missionaries and national Christian leaders in many lands. The central feature of the service is intercessory prayer. For many years a calendar of prayer has been used, indicating the person or persons to

---

[1] Until 1822 the office of the Board was in the home of the Corresponding Secretary, first Rev. Samuel Worcester of Salem, then Mr. Jeremiah Evarts of Charlestown. From 1822 to 1826 the office was on the second floor of a tenement building in Cornhill Street, then for four years in the Hanover Street Congregational Church nearby. That edifice burned in 1830. The office was moved back to Cornhill. More spacious quarters were needed by 1838. The Prudential Committee erected a three-story building in Pemberton Square on Beacon Hill which was occupied until 1873. Then quarters were rented at 14 Somerset Street, corner of Beacon. The Congregational Association of Boston built the eight-story building at 14 Beacon Street to house Congregational societies. It was dedicated in 1898.

be held in special remembrance each day of the year. Similar services are held each day in many mission stations throughout the world.

In recent years what has been known as *The Fellowship of Those Who Care* has caught up the spirit of this noonday service of worship at headquarters and by means of an occasional letter to all those who wish to receive it, including missionaries, active and retired, has been the bond of a deepening fellowship of kindred souls bent on the World Mission of the Church.

The Corporate Body

Quite naturally there has been a steady development of the organization of the Board. It has grown from very small beginnings to a complex operation. The essential features at first were nine "commissioners," one secretary, a treasurer and an administrative committee of three, called the Prudential Committee, in accordance with contemporary common usage in church circles in New England. The corporate body numbered twenty-four when the Board was incorporated in 1812.[1] Stage by stage it has been increased as supporting churches multiplied across the country. The Board was set up as a self-perpetuating corporation. As we have seen, neither denominational lines nor geography have been barriers to membership.

Periodically the annual reports have included printed lists of all corporate members classified by residence in states. A glance at the following figures confirms the statement often made by Board secretaries prior to 1910 that the Board had become a national body:

Year	Number of Corporate Members	Number of States Represented (In a few cases foreign countries)
1812	24	2
1822	33	8
1832	75	15

[1] See above, page 127.

1842	171	21
1852	192	22
1862	208	20
1872	201	20
1882	227	24
1892	251	32
1902	348	30
1912[1]	388	37
1922	662	37
1932	876	40
1942	1067	45
1952	1377	37[2]

In 1904 the provision was made that all male missionaries who had been seven years in service and were still holding the Board's commission should be elected corporate members.

Over the years corporate membership has proved a meaningful aspect of Board administration and support. One proof of that statement is the large number of laymen as well as of ministers who have actually participated in the affairs of the Board in one way or another. Another proof is the growth in the number of donors who contribute to Board support directly over and above their gifts to their local church budgets. Intelligent as well as sacrificial giving has deepened the spiritual life of all concerned and focused attention on the work abroad.

In addition, as we have seen (page 12, footnote) since 1821 the Board has numbered "honorary members" among its constituents. In 1835 the names of 1539 honorary members were recorded; in 1860, 7360. After 1860 the names of honorary members were published every five years. The basis of honorary membership was revised in 1938. Henceforth instead of being based on $50 or $100 subscriptions, honorary members were nominated from the list of those who had served at least twelve years as corporate members-at-large or others who had

---

[1] The following year (see page 147) the delegates to the National (General) Council became corporate members of the American Board.
[2] Differing methods of computation are responsible for the seeming decrease in areas represented.

rendered distinguished service to the cause of foreign missions. The category of Life Members instituted as early as 1884 was discontinued after 1902.

Secretarial Staff

The Board has been served by a distinguished line of executive secretaries from 1810 to 1930. The accent during these 120 years was on a staff that should be characterized not by a chain of authority but by the spirit of colleagues. As the Board's missions multiplied, it was evident that there should be a secretary or secretaries for foreign correspondence and supervision and a secretary or secretaries for home base correspondence and official relationships with the supporting constituency. It would be appropriate to call the roll of these secretaries and to provide sketches of their lives and activities. It would be invidious at this point to single out any names for special encomiums. In lieu of this the reader is referred to the files of the *Missionary Herald* in which, as they passed from the scene, their records and spirit are honored.

Reorganization in 1930

The Home Office underwent considerable reorganization in 1930. The merging of the three Woman's Boards with the American Board January 1, 1927 created a situation which called at once for consolidation and increased cooperation. The executive staffs of the four boards were brought together at 14 Beacon Street, Boston. The strictly administrative functions of the merged boards were consolidated. Over a period of several years the Board had to feel its way, as it were, toward more efficient methods of administration of the combined yet expanded enterprise. Prolonged consideration by various subcommittees resulted in a three-fold plan:

First, an executive leader to be called the Executive Vice President was chosen. His duties were not sharply defined at first but he was expected to consider and guide the work of the Board as a whole, represent the Board in major denominational and interdenominational circles, and study with special care Board policy, Board personnel (both staff and missionary) and Board finance.

Second, the three departments of administration were to be carefully coordinated: Foreign Department, Editorial Department, Treasury Department. What was formerly called the Home Department was absorbed in 1936 by the Missions Council, the unincorporated body jointly manned and maintained by the national boards for educational and promotional purposes. Utimately the Missions Council was given responsibility for all editorial work which did not belong strictly to administration. (See pages 151, 152)

Third, the Board increasingly shared with the homeland agencies, including the National (General) Council of Congregational Christian Churches, the task of broadening the understanding of church-folk regarding work beyond the immediate parish and securing for it adequate financial support. The essential problem in working out a new pattern of cooperation was how to reconcile apparently competitive interests and to win support for the total task of the churches in terms of world-wide effort. As we have seen, two main devices were successively tried: The Commission on Missions 1913-1936 and The Missions Council 1936 onward. In this effort the Executive Vice President of the American Board and a similar officer of the consolidated home agencies, under the name of the Board of Home Missions, were expected to play a major role.

District offices for information and promotional purposes had been maintained by the American Board for many years in New York, Chicago and San Francisco. After 1913 these offices were not strictly American Board responsibility.

The Foreign Secretary

It has long been recognized that the vital center of the Board's administration is the Foreign Department. The main function of Secretaries in this department is correspondence and conference with missionaries and missions. As the Board's work has grown, responsibility has been divided between two or more foreign secretaries. No one but a missionary on the frontier knows how helpful it is to maintain a confidential personal relation with a secretary in the home office who can be depended upon to consider carefully every question from the field and to follow through with such action as is in accordance with accepted principles and regulations. The foreign secretary is both judge and advocate, as it were, for many questions arising in the areas for which he is responsible, but he must take counsel frequently with the appropriate sub-committee of the Prudential Committee and with interdenominational committees. Normally all requests involving new missionary personnel, requests for funds (new or renewed), alterations in major policies and plans for mission activities must come to the foreign secretary through the responsible Mission body on a field, but the secretary is always glad to engage in correspondence with an individual missionary, or confer with a missionary when on furlough on any subject dear to the missionary's heart. There is no substitute for a high degree of understanding cooperation between a foreign secretary and the missionaries on the field.

The Prudential Committee

This account of the organization and operation of the Home Office would be inexcusably incomplete without reference to the present functions and record of the Prudential Committee. The service of ministers, laymen and laywomen on this "august body" has been unparalleled in Congregational history from the point of view of length and quality. As noted, the Committee began in 1810 with three members who agreed to meet three or four times a year to direct the affairs of the Board. One of these members was the "Corresponding Secretary" of the Board, Rev. Samuel Worcester of the Tabernacle Church in Salem, Massachusetts. He continued his ministry in Salem until he discovered that he could not carry successfully a double load. He resigned his pastorate in 1819 and until his death in 1821 gave his full time to the Board.

The members of the Prudential Committee were elected annually from among the corporate members of the Board. There was no limit placed upon the number of times a person could be re-elected. This fact led to prolonged service by several devoted members during the nineteenth century. From 1832 onward for many years the Committee met each week, year in, year out. The number of its members were increased from three to twelve. Meetings were held monthly. Reorganization in 1927 enlarged Committee membership to include twelve women, twelve laymen and twelve ministers. Terms of service were set at four years with eligibility for re-election for one term only, except after an interval of at least one year.

The records of the meetings of the Committee have been kept with scrupulous care. The volumes, numbering forty-four up to date, have been bound in leather and carefully indexed. The clerk of the Committee, upon election, is placed under oath for the faithful performance of his duties. It is interesting to turn the pages of these volumes. One has the feeling that he is glimpsing history in the making as he reads of the beginning of mission work among the Cherokee Indians (1817) in what is now Mississippi, Georgia and Tennessee but what was then Cherokee Land beyond the borders of the United States. Or again as one reads of the farewell service held in Park Street Church, Boston, on the occasion of the departure of the first group of missionaries for the Sandwich Islands in 1819. Or again as one reads of the debates and declarations within Board circles regarding the issue of human slavery, beginning with the missions to the Indians, some of whom owned slaves. Or again as one follows the developments in China during the Boxer uprising in 1900 and later the Communist regime in the nineteen-forties and fifties.

The agenda of the meetings of the Prudential Committee across the decades of the nineteenth century are eloquent evidence of the care and faithfulness with which the members of the Committee have carried their responsibilities. In items both great and small the secretaries and the members of the Committee have spared no effort to lay sound foundations, to develop worthy and efficient principles of Christian action, to select and send out and sustain competent, devoted missionaries, to disseminate information about the enterprise of foreign missions among the churches of the United States in such a way as to secure generous and adequate support, and to promote cooperation among all Christian bodies engaged in foreign missions.

Archives

The records of the official actions of the Prudential Committee are supplemented by the archives of the Board. By an arrangement consummated in the nineteen-thirties, the Board has deposited on permanent loan its voluminous archives with Andover Theological Seminary and with Harvard University. Houghton Library at Harvard houses over two thousand bound and indexed volumes of correspondence reaching back to 1810, covering letters to and from thousands of missionaries and others dealing with a great variety of subjects. Harvard Library authorities have included these archives and other items, such as printed material from the American Indian missions, in their card indices, so that they are at the disposal of authorized graduate students and scholars. Many requests for microfilming of certain sections of the archives come to the Board's librarian. The librarian of Harvard University in 1942 said that the Board's archives prior to 1865 were the best original source for information of which he knew relating to contemporary conditions in many foreign countries. Other materials have been deposited with Andover Theological Seminary at Newton Center, Massachusetts, a seminary with which the American Board has been in very close relationship since the very beginning and among whose graduates the Board has appointed hundreds of missionaries. Andover Seminary and the American Board were almost twins at birth and have grown up together!

One of the most interesting sections of the missionary museum at Andover-Newton Seminary is the collection of daguerreotypes of American Board missionaries in the first half of the nineteenth century.

Annual Meetings

The American Board has never failed to hold an annual meeting. Since 1910 these meetings have usually been held in connection with meetings of the General Council in the years when that Council meets and with the East or Midwest Regional Meetings of the Missions Council during the alternate years. For a hundred years it was the practice of the Prudential Committee and its officers to prepare well in advance reports on each mission or general area for submission as sections of the report to the annual meetings of the Board. The advance reports were considered by the Prudential Committee as a whole and then referred to subcommittees of the corporate body whose comments on these reports formed a part of the programs of the annual meetings. This duty was taken very seriously. Sometimes extended discussion resulted. The process was long considered a useful one, both for the soundness of administration and for the dissemination of information.

Reference has already been made to the remarkable series of "papers" by Board secretaries prepared for the annual meetings on various aspects and problems of Board affairs.[1]

Principles of Administration

The principles of Board administration, developed from a century and more of practical experience, may be summarized as follows:

1. Each Mission as an administrative unit is autonomous. It is expected to proceed with its work in democratic fashion with well understood and sincerely accepted procedures. It operates through such committees or agencies as are necessary for effective work on various lines. The Prudential Committee

[1] See pages 102, 108 and Appendix II.

at the home base reserves the right to determine the amount of funds to be placed at the disposal of a Mission, including the support of existing and of new personnel. It also reserves the right to act as a body of reference in all cases involving major changes in procedures or activities.

2. The Mission normally has the right to designate a new missionary to specific tasks within the mission or to transfer personnel from one function to another. In other words, personnel appointed by the Board is responsible in the first instance to the Mission.

3. The nature and range of the activities of a Mission are flexible within the general framework of the Board's charter and purpose. In interpreting the Board's purpose in terms of specific activities missionaries are responsible for conducting their work in ways which they believe would commend themselves to the church folk of the home base. This is never to be interpreted as a slavish procedure. On the contrary, it is to be regarded with as much prophetic Christian imagination and adaptation as possible.

4. The Board is fully disposed to "trust" its missionaries.[1] After appointment a missionary is thought of as an honored colleague, charged with the good name of the Board and, more importantly, with responsibility to witness as he is led by the Holy Spirit to the Christian Gospel as he understands it. The same attitude holds in relation to a Mission or an institution dependent upon or in affiliation with the Board.

5. When it is apparent that a situation in any mission or area confronts the Board with questions on which first-hand information is needed, the Prudential Committee usually arranges for the visit of a fact-finding team called a Deputation. A Deputation normally includes the secretary of the Board who bears special responsibility for the supervision of work in the area to be visited. Secretarial visits as such are much more frequent than deputations and are largely of an administrative nature.[2]

---

[1] See Chapter IV.

[2] The Board has been ably served by several deputations. The most notable are the

6. The autonomy of the indigenous churches is to be respected at all times. These churches, individually and in groups, are treated as autonomous however they may be organized. The function of the missionary in relation to these churches is to be defined by the appropriate responsible indigenous church bodies. When questions arise as to status or procedures, they are to be considered in the light of the policy of the Board which has consistently emphasized the responsibility of indigenous churches as self-directing, self-sustaining and self-propagating Christian communities.

7. Repeatedly the Prudential Committee has reaffirmed its policy of cooperation with other Christian bodies. It has not hesitated to encourage its missions and the indigenous churches overseas to stress the importance of mutual understanding, cooperative activities, and steps toward church union.

---

following:
Deputation to India, Ceylon and the Near East Missions in 1854-55, consisting of Messrs. Thompson and Anderson.
Deputation to the Turkish Missions in 1883, consisting of Messrs. Eldridge Torrey, I. S. Ely, A. L. Chapin, C. M. Mead, N. G. Clark and E. K. Alden.
Deputation to Japan in 1895 by Messrs. W. I. Ellison, J. G. Johnson, A. H. Bradford and James L. Barton.
Deputation to China Missions in 1898, consisting of Messrs. C. A. Hopkins, E. D. Eaton and Judson Smith.
Deputation to India and Ceylon Missions in 1901, consisting of Messrs. J. F. Loba, W. F. Whittemore and James L. Barton.
Deputation to Africa Missions in 1903, consisting of Messrs. Sidney Strong and Elnathan E. Strong.
Deputation to China Missions in 1907, consisting of Messrs. E. C. Moore, L. C. Warner and James L. Barton.
Deputation to West Africa Mission in 1911 by Messrs. Frederick B. Bridgman and Cornelius A. Patton.
Deputation to Marathi Mission, India in 1913 by Messrs. Samuel B. Capen, George A. Hall and William E. Strong.
Deputation to the Japan Mission in 1918, consisting of John C. Berry, James A. Blaisdell and Enoch F. Bell.
Deputation to India and Ceylon Missions in 1926, consisting of Mrs. Austin H. Decatur, Miss Amy Welcher, Rockwell H. Potter, William E. and Mrs. Strong.
Deputation to Mexico Mission in 1931 by E. D. Gaylord, A. D. Stauffacher, Mrs. E. B. Adams, and Alden H. Clark.
Deputation to India and Ceylon Missions in 1945, consisting of Miss Patty Lee Coghill, Albert B. and Mrs. Coe, and Raymond A. Dudley.
Deputation to the Philippine Mission in 1946 by Carl H. Kopf.

15

THE STORY OF THE TREASURY: I
1810-1910

The First Seventy-Five Years 1810-1885

The American Board began its work in 1810 with mingled faith and doubt. The faith of the founders was firm in God but their doubt concerned the response that the Christian public might give to their appeal for help in launching their mission. They knew their cause was worthy and in accordance with Scripture. But would the faith and vision of the young men of the Haystack Prayer Meeting at Williams College and of Rabbit Rock at Andover Theological Seminary be matched by the faith, love and gifts of people in the churches?

The first step of the founders looking forward to the securing of financial support was a brief "Address to the Christian Public." This Address closed with a form of subscription. The appeal was not made directly to the churches but to individuals of Christian conviction. After quoting pertinent passages of Scripture they said: "The Lord is shaking the nations; his friends in different parts of Christendom are aroused from their slumbers; . . . In our own country the missionary spirit is excited, and much has already been done for imparting the Gospel to the destitute in our new and frontier settlements. But for the millions on our own continent and in other parts of the world to whom the Gospel has never been preached, we have yet those exertions to make which comport with the Savior's emphatical directions." Then they called attention to the young men who were ready to go into any part of the unevangelized world. They put these two facts together and asked: "Is there, then, in those who are favored with the

Gospel, the same mind that was in Christ, when he freely gave
his own blood for the redemption of men?"[1]

The financial response to this appeal at the end of the first
year was $1,166.90.

The next year (1811) the Board addressed the Christian
public in similar fashion, adding considerable information
about "the Birman empire" and the pagan tribes in North
America to whom they tentatively proposed to send their first
missionaries. They maintained that "a great and effectual
door for the promulgation of the Gospel among the heathen
is now opened to all Christian nations; but to no nation is it
more inviting than to the people of New England." At the following annual meeting (1812) the treasurer reported receipts
for the year amounting to $13,611.90.[2] The first recorded gift
to the "Permanent Fund" also appears in this year's report.
The treasurer listed receipts in five groups: from individuals,
from foreign mission societies (in the churches), from other
charitable societies in local cities and towns, from ecclesiastical
societies, churches and congregations, and from profits on the
sale of books.

The Address to the Christian Public in 1812 stressed "two
great events" and "two great objects." The first great event was
"the actual commencement of a mission to Asia," the second
the incorporation of the Board by an act of the General Court
(legislature) of Massachusetts. The two great objects were
"the establishment and support of missions among the heathen"
and "the translation and publication of the Bible in languages
spoken by unevangelized nations." Appended to this Address
were two forms of bequest to the Board, one for property, one
for cash legacies. Total receipts for the year closing August 31,
1813 were $11,361.18.[3]

The 1813 Address to the Christian Public is an eloquent
document.[4] In it occurs a passage which has become famous.
"When it was objected on the floor of the Senate of Massachu-

[1] AR, 1811, p. 24.
[2] AR, 1861, p. 137.
[3] Ibid.
[4] AR, 1813, pp. 25-38.

setts to the act for incorporating the Board in whose behalf we speak, that it was designed to afford the means of exporting religion, whereas there was none to spare from among ourselves, it was pleasantly and truly replied that religion was a commodity of which the more we exported the more we had remaining."

Special tribute was paid to the response from interested women:

> The worthy and pious females in our country who have associated to contribute to the funds of this Board, are deserving of particular and affectionate remembrance. Nor would we pass over other females of like character, whose situation does not permit them thus to associate, but whose cordial regards to the cause have been expressed by individual donations. From the time of our Lord's crucifixion to the present day, probably from the patriarchal ages, the larger proportion of his most faithful and devoted followers have been found in the female sex. Here is a scene of action in which women may take a lively interest without overstepping the limits, which a sense of propriety has imposed on female exertion. Here is an occasion, in which thousands of pious females may exert the same affection with which the heart of Mary overflowed, when she annointed the feet of her Savior, and wiped them with the hairs of her head. *She* did it to honor the person of her Lord *before his burial;* they are invited to show the same affection, by furnishing the means of calling *to spiritual life in Him those who are dead in their trespasses and sins.*"[1]

The treasurer reported the total receipts for the year ending August 31, 1814 as $12,265.56.[2]

From 1810 through 1813 the device of an annual Address to the Christian Public, as widely circulated as possible, and the monthly *Panoplist* constituted the main reliance in the effort to secure funds for the enterprise. The Address in 1811, 1812, 1813 was signed by three persons representing the Board, Sam-

[1] AR, 1813, p. 37.
[2] AR, 1861, p. 137.

uel Worcester, clerk of the Prudential Committee, Jeremiah
Evarts, treasurer of the Board, and Jedidiah Morse, a corporate
member. Thereafter, for a number of years, the report of the
Prudential Committee was considered a satisfactory replace-
ment for an "Address" in imparting information and rousing
interest and response.

At first the Board adopted the plan of printing in the annual
reports the names of the donors. The last list of these donors
appearing in 1821 covers forty-two pages.[1] Thereafter the
Prudential Committee was authorized to give such "detail of
donations as may be deemed useful."[2] Acknowledgments of
all contributions were "published with exact particularity" in
the *Missionary Herald* (succeeding the *Panoplist*) which
became in 1820 the Board's property and chief tool for disseminating information.[3]

The first ten years of the Board's financial history were
obviously experimental. From 1810 to 1815 more money was
received annually than was expended. A surplus of approximately $16,500. was accumulated by 1815. The first operating
deficit occurred in 1816 ($3,433.97) but was cared for out of
the accumulated surplus. Operating deficits in 1818, 1819, and
1820 were likewise cared for by the accumulated surplus
account. In 1821 that surplus was reduced to $3.55.

Beginning in 1822 the Board had its attention sharply drawn
to the possibility of deficit financing. For seven successive
years, 1818-1824, receipts did not equal expenditures. The
missions were expanding. A debt of $14,275.65 was carried
on the books beginning September 1, 1824. This amount was
an alarming thirty percent of the total receipts for 1823-24.
The story was still more alarming for the decade 1834-1844.
Every year recorded an accumulated deficit.

Secretary Armstrong read a paper at the annual meeting in
Philadelphia in 1841 entitled "The Importance of Systematic
Organization in Raising Funds." At that time the Board's ac-

[1] AR, 1821, pp. 115-116.
[2] AR, 1822, p. 6.
[3] AR, 1822, p. 24. Some quaint items appear in the *Herald's* list of donations in kind.
For example, "A cheese secured in a tin case from Mrs. Porter (of Hadley, Mass.) for Mrs.
Bingham." (Sandwich Islands.)

cumulated deficit was $57,808.71. Secretary Armstrong's studies revealed some disturbing facts. "Nearly one-third of the churches professing to regard the Board as the channel through which their charities flow out upon the unevangelized world make no regular annual contributions to its funds." Moreover "in those churches where contributions are regularly made, the proportion of members who do not contribute varies from one-third to three-fourths. ... At least one-half (of the total church membership of the denominations) have done nothing for its support during the last year."[1] He urged *systematic* giving.

The Secretary called attention to the commendable fact that certain churches and certain groups of churches had formed auxiliary societies whose purpose was intelligent, increasing support for the Board. He outlined five steps essential to the operation of a successful auxiliary which sound very like the plan of an efficient twentieth century Every Member Canvass.

The Committee of corporate members to whom Secretary Armstrong's paper was referred offered nine resolutions aimed at substantial increases in effort and income. The resolutions did not entirely satisfy the assembly. "It was plain that there must be retrenchment at the missions, however disastrous the consequences might be, or a great advance in the receipts must be secured."[2] Each member of the Board, corporate and honorary, by vote was asked in person these questions:

1. Will you, in view of the facts presented, raise your subscription the coming year twenty-five percent?
2. Will you attempt to induce all others, upon whom it is, in your opinion, proper you should exert influence, to do the same?
3. Will you, with the leave of Providence, attend the meeting of this Board the next year and inform them what the Lord hath enabled you to do, and what He hath accomplished through your labors? or if necessarily detained, will you communicate such information?[3]

[1] AR, 1841, pp. 51-56.
[2] AR, 1841, p. 63.
[3] AR, 1841, p. 64.

The sequel was that in 1842 the treasurer reported that the accumulated deficit of $57,808.71 had been wiped out, largely through the receipt of legacies, and that there was only a small debit of $559.00 on current operations.

From 1844 to the beginning of the Civil War in 1861 when severe financial difficulties were anticipated, the treasury showed a surplus only seven out of eighteen years. A real crisis arose in 1859 when the accumulated debt rose to $66,374.13, approximately nineteen percent of the total receipts for the year.

The Jubilee year (1860) was an appropriate time to review with care the financial posture and practice of the Board. By a special appeal the debt was met through designated gifts of individuals, mainly from New England and New York. It is reported that the extinguishing of this debt "gave a cheerful tone" to the Jubilee meeting. Then the meeting optimistically adopted and "put on record a plan in accordance with which from that time onward, no appropriations would be made, which it might not be reasonably expected, after a careful estimate of the probable receipts, could be made without occasioning a debt, so that this encumbrance was henceforth, for all coming time, to cease."[1]

To make clear to its supporters the financial operations of the Board, the annual meeting of 1861 appointed a committee "to review the expenditures and finances of the Board, and report at the next annual meeting." The result was a most thorough review with a report on affairs at home and abroad that covers eighteen pages. In closing their report the Committee said:

> Your committee may be allowed to conclude this extended report with the statement of two significant facts which seem worthy of grateful commemoration:
> 1. The sum total of our receipts, from donations and legacies, in fifty-two years, is $9,103,276. — giving the average annual income of $175,063. It is with the material resources represented by these figures, that the Board has

[1] ABCFM Commemorative Volume, (Boston, 1885), p. 70.

accomplished, by the blessing of God on its labors, those great things for the advancement of the Gospel, which are already spoken of throughout the world to the glory of the Savior.

2. It does not appear that of this amount, contributed by Christian love and zeal for the foreign missions under our care, one dollar has ever been lost by unfaithfulness, incapacity, or negligence in the financial management of the Board. Let us thank God for the past and take courage for the future.

With the retirement of Secretary Rufus Anderson in 1866 after forty-five years with the Board, his colleagues had mingled feelings of gratitude for his remarkable service matched by astuteness and wide horizons, and feelings of anxiety especially regarding the Board's financial problems. The methods of dealing with the missions had become well standardized, but the matter of income from the churches gave grave concern. The Prudential Committee and the secretaries were greatly encouraged by such statements as the one made by President Bartlett of Dartmouth College, apropos of a financial crisis: "We have in our own minds not a particle of doubt," he said, "that it is within the duty, the privilege, and the power of our churches, to remove the indebtedness, and to make a decided advance upon the rate of expenditure. If the mass of our churches and church members even approximated, in their scale of benevolence, to the standard maintained by a large number of ministers and laymen, this result would be easily reached. What we imperatively need is a *movement all along the line*."[1]

Those who feared the Board would suffer severe setbacks in income during the Civil War were happily disappointed. Most remarkably the financial integrity of the Board was preserved throughout this trying period. After a temporary setback in 1861, another deficit of nearly $28,000. having been liquidated, there was not "a whisper of debt" for eight years. Then the unforeseen happened. Two events threw the Board again into

[1] AR, 1877, p. xxxi.

unwelcome financial uncertainty. First, the "New School" Presbyterians who for sixty years had been a part of the Board's supporting constituency withdrew to join their "Old School" colleagues in forming a united northern Presbyterian Foreign Board. Even though six of the smaller missions under the care of the American Board at that time were assigned to the new Presbyterian Board, uncertainty prevailed as to the total financial effect of Presbyterian withdrawal. Second, the Prudential Committee after much hesitation decided to recommend that the American Board undertake responsibility for the new missions in papal lands which for twenty years had been the special concern of the American and Foreign Christian Union. Up to 1871 the American Board had not operated in lands where Roman Catholicism was dominant but yielded in that year to a considerable body of its supporting churches and individuals who wished the Union to merge with the American Board. The anticipated additional support for this new work failed to materialize with the result that deficits began again to appear year by year: $26,086.25 in 1873, $30,441.07 in 1874, $44,323.96 in 1875, $31,050.22 in 1876, $47,985.94 in 1877. Secretary Alden joyfully refers to the annual meeting in 1877 at Providence, Rhode Island in these words: "The facts of the case were clearly stated to the Board . . . and such was the special interposition of Divine PROVIDENCE at that meeting that no one needs to be reminded where the meeting was held. In two hours the load was entirely lifted . . ." by subscriptions on the spot. For eight years following 1877, that is until the seventy-fifth anniversary in 1885, only in part due to appropriations from the munificent Otis bequest of $1,000,000. in 1879, no debt accumulated, "not indicating by any means, that all the needs and requests of the missions have been met, nor that many tens of thousands of dollars could not have been wisely appropriated, nor that the work abroad has not been kept under stringent limitations, but — indicating clearly what is desirable, the constituency of the Board should understand and appreciate, the resolute determination of the Prudential

Committee to follow the instructions presented twenty-five years ago, and frequently emphasized since, that the annual appropriations shall be kept within the annual receipts and no serious debt shall be henceforth incurred."[1]

It must be borne in mind that throughout the first one hundred years the responsibility for securing financial support for the missions rested squarely and solely upon the Board itself. This is in sharp contrast to the development of "unified promotion" which began to assume definite form in 1913.[2] There were a few "Missionary Societies" but few "State Conferences" as such anywhere until 1900. Moreover, the National Council of Congregational Churches was not organized until 1871. The national missionary societies whose major objectives were in the United States were in the same situation as the American Board as far as the responsibility for securing financial support was concerned. It was a case of "do it yourself." To this task decade by decade the Board set itself — (1) by developing district offices in New York, Chicago and San Francisco; (2) by extending as widely as possible the use of the *Missionary Herald* and other literature; (3) by making it possible for missionaries on furlough from various fields to visit churches and other groups to tell of their work abroad; (4) by developing a body of mission-conscious corporate members; and (5) by making the Annual Meetings of the Board focal points of insight and enthusiasm. To this end the amazing "papers" of the secretaries contributed heavily.[3]

The Accumulation and Use of Trust Funds

Shrewd Yankee Christian businessmen, laymen like Deacon Samuel H. Walley, the first treasurer of the Board, and Jeremiah Evarts who followed him as treasurer, (1811-1821), recognized the importance of some kind of a financial backlog for

---

[1] AR, 1877, p. 70.
[2] See above, p. 148.
[3] About 1840 it became the custom of the Prudential Committee to ask the secretaries to present "papers" at the annual meetings, laying frankly before the corporate members and interested friends both the opportunities and responsibilities faced by the Committee at home and abroad. These "papers" became a real feature of the annual meetings from 1841 to

Board operations. It is not known just when or in whose mind the plan took definite shape but, as already noted, in 1812 the treasurer reported an item of $16.20 "interest on a donation to the permanent fund."[1] This Permanent Fund thus has had a long history from its modest beginnings to the present (1957) when its book value is reported as $1,436,887.24. The income of this fund has continuously been at the disposal of the Prudential Committee, unrestricted as to use but applied for the most part to current obligations.

In 1823 due to the thoughtful and generous action of friends of the Board two other "permanent" funds were established, one "for the support of corresponding secretary" and one "for the printing press for Western Asia."[2]

Someone thought so favorably about the whole matter of permanent funds that in 1824 another permanent fund was set up, "for the support of treasurer."

The interest on the funds for the support of corresponding secretary and treasurer furnished in part the salaries of those two Board officials, kept separately until 1832, then combined, and later combined with the permanent fund which was designated as the General Permanent Fund. The following figures give an indication of the steady but slow growth of this Fund.

1897. They were printed in extenso in the annual reports and often reprints were made for wider distribution. Together they present a veritable history of the missions and of the Board's administration, albeit somewhat disjointed and fragmentary. On the matter of securing support the very titles of some of them suggest the nature of the financial struggles through which the Board passed in the middle and later decades of the nineteenth century:

1841 The Importance of Systematic Organization in Raising Funds — Secretary Armstrong.
1843 How Far the Amount of the Board's Indebtedness is Under the Control of the Prudential Committee — Secretary Anderson.
1850 The Churches Are Able to Furnish More Means — Secretary Pomeroy.
1852 The Importance of Adequate Support to Missions — Secretary Wood.
1859 Can the Board be Kept Out of Debt and in What Manner — Secretary Anderson.
1864 The Financial Policy of the Board — Secretary Treat.
1867 Provision for Disabled Missionaries and the Widows and Children of Missionaries — Secretary Wood.
1871 New Work in Nominally Christian Lands — Business Committee.
1871 The Duty of Congregationalists to Foreign Missions — Secretary Treat.
1874 The Financial Problem of the Board — Secretary Treat.
1877 Financial History of the Board — Prudential Committee.
1886 Constant Factors in the Missionary Problem — Secretary Smith.
1888 Our Financial Outlook — Secretary Alden.
1891 True and False Economy in Missions — Secretary Clark.
See below, Appendix II B, for other papers on other subjects.

[1] AR, 1812, p. 16.
[2] AR, 1823, p. 145. The fund for the printing press in Western Asia was not in reality a permanent fund but was available for its purpose whenever and as needed. The press was purchased and located at Malta in 1822 and removed to Smyrna in 1833.

General Permanent Fund

Year	Amount	Interest for Current Expense
1820	33,049.98	2,154.60
1830	41,126.75	2,218.71
1840	45,885.56	1,537.63
1850	56,460.00	2,073.64
1860	67,715.32	2,292.00
1870	117,571.96	6,415.56
1880	129,447.32	6,915.26
1885	172,047.32	9,101.72

The report of the treasurer for the seventy-fifth year of Board history (1885) reports only two permanent funds: "General Permanent Fund" ($172,047.32) and "Permanent Fund for Officers" ($59,608.00).

The next twenty-five years were to witness a remarkable awakening among Board members and officers as to the importance of "funds," the interest of which was to help sustain various projects abroad, mainly educational.[1] It is probably correct to say that during the first seventy-five years the Board relied heavily on legacies for supplementary support rather than upon invested permanent funds, but during the second seventy-five years, largely under the inspiration of Secretary James L. Barton's dynamic leadership, the receipts from legacies was more than matched by the income from a large number of restricted funds.

The Next Twenty-Five Years 1885-1910

The second half of Board financial history began and continued under prevailingly difficult economic conditions. The Victorian Age of world peace was drawing to a close at the beginning of the twentieth century. There were many bright passages, much to encourage. But there were multiple causes for concern, if not anxiety.

For a few years following 1885 the Andover controversy

[1] See Chapter Five.

shook the confidence of Congregational liberals in the Board's leadership. It is impossible to determine to what extent this episode expressed itself in decreased giving to the Board but it undoubtedly had some effect.[1]

Another factor which probably influenced the situation unfavorably as far as income from living donors was concerned, year by year for a decade at least, was the fact that the Board had received two large legacies, the Otis bequest in 1879 which totalled nearly one million dollars, and the Swett bequest in 1884 which amounted to nearly one half million dollars. Both these bequests were put at the disposal of the Prudential Committee for use, both principal and interest, over a period of years primarily for "new missions." The Committee with sober reflections and great conscientiousness carried out the desires of the donors, greatly to the joy of pioneer missionaries and those who had languished for lack of funds for pioneer projects in older fields. By 1895 the unused balance of the Otis bequest was $17,769.96, and of the Swett bequest $889.61. The use of these bequests in itself is a thrilling story of success and progress in well planned work. One thinks especially of the West Africa Mission (Angola) founded in 1880, and the East Africa Mission (Southern Rhodesia) founded in 1882. In part these two missions are glorious memorials to Otis and Swett. But paralleling the use of this special legacy income, receipts from living donors were showing relatively little increase.[2]

[1] See Manuscript by Enoch Bell, The Andover Controversy, in Board Archives, AB 12Z9, pam. box.

[2] The figures showing the use of the Otis and Swett bequests and the income from living donors year by year for the period 1879 to 1895 are as follows:

	Otis Bequest	Swett Bequest	Income from Living Donors
1879	166,459.15		283,627.35
1880	182,787.05		347,423.83
1881	240,031.06		349,424.74
1882	189,705.63		348,374.80
1883	67,568.75		393,319.38
1884	34,894.70		392,864.99
1885	43,884.55	52,992.17	387,013.15
1886	41,144.94	116,000.00	384,247.98
1887	48,808.31	154,319.96	366,958.40
1888	51,032.58	62,500.00	394,568.37
1889	43,664.98	82,110.90	395,044.90
1890	61,482.16	72,707.89	417,921.74
1891	80,907.85	42,000.00	484,463.78
1892	35,185.38	°°	545,097.49
1893	30,864.73	7,000.00	483,187.78
1894	30,952.28	°°	483,108.25
1895	41,366.88	°°	516,003.47

At the turn of the twentieth century, therefore, the Board was in deep trouble financially. Beginning in 1893, a year of economic depression, a serious deficit was reported every year until 1901 except in 1896. The accumulated deficit in 1900 was $82,631.16. Obviously something constructive had to be done to avert still further trouble. With the crisis came a consecrated and astute business man into the presidency of the Board, Samuel Billings Capen of Boston. He was ably seconded by secretaries James L. Barton and Cornelius H. Patton, foreign secretary and home secretary respectively. With urgent calls from the field, particularly from the new mission in the Philippines (1901), with the pressures of expanding denominational programs among the home churches, and with the complications due to industrial expansion in the United States as a whole, there was little likelihood of financial smooth sailing, but the Board was fortunate in its leadership.

Two major developments equipped the Board for the stormy days ahead, one within the Board's financial set-up (the Twentieth Century Fund), and one in common with several major denominations (the Conditional Gift Plan). Both were major factors in maintaining stability and solvency, especially during the first ten years of the century.

So it came about that within the Board's financial set-up two new "funds" were established, the Twentieth Century Fund in 1900 and the Conditional Gift Fund in 1902. Though these two funds did not solve the Board's financial difficulties, they laid the foundation for a long-range policy that has brought immeasurable blessing.

President Capen and Vice President D. Willis James of New York proposed the establishment of a Twentieth Century Fund of $250,000.00. This had the two-fold purpose of equalizing unrestricted legacy receipts and, as far as possible, preventing annual deficits. The essential feature of the plan was to have a reserve fund available from which appropriations could be made when necessary to stabilize or equalize the receipts from legacies year by year. The average annual income from legacies for a number of years had been approximately $125,000.00. It was proposed to establish a reserve fund of twice this amount. The unrestricted legacies of each current year plus interest on the fund were to be added to the principal. One third of the total sum was to be used for the current budget. Thus the unrestricted legacies received in any one year were not to be used *in toto* during that year, but were to be divided into three parts, one third to be used each year for three years in connection with this equalization fund.

The plan of the proposed Twentieth Century Fund was presented in detail to the corporate members of the Board. Many questions were asked. Some members expressed serious doubts as to the wisdom of the plan, fearing that the raising of the Fund would detract from regular annual income. It was explained that contributions for this Fund would be sought solely from donors of relatively large means and that there would be no appeal to the general church public. The members of the Prudential Committee were solidly behind Messrs. Capen and James and had indicated their hearty approval by subscribing "on the spot" $37,000.00 to start the Fund. The annual meeting of 1900 adopted the plan by an overwhelming vote.

It took several years to reach the goal of $250,000.00. The treasurer's reports for the next few years indicated the progress made:

1901	78,363.84
1902	98,426.94
1903	109,183.44
1904	122,587.14
1905	136,178.30
1906	142,999.76

On July 3, 1906, the Prudential Committee, with the approval of the donors to this Fund, voted that it should become operative during the fiscal year beginning September 1, 1906.

The story of the completion, and use of this Fund is an exciting one.

In closing the Board's books in September 1907, the Prudential Committee instructed the treasurer to make the Twentieth Century Fund operative for the first time even though its modified goal of $240,000.00 had not been reached. The usefulness of the fund was soon apparent. For instance, without the fund there would have been a sharp drop in the receipts column from legacies from $207,738.12 in 1906-1907 to $120,263.44 in 1907-1908. By the operation of the plan $149,246.04 was available in the former year and $142,256.82 in the latter.

In closing the books August 31, 1909, the treasurer made the following calculations:

(1) Amount of Twentieth Century Fund
    August 31, 1908 .... $284,513.65

(2) Interest on item (1) during 1909 .... 8,810.38

(3) Gifts to the Fund during 1909 .... 50.00

(4) Unrestricted legacy receipts during 1909 .... 113,568.14

(5) Total of items (1), (2), (3), (4),
    August 31, 1909 .... 406,704.43

(6) According to plan, one-third of item (5)
    to be used in 1908-1909 budget 135,568.14

(7) Difference between items (4) (current
    legacy receipts) and (6) (anticipated
    income from legacies) 22,237.74
    to be drawn from item (1) in order to
    stabilize receipts from legacies

(8) Basis for new reckoning in 1910, sum of items
    (1), (2), and (3) minus item (7) 271,136.29

Another interesting year's record of the Twentieth Century Fund is as follows:

1913

(1) Amount of Twentieth Century Fund
    August 31, 1912 .... $257,910.20

(2) Interest on item (1) during 1913 .... 10,787.77

(3) Unrestricted legacy receipts 1912 .... 131,625.08

(4) Total of items (1), (2), (3)

August 31, 1913 .... 400,323.05

(5) According to plan one-third of (4) to be
used in 1912-1913 budget 133,441.01

(6) Difference between item (3) (current
legacy receipts) and item (5) (anticipated
income from legacies) to be drawn from
item (1) to stabilize receipts from legacies   1,815.93

(7) Basis for new reckoning in 1914:
sum of items (1) and (2) minus item (6)   266,882.04

Year by year the same plan of operation was followed resulting in a steadier amount of legacy receipts, thus making
possible better budget planning.

It is to be noted that the actual completion of the Twentieth
Century Fund was due to the generosity of D. Willis James
who with Samuel B. Capen had initiated the plan. D. Willis
James served the Board as Vice President from 1897-1900 and
became deeply interested in the total enterprise. He observed
the slow growth of the Fund toward its goal and left a bequest
of $95,250.00 in 1908 to complete it.

From 1908 until 1928 the plan of the Fund was consistently
carried out with two exceptions. In 1922 when the Fund was
larger than twice the average annual income from legacies
the sum of $50,000.00 was taken from the Fund and used in
the current budget. In 1927 a large legacy of $90,000.00 was
not equalized through the Fund, but used for the current
budget.

In spite of these operations the principal of the Fund had
increased to $615,333.20 in 1928. This increase was due to the
increase in the current legacies and the merging with the
Twentieth Century Fund of the Legacy Equalization Fund of
the Woman's Board of Missions which united with the American Board in 1927.

At the same time the receipts for the current budgets of the
Board were lagging behind the expenditures and there was the
ever-present pressure of unmet needs on the field.

After a study of the matter by the Finance Committee and

on their recommendation, the Prudential Committee voted that beginning with the fiscal year ending August 31, 1929, forty percent instead of thirty-three and one-third percent of current legacies and of the Twentieth Century Fund be used for the current budget. A further action in 1929 was taken authorizing the transfer from the Twentieth Century Fund of such amount as was necessary to clear the accumulated deficit, provided it left in the Twentieth Century Fund an amount equal to one and one-half times the current legacy income average of the previous five years. As a result the sum of $113,009.66 was transferred.

This change resulted in a larger amount of legacy income being available for current budget than would have been possible under the thirty-three and one-third percent plan previously in operation. This, however, was at the expense of the Twentieth Century Fund. This Fund was thereby reduced to an amount substantially less than the one and one-half times the current legacy figure.

In 1938 the matter was reconsidered by the Prudential Committee and the old plan of thirty-three and one-third percent re-instated. In order to raise the depleted Twentieth Century Fund to twice the current legacy average there was added to it $250,000.00 from the Elizabeth Garrett legacy.

From 1938 to 1951 the Twentieth Century Fund operated on the thirty-three and one-third percent basis. In 1951 another modification was voted by the Prudential Committee. This provided that in the equalization process instead of using the full amount of current legacies and matured Conditional Gifts, only $100,000.00 be used and any excess over that amount be held in reserve. At the time this action was taken, it was thought that this would result in a reserve which could be called on when and if a period of sharply reduced receipts occurred and so save the necessity of too rapid and radical budget adjustment. Since that time the Board has received the matured Conditional Gift of $425,000.00 from Mr. McKerchey which is held as an invested fund and is available at the discretion of the Prudential Committee for any emergency use. Because this fund can act as a reserve, the excess over $100,000.00 of current legacies has been called the Legacy Equalization Fund. In 1955 the figure of $100,000 was increased to $125,000. This fund is to be used primarily in case current legacies and matured Conditional Gifts fall below $125,000. but it is to be available for any purpose which the Prudential Committee may decide.

The second major development in common with several other denominations initiated shortly after the turn of the century was the Conditional Gift Fund. The more common name for a fund of this kind is Annuity Fund. The main feature is an agreement between the individual donor and the Board by which the donor makes an absolute gift to the Board and the Board agrees to pay to the donor during his lifetime a fixed income at a rate determined by the age of the donor at the time the gift is made. On the decease of the donor the principal of the gift or such part as remains is available for the work of the Board and is handled on the same basis as unrestricted legacies. The rates used are based on actuarial tables. These tables, the result of average experience, furnish reason for the judgment that during the lifetime of the donor thirty percent of the principal gift would be used to supplement the earned income of the fund to provide the guaranteed return to the donor. The experience of the Board has proved much more favorable. In the period from the beginning of the Fund in 1902 until 1932 the earned income was sufficient to make the guaranteed payments to the donor. For the period from 1932 through 1956 only ten percent of the maturing gifts had to be taken from the principal, leaving ninety percent available for the work of the Board.

The Conditional Gift Fund is first listed in the treasurer's report of 1902. The item bears the legend "Income used for payments to living donors." The sum reported at that time is $370,671.51. The sum reported in 1957 was $2,285,971.57.

A vital feature in the Board's operation of this Fund is the provision in the by-laws of the Board that the principal of the gift shall be held as an invested fund during the lifetime of the donor. Thus a high degree of confidence is assured to donors. Consistently the Board's practice is to pay interest at the agreed-upon rate, regardless of market conditions. The Board has never failed to observe this rule even though at times it has seemed costly.

16

THE STORY OF THE TREASURY: II
SINCE 1910

As it gathered for the centennial meeting in Boston, October 11, 1910 the Board was reminded that the previous year had closed with an accumulated deficit of $35,585.38. Everyone concerned had hoped that one feature of the centennial might be a balanced budget. When the auditors examined the accounts they found that the accumulated deficit had been reduced to $6005.62. One of the auditors, Mr. William B. Plunket, volunteered a gift of $5000.00, hoping that the balance of the deficit would be subscribed before the report was presented to the Board. This was very quickly done and it was announced that the century had closed with all bills paid. Thus the second century began most auspiciously, financially speaking.

For ten years this auspicious beginning was emulated, though relatively small deficits occurred in 1913 (one percent) and in 1918 (two percent). But in 1920 serious trouble began. World War I was taking its heavy toll. Depression followed war. In spite of devoted and shrewd administration, and energetic, even imaginative promotional efforts, the next two decades were to register dark depths of concern. Finances were only a part of the picture. In other words, there was mingled tragedy and triumph from 1920 to 1940. The deficit figures for these years help to tell the story:

	Operating Deficit	Accumulated Deficit
1920	257,831.58	242,544.36
1921		161,929.89

1922	10,279.12	180,039.94
1923		180,103.41
1924	31,039.43	149,660.52
1925	115,277.12	213,837.72
1926	14,901.10	213,242.13
1927	147,956.46	161,387.59
1928		113,009.66
1929	50,204.28	
1930	29,402.90	79,607.18
1931	74,125.84	162,733.02
1932	89,430.14	251,954.71
1933	59,759.32	311,714.03
1934		136,714.03
1935		111,714.03
1936		111,714.03
1937	51,511.26	142,603.75
1938	40,417.28	133,726.61
1939		57,528.66
1940		27,775.30

It will be noted that every year from 1920 to 1940 closed with a deficit, either operating or accumulated. In thirteen of the twenty-one years current expenditures exceeded current receipts. In every year except 1929 accumulated deficits were recorded, running from twenty-two percent of current income or $311,714.03 in 1933 to two and one-half percent in 1940. During five of these years the accumulated deficits exceeded $200,000. The reader quite naturally will ask how the Board weathered this prolonged financial hurricane. There is no one answer to this inquiry. Basically there were seven lines of effort to remain solvent, operative and creative.

First, repeatedly the foreign secretaries reviewed field budgets, recommending, however reluctantly, reductions in appropriations where least likely to cause disruption. No words can adequately convey the feelings of secretaries and field committees, especially during the nineteen-thirties when the Board's income dropped almost fifty percent,[1] entailing stunning losses in personnel and momentum.

Second, the situation year by year was made known in all its urgency to a large number of friends. Occasionally gifts were received to apply directly to the accumulated deficit.[2] At times urgent needs on the field were stressed and explained, resulting in special contributions. Those engaged in securing support for the Board intensified their efforts, laying the situation before conference superintendents and other state officials, as well as before churches and individuals. Likewise the committees of the Commission on Missions (later of the Missions Council) dealing with appraisals of projects and with percentage distribution of the benevolence dollar, were fully informed of the Board's needs.

Third, the Prudential Committee asked its Finance Sub-Committee to review the assets of the Board, especially funds not restricted to specific projects by terms of the donor. Repeatedly relief came from this source as the Prudential Committee wrestled with deficit after deficit.[3]

Fourth, the Twentieth Century Fund and Conditional Gift Fund set up at the turn of the century, proved to be financial sheet anchors for Board finances during these years of terrific stress.[4] Occasionally the Prudential Committee would specifically assign a legacy or a sizable matured conditional gift to the cancellation of a deficit or major part thereof.[5]

Fifth, the havoc of the first World War in the Near East had compelled the Board to abandon operations in several areas, especially in eastern Asia Minor (Turkey). Dr. W. W. Peet, the Near East treasurer for forty years (1881-1925), had done a remarkable piece of work in securing Board title to almost all the property used by missionaries in their work or as

---

[1] From $2,132,375.02 in 1930 to $1,105,274.63 in 1939.
[2] For instance, in 1925, $20,517.30 was given specifically to reduce accumulated deficit of $149,660.52. In 1928 $36,938.46 was given specifically toward the accumulated deficit of $161,387.59.
[3] For instance, in 1934 $150,000. of capital assets were applied to the accumulated deficit of $311,714.03.
[4] For instance, in 1922 $50,000. was taken from the Twentieth Century Fund and used in the current budget. Again in 1929 the entire accumulated deficit of 1928 of $113,009.66 was met by the transfer of an equal amount from the Twentieth Century Fund.
[5] For instance, in 1926, two legacies totalling $100,000. were assigned to the current budget. Again in 1927, a legacy of $90,000. was used for the current budget.

residences. This involved hundreds of buildings and many plots of land. In the early twenties Dr. Peet supervised the preparation of lists of war damages or losses to present to the Turkish Government. These lists were not complete, partly because the necessary data were not obtainable. But from what was submitted to the Government of the Turkish Republic, a new constellation in the Near East sharply in contrast to the Government of the old Ottoman Empire, indemnities were received, payments being made over a period of three years amounting to $180,000.00.[1] The Prudential Committee was free to use these funds in the best interests of the Board.

Sixth, related somewhat to the question of war indemnities was the question of the sale of certain pieces of property which the Board could no longer profitably use. Considerations of this nature were referred to the Property Sub-Committee of the Prudential Committee with the result that substantial returns were put at the disposal of the Board.[2] Approximately $387,234.68 was realized from the sale or rental of Board property during the two decades 1920 to 1940.

Seventh, the Board sought in every possible way to reduce administrative expenses. Staff salaries were cut, the staff was sharply reduced and every effort made to conserve resources, maintain morale and deepen dedication to a high purpose.

Thus along those seven lines of effort, steps were taken during the 1920's and 1930's to meet obligations and to maintain the credit of the American Board Treasury.

During the days of depression and war the officers and missionaries of the Board consistently sought to maintain the glow of faith and hope and love. The truly herculean efforts of dedicated personnel, always under the scrutiny and by the grace of a just as well as loving Heavenly Father, saved the Board from irretrievable disaster during the years from 1920 to 1940. In the longer perspective of time it may be possible

[1] For instance, in 1938 $20,639.90 and in 1939 $15,571.97 were received as annual payments from the Turkish Government toward the total indemnity figure of $180,000.00.

[2] For instance, in each of the following years, the current budget was credited with substantial sums from the sale of mission property: 1937, $18,596.54; 1938, $25,000.00; 1939, $25,000.00; 1940, $25,000.00; 1941, $27,775.34.

to point to gains and values which those years of tragedy and triumph brought in their train.

The relief from extraordinarily severe financial burdens which came with the nineteen-forties and nineteen-fifties was very welcome even though there were all too frequent reminders of the losses sustained and the opportunities neglected. The great unpredictable fact of the nineteen-forties was the outcome of revolution and change in China. Little did anyone related to the work of our three missions in China (North China, Foochow, and Shaowu) dream that by 1950 all Protestant missionaries, including our own, would either be out or on the way out of that strife-ridden land.

The story of the treasury from 1941 to the present (1956) began with what seemed to be a strange new fact, namely a small surplus at the end of a fiscal year. This was true in 1941 and in every year up to and including 1946 except 1942 when there was a small operating deficit. The broad explanatory fact seems to be that two currents of thought and effort met: the one, the increased giving of the churches, spurred by work for war victims, the other, the effects of the severe cuts in appropriations for the missions abroad from 1930 to 1940 which became increasingly operative. The sequel of depression — war and the evacuation of China — spelled out in terms of Board administration, initiated a series of years when the treasurer's books were balanced with the single exception of 1949.

Personnel

Two names stand out when one reviews the story of efforts to secure funds with which to sustain and expand the work of the American Board — James Levi Barton and David Brewer Eddy. Among all the men and women who with great faithfulness have pleaded the cause of foreign missions as carried on by the American Board, these two men deserve the highest praise.

Dr. Barton joined the staff of the Board in 1893 after seven years as a member of the Eastern Turkey Mission, with head-

quarters at Harpoot. He served continuously until 1927. After
a few years as Foreign Secretary associated with Dr. Judson
Smith, he espoused with unique enthusiasm the cause of higher
education on all the Board's fields.[1] He saw that it was unreasonable to expect to secure the necessary financial support
for colleges abroad from the current contributions of churches
in the United States. He made it, therefore, a matter of policy
to encourage the institutions which had made a beginning
under Prudential Committee auspices to secure independent,
separate though sometimes interlocking, boards of trustees in
America. Their chief duty should be to sponsor the search for
funds, both for current expenses and for endowment, mainly
from non-Board sources. He further advocated the plan that
these institutions should be genuinely interdenominational, international and non-sectarian Christian projects. His friends
who knew the facts said that he was the motivating force that
put higher Christian education on the missionary map and that
funds of approximately $33,000,000. for twenty-one colleges
were raised before he retired in 1927.

Dr. Eddy, as a Secretary of the Board, worked several years
beginning in 1909, in close partnership with Dr. Cornelius A.
Patton, Home Secretary. They developed a plan for appeals to
individuals, both by personal visit and by correspondence,
which proved to be unique and uniquely successful. Dr. Eddy's
ideas and efforts grew out of what seemed to many friends a
remarkable degree of self-dedication to a great cause. He said
on one occasion "My sense of obligation to our missionaries on
the field . . . has underlain my thought and my addresses." He
became an acknowledged genius in the field of securing funds
for foreign missions. He tells a moving story which illustrates
his devotion, directness, and intensity of feeling. A potential
donor's name had been given him with the comment that this
man was rich but eccentric. In his unpublished memoirs, Dr.
Eddy wrote:

A letter was written asking for a substantial gift of

[1] See above, p. 56 ff.

$500., describing the Board's work, with total figures of pupils in the schools, treatments in the hospitals and members of the churches abroad and with due mention of the Board's age and record and its wide-flung work. A letter hot with impatience came by return mail, somewhat to this effect: "Not one dollar for your kind of work. I know the soft polish of your desk, the easy comfort of your chair, the thick nap of your rugs and the luxurious appointments of an office like yours, etc." Astonished at such an unkindly answer and after a delay of a week, my letter pleaded "not guilty" to his four indictments. The desk was rescued from the basement with two legs off and now mended with angle irons, but with so marred a surface that a plate glass had to be added, and the easy chair was bought for five dollars, third hand from the widow of a man who had an office in the building. The thick nap of the rug had disappeared eight years ago and we now had shellacked the floor every four years. The luxurious appointments of the room centered in the twenty pictures before me for which I had personally paid for the photographing and the framing and contained 569 missionaries who had gone out in those annual groups to a work of sacrifice and devotion and under whose eye the routine of each day was performed. I spoke of their life, their sacrifice, their heroism and the soundness of the results of their life investment. I asked him to compare his comforts with theirs, his Christian loyalty with theirs.

Back came a letter of profound apology, not knowing why he wrote any such thing and with a check of $500. The next was $1000. and the year after that $1500. By this time we were becoming acquainted.

It is very difficult to convey the intensity and earnestness with which Dr. Eddy threw himself into the search for funds for the Board's work. His manner of speaking both in private and in public was dramatic and climactic. He often spoke in superlatives because he believed in the superlative value of Christian missions. From his days with the famous "Yale Band" in 1890 which took him and fellow students into thirty-six large cities, pleading for Christian missions, to the last years of his service with the American Board in the early nineteen-forties, Dr. Eddy often electrified his hearers and brought many individuals to a new and conclusive sense of their Christian obligation to give to the missionary enterprise. It is safe to say that by this ingenuity, faithfulness, tireless effort in season and out of season, he brought many millions of dollars into the treasury of the Board during his thirty-five years of active service.

Signposts Along the Way

What broad conclusions can be drawn from our study of the Board's financial history?

Perspective and wisdom are to be gained by a careful study of two "papers" presented to the Board by Secretary Rufus Anderson in October, 1843. For ten years, beginning in the third year of his tenure of the office of major secretary, an annual deficit had occurred. The accumulated debt had reached the then alarming proportions of $21,000.00 or nine percent of the current receipts. For a Board which prided itself on its solvency and gilt-edged credit, this was too much for complacency.

One can almost see the serious look on Dr. Anderson's face as he looked out from under his heavy eyebrows upon the assembly. He spared his hearers no aspect of the seriousness of the situation. He rang the changes on the motive justifying missionary work as he understood it. Then he uttered these words revealing both his idealism and his realism:

It will be necessary to have a distinct apprehension of the object for which the church of Christ exists contemplating the church in its largest signification — not as the result of any particular form of organization, but as the whole body of believers, with Christ for their head. We should have a very inadequate view of the object of this church, if we regarded it as being merely to transmit the Christian religion from generation to generation. No doubt it is bound to take all suitable measures for its own preservation; but its main object (as it should be of every member) is to *propagate* this religion as fast as possible, throughout the world. The Christian church exists for conquest. It is not a fortress, nor a garrison, but an army, a church militant, in the field of conflict, and that field the world. And from this view we gather the weightiest and most conclusive arguments in favor of home missions and all other measures for increasing the strength and resources of the churches. And the more deeply the churches are engaged in this spiritual warfare in all parts of the world, the more will they feel the need of means for the conflict, and of taking the effectual measures to secure them.[1]

One is led to reflect upon a statement made by Dr. Leonard Bacon of New Haven, chairman of the Committee appointed by the Board in 1861 to "review the expenditures and finances of the Board" at a time of crisis: "The true financial policy for an institution like ours, is that which relies not on transient excitement, but on the steady force of religious principle. 'Our ways and means' of revenue are all summed up in the one expedient of making known, as widely as possible, our plans, our operations, our successes, and our embarrassments, and of taking care that every friend of our work shall have all needful opportunities of making his contributions to our treasury, according to his willingness and his ability."[2]

One is also reminded of the remark by the great Scotch theologian, Dr. James Denney of Glasgow: "All works of love, from Christian missions down, are carried on under the pressure of perpetual deficit. When people say they have not anything to give for such causes, they are as a rule telling the truth. They have nothing to give because they have already spent everything. But the true moral of this is that the call for charity is often also a call for self-denial and thrift."[3]

Next in importance to "a distinct apprehension of the object for which the Church of Christ exists" is the understanding of the process by which a Christian community comes into exist-

---

[1] AR, 1843, pp. 52-54, 61-64.
[2] AR, 1862, p. 38.
[3] James Denney, *The Way Everlasting*, (London, Hodder Stoughton, 1911), p. 173.

ence and grows. One comes to appreciate the truth of Jesus'
parable of the leaven. The Church, the body of God's people,
in any area comes into existence, as the Board's record has
proved, by personal contact.

A teacher, a preacher, a close friend, a member of the family
may be the bearer of the arresting word of witness. In very
few cases is the Word meditated in any other way, although
instances of conversion due to the reading of the New Testament in prison or in other forms of isolation have occurred.
This means that the Church normally grows by geometrical
progression. Rufus Anderson was right when he said "Foreign
missions are essentially progressive." The part therefore which
money plays in the whole movement is vital in so far as it
provides for an ever-widening dream of Christian witness.

Secretary Anderson prepared the Memorial Volume published by the Board in 1862. Among other aspects of the history
of the Board he reviewed its finances. The tables of receipts
and expenditures and other tables of statistics which he prepared were the basis of his clear-cut ideas about Board finance.
His main conclusions can be summed up in these sentences:
"Foreign missions are essentially progressive, as much so as a
family. Experience shows that an invariable yearly increase
in the receipts is not to be expected. One of the unsolved
problems in foreign missions [is] how to provide against these
[variations in receipts]. Perhaps our only solution is the principle of faith. The main ground of confidence in the success
of missions . . . is in that principle. To the missionaries on the
ground, a great increase [in expenditures] may seem a matter
of obvious necessity . . . [but] . . . it unquestionably belongs
to the Prudential Committee to regulate the expenses of every
mission, and of every missionary. The cost of printing the
Annual Report has ever been regarded as a judicious expenditure. . . . A thorough digest was the thing needed, a careful
resume, an intelligent exhibition of the proceedings and events
of the year; and such has been the Annual Report. It has put
the Board and the churches in communication with the execu-

tive and the missions. Its influence upon the officers in
preparing it, has been like taking an account of stock with the
merchant. It has been the winding up of the mainspring. The
foundations of the General Fund were laid in Mrs. Norris's
legacy of $30,000. at the outset of the Board's history. . . . It is
deemed prudent to retain such permanent funds . . . in order
that there may be a sure reliance in case of emergency. In two
or three instances, owing to unusual prosperity in some of the
missions, and it may be to commercial distress at home, the
indebtedness has become such as to occasion some uneasiness.
But it has always been paid without impairing the credit of the
Board, or bringing any damage on the Christian community.
. . . The missions cannot be healthy, contented, prosperous,
without a free growth and expansion. The public admission
of debt on the part of the Board has never affected its credit."

The question is sometimes raised as to whether the receipt
of legacies or the expectation of income from that source does
not influence unfavorably the income year by year from living
donors. Interestingly enough in 1868 the treasurer of the
Board, Mr. Langdon S. Ward, has this to say in his report
regarding the income from the largest legacy which the Board
had received up to that time:

> For ten successive years, the Treasurer has enjoyed the
> privilege of acknowledging in the Herald the sum of
> $10,000. from the estate of one who had long been a gen-
> erous friend of this institution, the late Anson G. Phelps,
> Esq. As the last installment of this munificent bequest has
> been received, the Committee deem it proper to bear
> witness, on this occasion, to its great value in two particu-
> lars: (1). Every dollar of it has been helpful to our
> treasury. By recurring to the balance reported during
> these ten years, it will be seen that five were against the
> treasury, amounting to $115,978, and five were in favor
> of it, amounting to $12,725. Deducting the latter from the
> former, we have a residual adverse balance of $103,253.
> Without the legacy of Mr. Phelps, therefore, the residual
> adverse balance would have been $203,253; and we should

have been obliged to report, unless deliverance had come from some other quarter, a constant succession of enormous debts. (2). It is apparent, now, that a very large legacy, paid by installments, (and paid, moreover, at the close of our financial years), will not materially reduce the contributions of the churches. In having established this fact, our honored and departed friend has performed a service of signal value for the benevolent institutions of these United States.

Several times in the course of the first hundred years, the officers of the Board seemed to rely upon the enthusiasm engendered at annual meetings to provide what was needed to wipe out an accumulated debt. Thus in the jubilee year, 1860, at Boston the friends of the Board completed the raising of the debt of $66,374.13. Again in 1877 at Providence a debt of nearly $48,000. was raised at the meeting even though it required extra sessions. Expectations of this nature were gradually given up, especially after the denominational effort to coordinate the benevolence giving of all the churches. Increasing emphasis was laid upon the principle already quoted as: "The true financial policy for an institution like ours is that which relies not on transient excitement, but on the steady force of religious principle."[1]

Throughout the years since 1913 "the steady force of religious principle" has been increasingly the reliance of the Board for adequate support and the basis of the manifold and varied efforts at what has been called "missionary education" in the local church.

A Final Word

That prince of preachers and man of prophetic insight, Jay T. Stocking, Moderator of the General Council from 1934 to 1936, coined the term "immortal money." He spoke to his people about the privilege of helping to sustain the work of the Christian Church at home and abroad.[2] On the highest levels

---

[1] AR, 1862, p. 38.
[2] See "Immortal Money," reprint by Missions Council, New York, April 1956.

of Christian stewardship in giving your money you give your-self. That makes it immortal.

Across the decades the American Board has fulfilled the trust placed in it by those who have enabled it to send Christian heralds around the world. The signposts on the King's High-way may be such things as buildings and books, but the vistas of beauty reach out endlessly in the transformed lives of God's children of many races and in their visible bonds of fellowship in faith and service which constitute the Church, the people of God in Christ.

17

THE PAST IS PROLOGUE

Where Are We Today?

Along the upper reaches of the rugged trail that leads from the village of Zermatt, Switzerland, to the summit of the Matterhorn (nearly 15,000 feet elevation) there are several spots from which the climber can get a good view of the terrain he has covered even though he cannot be sure of what lies ahead. The Solway Hut is such a point. At these points he can take his bearings, breathe deeply, dream a bit and mobilize his strength and courage for the upward trail. Incidentally it should be noted that few climbers try to make the ascent alone. Often the best part of the experience centers in companionship on the way and in sharing the glories of creation.

The enlarged meeting of the International Missionary Council at Tambaram, near Madras, India, in December 1938 was for many who were there the opportunity to recall the main features of the spiritual landscape through which mission boards had passed since William Carey said in 1792: "Expect great things from God; attempt great things for God." After he said that he went to India to witness to Hindus, indeed an attempt in a great cause! It is likely that the insights of the Tambaram Assembly will be recognized in centuries to come as truly creative, even revolutionary.

The year 1938 is a good dividing line between the old and the new in modern Protestant missionary experience. To be sure, the atom had not yet been split and outer space was still inviolate, but the new die of the missionary movement had been cast. The inescapable fact which announced that a new era had begun was as momentous as it was simple: The assembly visualized as no previous assembly of Christians had ever done in the history of the world that the Christian Community is world-wide. Delegates had come from the East and the West, from the North and the South, from all continents and many islands, from the midst of all sorts and conditions of men and had sat down to take counsel as colleagues in the name of Christ. The key word of that Assembly was *colleagues.* To be sure, the not-all-together felicitous term "older and younger churches" was on everyone's lips but deeper than their time-bound implications were the realities of fellowship and comradeship in the Church of Christ which obliterated distinctions of time and place, race and culture.

The next three assemblies of the International Missionary Council, Whitby 1947, Willingen 1952, and Accra 1957, developed the concept of "colleagues" in the world mission of the Church but in the nature of things could not go beyond it. Whitby coined the phrase "partners in obedience." That is what Christian colleagues are. Willingen stressed the nature of the Church as essentially a body of witnesses united in their sense of mission. That is what Christian colleagues are and do. Accra (Ghana) worked over both these emphases, rejecting unhesitatingly the phrase "older and younger churches" and accepting the "fact of the one Church sent to the world in obedience to Christ."[1] One delegate at Accra put it this way: "They (the churches of Asia) are now saying, in no uncertain terms, that they feel called by Christ to take their share in the world-wide mission of the Church, not simply through the evangelization of their own countries, but in other lands as well. They realize that mission is of the essence of the Church and as churches now grown to maturity they, too, want to fulfill their responsibilities."[2] Thus arose the aptness of the phrase "The World-wide Mission of the World-wide Church."

There is proof that the churches and many of the mission boards of America, including the American Board, have shared this new vision. ..

[1] *International Review of Missions,* April 1958, p. 144.
[2] General Secretary's Letter, London Missionary Society, No. 174, March 1958, p. 3.

Once the missionary went from a church that sent to a people who received. Now the churches both send and receive. Once the missionary went largely from one part of the world to another. Now he goes from all parts unto all. Men and women go without regard to direction, or culture, or continent in order that people everywhere may hear in their own tongues the wonderful works of God. Missionaries not only bring their hope, their faith, their love; they also receive the treasures of God in churches in other lands.[1]

The modern missionary movement began in the West when the West was hardly conscious of the rest of the world. The psychological distance traveled during the eighteenth and nineteenth centuries by the leaders of Protestantism both in Europe and in America was astonishing. At last Protestantism caught up with the enthusiasm and missionary achievements of the Roman Catholic Counter-Reformation and began to think in terms of the whole world as the field.

Mobility and Adaptation

"New occasions teach new duties. Time makes ancient good uncouth." The insight of the poet should inspire the artistry of the missionary. For the missionary, as Bishop Hall so well insists, is or should be an artist in the presentation of truth embodied in personality.

One cannot survey, even cursorily, the history of the American Board from its beginning in 1810 without coming to the conclusion that the Board has carried on with consistency through the thick and thin of fifteen decades, meeting crisis after crisis with faith and singleness of purpose. But one is even more impressed with the grace that has been given to its officers and missionaries to explore and to experiment, to adjust and to adapt, to cancel and to construct where circumstances well beyond their control have seemed hostile or even mildly adverse.

[1] Division of Foreign Missions, National Council of Churches of Christ in the U. S. A., *The Missionary Responsibility in Our Time*, 1957.

Many examples of this capacity for mobility and adaptation could be given. Consider these instances.

The war of 1812 between the United States and Great Britain was going on when the first American Board missionaries sailed in 1812 from Philadelphia and Salem for India. The East India Company of Britain had been for some time and was still the ruler in India. The opposition of that Company to the presence and activity of missionaries from the West, even from Britain itself, was well known. To be sure, clergy from the Church Missionary Society and the Society for the Propagation of the Gospel were allowed to function as chaplains among British subjects in India but missionary activity as such was forbidden. Consider then the effrontery of American missionaries in approaching India under those circumstances! None but foolhardy fanatics would undertake such a mission and those who sent and sustained them could hardly be considered less visionary. The missionaries who landed at Calcutta probably expected to be deported. They had to flee but they were only diverted, not defeated. Bombay was only a shade more hospitable than Calcutta. Illness and even death were part of the toll of their effrontery. Then without losing sight of the mission to the people of India one of the missionaries, Rev. Samuel Newell, who had been deported from Calcutta, chanced to land at Colombo, Ceylon. He soon made friends with Wesleyan missionaries there and in conference with them and with Government authorities recommended to the Board at Boston that a mission among the Tamils of northern Ceylon would perhaps become a providential stepping stone to India. In the meantime, missionary colleagues had won a foothold in Bombay. Then in 1816 the first contingent of missionaries arrived at Colombo, soon to go as agreed to the Jaffna area in northern Ceylon. These missionaries in Ceylon went to work with a will among the Tamils, ethnically of the same stock as the Tamils of South India. They never lost sight of their purpose to witness in India. That purpose was fulfilled in 1834 when the Madura mission in South India was established. They had been flexible enough to adapt readily to the needs and demands of the time.

Consider another situation calling for mobility and adaptation. In 1922 Mustafa Kemal — later called Ataturk — rallied the Turks after the crushing defeats of the first World War in which Turkey had been allied with the Central European powers. The story of his daring exploits and of his magnetic and farseeing leadership has become widely known. "The sick man of the old Ottoman Empire" died but "the strong man of the new Turkish Republic" was born. The American Board had sent its representatives to the Ottoman Empire in the early decades of the nineteenth century. The story of their activities, including many failures and many successes, is a long one, but suffice it to say that their lines of churches, educational and medical institutions and translation and publication work penetrated every part of the Near East. Muslim public opinion prevented Muslim youth and others from responding to the services in which these missionaries pioneered. Yet the minority populations, chiefly the Armenians, took advantage of these new opportunities for physical, moral and spiritual welfare. The war years 1914-1918 wrought sad havoc among the minorities. People perished by the thousands, and in the suffering and confusion, missionary institutions of all kinds were wholly or partially ruined. The mood of the defeated Turks was morose but their despair was turned to hope by the indomitable and ingenious Ataturk. At Lausanne in Switzerland, following his victorious counter-attack, the diplomats of Europe met the emissaries of the new Turkey to salvage what they could of Western "interests," prestige and institutions.

What attitude should the American Board missionaries take under the new circumstances? Secretary James L. Barton, a master builder of American Board institutions in many areas of the world, visited Turkey in 1922 to discover the thought and test the temper of the missionaries on the spot. Then he went to Lausanne to plead for such tolerance and understanding as would allow the continuance of missionary service in the new Republic of Turkey. He faced hard facts but he faced them conscious of the desire of missionaries to carry on, to adapt themselves to new conditions, to serve the new Turkey with devotion and loyalty to the spirit of Christian pioneers. Here was not only singleness of purpose and courage, but also mobility and adaptation.

There have been other instances of the same qualities which might be cited. They have appeared in each generation.

To What Is the Past Prologue?

After two world wars and their accompanying suffering and upheavals through the whole area of human living and thinking, at the middle of the twentieth century the American Board faces major questions of policy and practice.

Has the foreign missionary enterprise of American Christians reached the end of its usefulness or calling? Have the revolutions in every part of the world spelled decline, perhaps defeat, for the world mission of the Christian Church so far as Americans are concerned?

"The American Board must do vastly more than it has already done or it has already done too much," said Dr. John R. Mott in an address to the Prudential Committee, September 11, 1945. This characteristic utterance of the chief architect of the ecumenical movement of our day is a challenge to every foreign mission board. It is the spiritual counter-part of that famous word of one of our American naval heroes: "I have not yet begun to fight." However one may try to peer into the future of the World Christian Community and the relation of the mission boards which burgeoned in the nineteenth century to that nascent world-wide Community, unfinished tasks sway the imagination. Hope vies with memory. There can be gratitude to God for His patience and blessing in the past but gratitude is best expressed in renewed dedication to present and future obligations.

To what is the past prologue in the history of the American Board? For what larger purpose has God our Father led us

thus far? Can we spell out in concrete terms, relevant measures, and specific next steps the attitudes and programs which
are the logical developments of our 150 years of history? Can
we dream with the prophetic souls and seers among us of the
glory that is yet to be as the Christian Gospel gains deeper
rootage, provided we, our comrades in every land and our
successors are faithful to the heavenly vision? What are the
signboards for the future along the King's Highway?

Certainly the God of history is speaking to us out of 150
years of our effort to respond to the imperative implicit in the
Christian Gospel to communicate the Good News to every
creature. Call God's voice in this case the logical implications
of what we have learned as a board in the effort to do His Will.
The future must take account of the past even as it seeks to
avoid its mistakes and pitfalls, and to evaluate what we are
wont to call its successes. Whether or not we believe that the
Kingdom of God will come in its fullness within human history,
as Christians our foundation rock is Jesus Christ, our touch-
stone is His Spirit, and our goal His beloved Community.

There has been a refinement of motive as the American
Board has gone about its work. The deepest impulse from the
beginning has been loyalty to Christ. What that loyalty on its
highest levels has been understood to require generation after
generation has been expressed in various terms. Today we say
that the Gospel of God in Christ is relevant to every human
need. Our sensitivity to human ill fortune of every description
drives us to a deeper understanding of God's loving purpose
for humanity as a whole. Christ came that men might have
life — unfathomable life. We ponder the memorable words of
the Jerusalem meeting (1928) of the International Missionary
Council:

> We believe in a Christ-like world. We know nothing
> better; we can be content with nothing less. We do not
> go to the nations called non-Christian, because they are
> the worst of the world and they alone are in need; we go
> because they are a part of the world and share with us in

the same human need — the need of redemption from ourselves and from sin, the need to have life complete and abundant and to be remade after this pattern of Christ-likeness. We desire a world in which Christ will not be crucified but where His Spirit shall reign.

We believe that men are made for Christ and cannot really live apart from Him. Our fathers were impressed with the horror that men should die without Christ — we share that horror; we are impressed also with the horror that men should live without Christ.

Herein lies the Christian motive; it is simple. We cannot live without Christ and we cannot bear to think of men living without Him. We cannot be content to live in a world that is un-Christ-like.[1]

As we survey the past and look toward the future we believe that God's purpose for humanity has never changed and will never change. However the motive for witness or service in the name of Christ may be described, it will be essentially the desire to declare God's loving purpose for his children.

Pressures for change in structure, relationships, and methods of work have arisen sometimes from within, sometimes from without the Board's fellowship. The Christian movement in every part of the world today is under the terrific pressures of both wholesome and unwholesome physical developments, such as accelerated transportation and communication, war potential and industrial achievement. It is likewise under the pressure of developments in the social sciences, chiefly psychology, sociology, anthropology and the philosophy of religion. The most dynamic of these pressures is matched by communism, nationalism and the revolt against colonialism all over the world. Economic and political trends supplement all other forces to produce unrest among people, East and West, who regard themselves as underprivileged and who therefore covet the creature comforts which they identify with progress.

But it must not be imagined that all the pressure for change

---

[1] Jerusalem Series, International Missionary Council, (New York 1928), Vol. I, p. 406.

in policies or methods of work by the American Board stems from without the Christian movement. The developing self-consciousness of the churches and their leaders in many lands spearheads demands for self-determination with its accompanying privileges and duties. It seems to make little difference in the face of these inner pressures to assert that this or that community is not yet ready for autonomy. The vortex of problems connected with the pain of growing up has to be experienced to be appraised at its true complexity.

Some missionaries of the Board have learned the hard way that Secretary Rufus Anderson's emphasis upon the self-governing, self-supporting and self-propagating church sets a standard and dictates a program analogous to those faced by the parents of teenagers in present day America. The future of the Christian movement around the world, believe it or not, like it or not, is in the hands of national Christians and their spokesmen. By every conceivable worthy standard this must be reckoned as success.

This brings one to the concrete question of what changes in structure, relationships and methods of work should logically and advisedly be made as the American Board faces a new century of effort in pursuit of its major objective, the strengthening of the witness of the Christian churches in other lands.

The question when analyzed leads one not only deep into the heart of the Christian faith itself but also deep into the practical and often baffling problem of how to help people grow.

We must act in accordance with a clearer understanding of the unity we seek in Christian worship and work. This means, for instance, heeding the voice of the leaders of the younger churches who insist that unity, organic unity in many cases, on the so-called mission fields is an imperative. The outworn regalia of American denominationalism must be discounted and cast away as rapidly as Christian communities abroad have the insight and courage to unite with other communities in tradition-breaking but loyal-to-Christ comradeship.

We must act in accordance with the fact that the Christian World Mission to be served by the American Board is definitely a multiple mutual affair from now till its end. The people of the United States need the Christian witness of non-white Christians from abroad in the same way and according to a developing program as other nations need the Christian witness of Americans whatever their racial origin. This principle can make ample provision for non-white American missionaries of which there ought to be many more than there are now.

One might mention several corollaries to the thesis that missions today are a multiple, mutual affair. The International Missionary Council, following a recommendation of the Willingen meeting (1952) has sponsored interdenominational, interracial Missions of Fellowship or Deputations for specific purposes, all carrying further into action the spirit of Christian unity and mission on a world-wide scale. Fuller development of this method cannot fail to be richly productive. Closely associated with this principle and the purpose of this plan is the basic need, now in its early stages of realization, for missions from one younger church area to another. There is properly no such thing as a home base church or a home base country except as every country and every church is a base for extending the influence of the Gospel. The next generation, we can be reasonably confident, will see a leveling up of missionary service upon the principle that all churches in all lands are called to be active missionary centers. Christian missionaries of all races and churches are fraternal workers, serving the Church or Christian movement in the areas they visit and under its direction.

Once again, we must act as Christian brothers in stewardship both in giving personnel and substance and in committing the use of such resources to the responsible persons or groups in other lands. Concretely, this suggestion involves the end of the authority of the foreign missionary or a group of foreign missionaries functioning as a "mission" or committee in the matter of the allocation of funds from abroad. All too often in the past the foreign missionary has claimed the right to allocate funds appropriated by his board on the principle that the donors expect that function to be performed by "someone they know and can trust." No one would excuse delinquency wherever it occurs but the time has come for American donors and the American Board to "trust" their indigenous colleagues in other lands with complete authority in money matters. There are devices in use already which are calculated to lift the burden from the shoulders of any one individual national leader. This method of administration can put new life into a stagnant church group because it places responsibility where it belongs. After all, in many cases the members of the indigenous churches and communities are putting far more proportionately of their own resources into their Christian enterprises than many donors to the American Board.

Likewise, there must be a wide extension of the principle already followed in many cases whereby personnel from abroad, that is, missionaries, will be designated to posts of service by the proper bodies of the indigenous churches, whether it be evangelistic, educational, medical or other lines of service.

These developments pose a problem of a somewhat different nature. It may be stated in this way: If the logic of growth in the areas of the younger churches demands, according to their own judgment, a high degree of unity and freedom from denominational impediments, how shall the churches of America, associated with the different denominational boards, operate? Does not unity "on the field" demand "unity at home"? We may recognize that the required unity is not necessarily organic at home or abroad. We may also recognize that, humanly speaking, it will be difficult for an indefinite period to secure adequate income for projects or causes not immediately related to specific denominations or groups of churches. Nevertheless, churches and Christian communities abroad mean business in this matter of unity. What shall we American Christians do about it? Do we see God's hand in that demand?

Are we not ingenious and devoted enough to find a way? The experiments already in process in connection with the work of ten boards in Japan, of which the American Board is one, and of a similar set-up in the Philippine Islands, have much to offer as this problem is seriously faced.

This problem is related to the Congregational Christian churches of America in a very challenging fashion. As we have reviewed the main features of the history of the American Board in relation to the Congregational churches, we have noted the tendency of the churches in their organized capacity to claim the Board as a distinctly denominational agency. That tendency actually has not seriously restricted the freedom of the Board in its operations abroad, but it has increasingly put the denominational stamp on the Board in its structure and relationships at home. This is in sharp contrast to the facts and spirit prevailing in the earlier decades of its history. The logic of events abroad today demands less rather than more emphasis upon the denominational spirit. Shall we Congregational Christians find a way to help Christian movements toward unity abroad especially where the American Board is heavily involved? Or will the virus of resurgent denominationalism vitiate our influence and efforts?

Another problem presses for a wise solution in the not-distant future. It is not unrelated to the foregoing points but concerns what one may call the supporting fabric of the younger churches. Since the eighteen-eighties American Board operations abroad have become heavily institutionalized. After the great debate regarding higher education precipitated by the Board's Deputation to India, Ceylon and the Near East in 1854-1855 had been settled in favor of a program of higher education, the Board entered upon a long period of institution building. As already related, Dr. Barton came to the conclusion, after a decade of wrestling with the problem of support for a score or more of higher educational institutions, that the usual annual benevolence giving of the churches and interested individuals would not prove adequate. Institutions are relatively expensive parts of a foreign missionary program. Questions arise in connection with their needs and operations which do not easily fit into a church-centered enterprise. Furthermore, while indigenous churches and communities, both Christian and non-Christian, warmly approve, patronize and to a considerable extent support these institutions, far greater subsidies from abroad are required for them than for other lines of mission work. It is manifestly unwise — in fact, under prevailing circumstances, impossible — to demand that indigenous communities provide all that is needed for these institutions. Broadly speaking, one of the greatest services which American Christians have rendered communities in Asia, Africa and Latin America during the last one hundred years has been the founding and maintenance, including a large measure of financial support, of these institutions of higher learning.

The problem becomes acute as institutions grow and meet with substantial success. The usual answer throughout recent years has been the organization of separate boards of trustees in America for institution after institution. The main purpose of an American board of trustees of an institution overseas is not academic control but interest and financial support. This plan has worked surprisingly well. The American Board has supplemented this plan with its Higher Educational Fund, as we have seen. The dilemma that faces the Board today as costs increase so rapidly is greater support or practical desertion of institutions like secondary schools, hospitals, and theological seminaries as well as colleges to which the Board has long been related.

On the one hand, it is estimated that over one half of the present missionary staff of the Board are engaged in educational work.

On the other hand, we are moving rapidly toward a church-centered policy. It is not without significance that at the Tambaram meeting of the International Missionary Council in 1938, "the Church" was stressed beyond all previous emphasis as the instrument by which God in Christ was to bless the world. "The Christian Church today is called to live, and to give life, in a world shaken to its foundations. . . . It is in and to this world that the Church must conduct its mission, seeking to repossess and proclaim its God-given message in all its truth and power. . . . We must come in deep humility, knowing that no merely human deed or word of ours will suffice to meet humanity's need. God's words and deeds alone are the healing of its sickness. Yet it is still His Will to utter and accomplish them through His Church. His promise is still that His strength shall be made manifest in our weakness."[1]

Broadly speaking, the major question before the American Board today is: How can we serve effectively in the new era in these two interrelated areas of concern — church-to-church help, and Christian education? The Board must not fail to adjust its organization and administration to the realities of the growth of the World Christian Community.

In a great many areas the patterns of the future are not yet altogether clear. In a real sense, we look out, as did our fathers, into an unknown world. Unlike them, we have behind us a century and a half of experience in the Christian world mission. This provides some measure of wisdom and a great measure of momentum. And unlike them there stand with us a great multitude in the churches of America and overseas who seek unity and share the sense of mission with all Christians. Yet we are called in the new era, as our forebears were called 150 years ago, to be His witnesses throughout the world. "You shall receive power when the Holy Spirit has come upon you; and you shall be my witnesses in Jerusalem, and in all Judea, and Samaria, and to the ends of the earth." (Acts 1:8)

---

[1] *The World Mission of the Church,* (New York, International Missionary Council, 1939), pp. 13, 14.

APPENDICES

Appendix I
Bibliography

It is obviously undesirable to attempt here a comprehensive bibliography dealing with the subject of this volume and related matters. What is attempted is a list of books and other records which may be of interest to the reader who would like to examine sources or to continue studies suggested by what is written.

A
DOCUMENTS

Barton, James L. Memoirs. Manuscript in American Board Archives: AB 55 B 28, 1936.

Bell, Enoch Frye. The Andover Controversy. The Hyde Lecture. Andover Theological Seminary, 1943. Manuscript copy in American Board Archives.

Berry, John C. (M.D.) History of the Medical Work of the Japan Mission 1919. Manuscript in American Board Archives: Japan 12 Z 9.

Capen, E. W. American Board History (Beginnings). Manuscript in American Board Archives: 1908.

Eddy, David Brewer. Raising Money for the American Board. Manuscript in American Board Archives: 1942.

Goertz, Peter Siebert. A History of the Development of the Chinese Christian Church under the American Board in Fukien Province. A dissertation presented to the faculty of the graduate School of Yale University in candidacy for the degree of Ph.D., 1933. Typescript copy in American Board Archives.

Hazen, William. History of the Marathi Mission 1910-1943. Boston: Manuscript in American Board Archives.

Lamson, Kate G. History of the Woman's Board of Missions. Manuscript in American Board Archives: AB 16 L 21 H, 1927.

Leamon, John H. The Christian Approach to Islam. Manuscript: A Paper read by John H. Leamon at the Cambridge, Mass. Ministers' Meeting, October 1957.

Learned, Dwight Whitney. Three Score Years and Ten (1848-1918). Manuscript in ABCFM Archives: Jap 24 L 47 Boston.

Lombard, F. A. A History of the Japan Mission of the American Board. Typescript original (3 vols.) in ABCFM Archives: Jap 10 L 83 H.

Manuscript Sources in American Board Archives: (Approximately 2500 bound volumes) Original Minutes of the Prudential Committee 1810-1959. Collection of original letters from secretaries of the American Board to its missionaries and others, 1810 to the present. Collection of original letters from missionaries of the

American Board to the secretaries at Boston, 1812 to the present.

Phillips, C. J. The American Board 1810-1860. Thesis presented to Harvard University in partial fulfillment of requirements for the Ph.D. degree, 1953. Typescript copy in American Board Archives.

Stock, Harry Thomas. A History of Congregational Missions Among the North American Indians. Thesis presented to the University of Chicago for the M.A. degree, 1917. Typescript copy in Library of Chicago Theol. Sem'y.

B
HISTORY

American Board History

Anderson, Rufus. History of the Missions of the ABCFM in India. Boston: Cong'l Pub. Society, 1875.

————. History of the Missions of the ABCFM to the Oriental Churches (in two vols.). Boston: Cong'l Pub. Society, 1872.

————. History of the Sandwich Islands Mission. Boston: Cong'l Pub. Society, 1870.

Annual Reports of the American Board of Commissioners for Foreign Missions. Boston: American Board, 1810 to 1958.

Commemorative Volume in Connection with the Seventy-fifth Anniversary of the ABCFM, held in Boston, October 13-16, 1885. Boston: American Board, 1885.

Davis, Grace T. Neighbors in Christ. Chicago: James Watson & Co., 1926.

Deputation Report. Boston: American Board, 1855.

Deputation Report. Boston: American Board, 1901.

Memorial Volume of the First Fifty Years of the ABCFM. Boston: American Board, 5th ed., 1862.

One Hundredth Anniversary of the Haystack Prayer Meeting, celebrated at the Ninety-seventh Annual Meeting of the American Board in North Adams and by the Haystack Centennial Meetings at Williamstown, Mass., October 9-12, 1906. Boston: American Board, 1907.

Prudential Committee's Instructions. Boston: Samuel Armstrong, 1819.

Strong, William E. The Story of the American Board, An Account of the First Hundred Years of the ABCFM. Boston: Pilgrim Press, 1910.

Tracy, Joseph. History of the ABCFM. New York: M. W. Dodd, 2nd ed., 1842.

View of the Missions of the AMCFM, November 1823. Leaflet in American Board Archives: AB 90 Z 10.

Winslow, Miron. Sketch of Missions, or History of the Principal Attempts to Propagate Christianity Among the Heathen. Andover (Mass.): Flagg and Gould, 1819.

Mission Boards (other than American Board)

Armstrong, M. W., Letscher, L. A., and Anderson, C. A., Editors. The Presbyterian Enterprise, Sources of American Presbyterian History. Philadelphia: Westminster Press, 1956.

Barclay, Wade Crawford. History of Methodist Missions (six vols.). New York: Board of Missions of the Methodist Church, 1957.

Barton, James L. Story of the Near East Relief (1915-1930), An Interpretation. New York: The Macmillan Company, 1930.

Brown, Arthur Judson. One Hundred Years, A History of the Foreign Missionary Work of the Presbyterian Church in the U.S.A. New York: Fleming H. Revell, 1936.

Brown, Stephen J., and McDermott, Editors. A Survey of Catholic Literature. Milwaukee: Bruce Publishing Company, 1945.

Drury, Clifford Merrill. Presbyterian Panorama, One Hundred Years of National Missions History. Philadelphia: Board of Christian Education, 1952.

Fifty Years of Foreign Missions (German Reformed Church). Philadelphia: Board of Foreign Missions, 1927.

Goodall, Norman. History of the London Missionary Society, 1895-1945. London: Oxford University Press, 1954.

Lovett, Richard. History of the London Missionary Society 1795-1895 (two vols.). London: Oxford University Press, 1899.

Schmidlin, Joseph. Catholic Mission Theory. (A translation from German). Techny, Illinois: Mission Press, SVD, 1931.

Torbet, Robert G. Venture of Faith (The Story of the American Baptist Foreign Missionary Society). Philadelphia: Judson Press, 1955.

Congregationalism and Congregational Churches

Atkins, Gaius Glenn. Fagley, Frederick L. History of American Congregationalism. Boston: Pilgrim Press, 1942.

Baldwin, Simeon. The Genius of Congregationalism. New Haven: Tuttle, Morehouse and Taylor, 1886.

Debates and Proceedings of the National Council of Congregational Churches held at Boston, Mass., June 14-24, 1865. Boston: American Congregational Association, 1866.

Fagley, Frederick L. (see Atkins).

Merrill, Charles C. The State Conference. Boston: Pilgrim Press, 1946.

Miller, Perry. Errand in the Wilderness. Cambridge: The Belknap Press of Harvard University, 1956.

Minutes of the National Council of the Congregational Churches of the United States of America at the first session held in Oberlin, Ohio, November 15-21, 1871. Boston: Cong'l. Pub. Society, 1871.

Proceedings of the General Convention of Congregational Ministers and Delegates in the United States. New York: S. W. Benedict, 1852.

Simpson, Alan. Puritanism in Old and New England. Chicago: University of Chicago, 1955.

Sweet, William Warren. Religion on the American Frontier. (Vol. iii: The Congregationalists). Chicago: University of Chicago Press, 1939.

Upham, Warren (Ed.) Congregational Work in Minnesota. Minneapolis: Congregational Conference of Minnesota, 1921.

Walker, Williston. A History of the Congregational Churches in the United States. New York: Christian Literature Company, 1894.

General Historical Items

Burton Commission: Christian Education in China. New York: Committee of Reference and Counsel, 1922.

Latourette, Kenneth Scott. History of the Expansion of Christianity. New York: Harpers (seven vols.), 1943.

Lindsay Commission: The Christian College in India. London: Oxford University Press, 1931.

Padelford Commission: Christian Education in Japan — A Study. New York: International Missionary Council, 1932.

Sherring, M. A. The History of Protestant Missions in India: from their commencement in 1706 to 1881. London: Religious Tract Society, 1884. New Edition, carefully revised by Edward Storrow.

Teggart, F. J. The Circumstance and Substance of History. Reprint from the American Historical Review, Vol. xv, No. 4, 1910.

Toynbee, A. J. A Study of History. Abridged by D. C. Somervell. London: Oxford University Press, 1946.

Usher, R. G. The Pilgrims and Their History. New York: Macmillan, 1920.

Warneck, Gustav. Outline of the History of the Protestant Missions from the Reformation to the Present Time. (George Robson, editor). Halle: Advent, 1904. (Third English edition, being authorized translation from the eighth German edition).

C
BIOGRAPHY AND AUTOBIOGRAPHY

Alexander, Mary Charlotte. Dr. Baldwin of Lahaina. Berkeley (Cal.): Privately printed by the Stanford University Press, 1953.

Anderson, Courtney. To the Golden Shore (Biography of Adoniram Judson). Boston: Little Brown, 1956.

Berry, Katherine Fiske. A Pioneer Doctor in Old Japan, The Story of John C. Berry, M.D. New York: Revell, 1940.

Bliss, Daniel. The Reminiscences, Edited and Supplemented by His Eldest Son. New York: Revell, 1920.

Bridgman, Eliza J. G. (Ed.). The Life and Labors of Elijah Bridgman. New York: Anson D. F. Randolph, 1864.

Carter, Franklin. Mark Hopkins. Boston: Houghton Mifflin, 1892.

Clapp, Frances Benton. Mary Florence Denton and the Doshisha. Kyoto, Japan: Doshisha University Press, 1955.

Cormack, Maribelle. The Lady Was a Skipper, The Story of Eleanor Wilson, Missionary Extraordinary to the Marshall and Caroline Islands. New York: Hill and Wang, 1956.

Cushman, Mary Floyd. Missionary Doctor. New York: Harpers, 1944.

Davis, J. Merle. Davis: Soldier Missionary. A Biography of Rev. Jerome D. Davis. Boston: Pilgrim Press, 1916.

DeForest, Charlotte B. The Evolution of a Missionary. A Biography of John Hyde DeForest. New York: Revell, 1914.

Drury, Clifford Merrill. Marcus Whitman, Pioneer and Martyr. Caldwell, Idaho: Caxton Printers, 1937.

Eells, Myron. Marcus Whitman, Pathfinder and Patriot. Seattle: The Alice Harriman Company, 1909.

Emerson, Oliver Pomeroy. Pioneer Days in Hawaii. Garden City: Doubleday Doran, 1928.

Fosdick, Raymond. John D. Rockefeller, Jr., A Portrait. New York: Harpers, 1956.

Frear, Mary Dillingham. Lowell and Abigail, A Realistic Idyll. New Haven: Privately printed, 1934.

Gabriel, Ralph. Elias Boudinot, Cherokee and His America. Norman (Oklahoma): University of Oklahoma Press, 1941.

Gates, Caleb Frank. Not to Me Only. Princeton: Princeton University Press, 1940.

Gladden, Washington. Recollections. Boston: Houghton Mifflin, 1909.

Good, James I. Life of Benjamin Schneider. Philadelphia: Board of Foreign Missions, 1897.

Gordon, Elizabeth Putnam. Alice Gordon Gulick. Her Life and Work in Spain. New York: Revell, 1917.

Greene, Evarts Boutelle. A New Englander in Japan: Daniel Crosby Greene. Boston: Houghton Mifflin, 1927.

Hamlin, Cyrus. My Life and Times. Boston: Pilgrim Press, 6th Edition, 1921.

————. Among the Turks. New York: Robert Carter, 1878.

Hawkins, Chauncy J. Samuel Billings Capen: His Life and Work. Boston: Pilgrim Press, 1914.

Hayden, H. C. (Ed.). American Heroes on Mission Fields. New York: American Tract Society, 1890.

Jewett, Frances (Gulick). Luther Halsey Gulick: Missionary in Hawaii, Micronesia, Japan, and China. Boston: Cong'l S. S. and Pub. Society, 1895.

Moore, Edward Caldwell. Twenty-five Years with the Board. Boston: American Board, Envelope Series, April, 1925.

Myers, J. B. William Carey. New York: Revell, 1887.

Padwick, Constance E. Call to Istanbul. London: Longmans Green & Company, 1958.

Peet, Louise Jennison. No Less Honor. The Biography of William Wheelock Peet. Chattanooga: Privately printed, 1939.

Pierson, H. W. American Missionary Memorial (including biographical and historical sketches). New York: Harpers, 1853.

Porter, Henry D. William Scott Ament, Missionary of the American Board to China. New York: Revell, 1911.

Pye, Ernest. Charlotte R. Willard of Merzifon — Her Life and Times. New York: Revell, 1923.

Richards, Linda, Reminiscences of. Boston: M. Barrows & Company, 1929.

Riggs, Alice Shepard. Shepard of Aintab. New York: Interchurch Press, 1920.

Riggs, Stephen Return. The Gospel Among the Dakotas. Boston: Cong'l Pub. Company, 1869.

————. Mary and I, Forty Years Among the Sioux. Chicago: W. G. Holmes, 1880.

Rudolph, Frederick. Mark Hopkins and the Log. New Haven: Yale University Press, 1956.

Speer, Robert E. George Bowen of Bombay — Missionary, Scholar, Mystic, Saint. Privately printed, 1938.

Stevens, George B. The Life, Letters and Journals of the Rev. and Hon. Peter Parker, M.D. Boston: Cong'l S.S. and Pub. Society, 1896.

Tharp, Louise Hall. Three Saints and a Sinner. Boston: Little Brown & Company, 1956.

Tilak, Lakshmibai. From Brahma to Christ, the Story of Narayan Tilak and Lakshmibai, His Wife. London: Lutterworth Press, 1956.

Tracy, Ebenezer C. Memoirs of the Life of Jeremiah Evarts. Boston: Crocker and Brewster, 1845.

Tyler, Josiah. Forty Years Among the Zulus. Boston: Cong'l and Pub. Society, 1891.

Ussher, Clarence D. (Grace A. Knapp collaborating). An American Physician in Turkey. A Narrative of Adventures in Peace and War. Boston: Houghton Mifflin, 1917.

Walker, Williston. Ten New England Leaders. New York: Silver, Burdett & Company, 1901.

Waterbury, Jared Bell. Memoir of the Rev. John Scudder, Thirty-six Years Missionary in India. New York: Harpers, 1870.

Willard, Frances E. Livermore, Mary A. A Woman of the Century. Buffalo: Charles Wells Moulton, 1893.

Winslow, Harriet Wadsworth (Lathrop). Memoir of Mrs. Harriet Wadsworth Winslow, Combining a Sketch of the Ceylon Mission by Miron Winslow. New York: Leavitt, Lord and Company, 1835.

Worcester, Samuel Melanchton. The Life and Labors of Samuel Worcester, D.D. Boston: Crocker and Brewster, 1852.

D
THEOLOGY

Allen, Geoffrey. Christ, The West and the East. London: SPCK, 1952.

Allen, Roland. The Spontaneous Expansion of the Church and the Causes Which Hinder It. London: World Dominion Press, 1949.

Anderson, Rufus. Foreign Missions, Their Relations and Claims. New York: Charles Scribner and Company, 1869.

Anderson, Wilhelm. Toward a Theology of Mission. London: SCM Press, 1955.

Andover Theological Seminary. General Catalogue, 1808-1908. Boston: Thomas Todd, 1908.

Ashby, Philip H. The Conflict of Religions. New York: Scribners, 1955.

Bainton, Roland H. Yale and the Ministry. New York: Harpers, 1957.

Baker, A. G. The Christian Mission in a New World Culture. Chicago: Willett Clark, 1934.

Bavinck, J. H. The Impact of Christianity on the Non-Christian World. Grand Rapids (Mich.): Eerdmans, 1948.

Benedict, Ruth. Patterns of Culture. Boston: Houghton Mifflin, 1934.

Bennett, John C. Christianity and Our World. New York: Association Press, 1936.

Buttrick, G. A., ed. Interpreters' Bible. New York: Abingdon-Cokesbury Press (12 vols.), 1951.

Calkins, Raymond. "The Finality of Christ." (One of several sermons in Religion and Life.) New York: Harpers, 1935.

————. The Holy Spirit. New York: Abingdon Press, 1930.

Cragg, Kenneth. The Call of the Minaret. London: Oxford University Press, 1956.

Denney, James. The Way Everlasting. London: Hodder Stoughton, 1913.

Dewick, E. C. The Christian Attitude to Other Religions. Cambridge: Cambridge University Press, 1953.

Douglass, Truman. Preaching and the New Reformation. New York: Harpers, 1956.

Durant, Will. The Reformation. New York: Simon and Schuster, 1957.

Fahs, Sophia Lyon. The Old Story of Salvation. Boston: Beacon Press, 1955.

Fingesten, Peter. East is East: Hinduism, Buddhism, Christianity, A Comparison. Philadelphia: Muhlenberg Press, 1956.

Fleming, D. J. Attitudes Toward Other Faiths. New York: Association Press, 1928.

————. Contacts With Non-Christian Cultures. New York: Doran, 1923.

Foster, John. Beginning at Jerusalem. New York: Association Press, 1956.

Geer, Curtis Manning. The Hartford Theological Seminary 1834-1934. Hartford: Hartford Seminary Foundation, 1934.

Hays, H. R. From Ape to Angel; An informal history of social anthropology. London: Methuen, 1958.

Heim, Karl. Spirit and Truth, the Nature of Evangelical Christianity. London: (trans. by Rev. E. P. Dickie) Lutterworth Press, 1935.

Hocking, William E. Living Religions and a World Faith. New York: Macmillan, 1940.

————. The Coming World Civilization. New York: Harpers, 1957.

Horton, Walter. Toward a Reborn Church. New York: Harpers, 1949.

International Missionary Council. The Missionary Obligation of the Church. New York: International Missionary Council, 1952.

Kraemer, Hendrik. Religion and the Christian Faith. London: Lutterworth Press, 1956.

————. The Communication of the Christian Faith. Philadelphia: Westminster Press, 1956.

Latourette, K. S. Introducing Buddhism. New York: Friendship Press, 1956.

MacNicol, N. Is Christianity Unique? New York: Macmillan, 1936.

McGaran, Donald. The Bridges of God, A Study in the Strategy of Missions. New York: Friendship Press, 1955.

Moore, Edward Caldwell. East and West, The Expansion of Christendom and the Naturalization of Christianity in the Orient in the XIXth Century. New York: Scribners, 1920.

Morgan, Kenneth W. Islam — The Straight Path; Islam Interpreted by Muslims. New York: Ronald Press, 1958.

Mott, John R. Five Decades and a Forward View. New York: Harpers, 1939.

————. The Evangelization of the World in This Generation. New York: Student Volunteer Movement for Foreign Missions, 1900.

————. The Larger Evangelism. New York: Abingdon-Cokesbury Press, 1944.

Newbigin, Leslie. The Household of God. London: SCM Press, 1953.

Niebuhr, H. Richard. Christ and Culture. New York: Harpers, 1951.

————. The Purpose of the Church and Its Ministry. New York: Harpers, 1956.

Niebuhr, Reinhold. The Self and the Dramas of History. New York: Scribners, 1955.

Niles, D. T. The Preacher's Task and the Stone of Stumbling. New York: Harpers, 1958.

Orr, Grace Douglass. A Layman's Guide to Ecumenicity. Privately printed: 1956.

Paton, David M. The Christian Mission and the Judgment of God. London: SCM Press, 1956.

Pope, Liston. The Kingdom Beyond Caste. New York: Friendship Press, 1957.

Ranson, Charles W. That the World May Know. New York: Friendship Press, 1953.

Rethinking Missions: A Layman's Inquiry After One Hundred Years. New York: Harpers, 1932.
Rethinking Missions with the American Board. Boston: American Board, 1932.
Smith, Wilfred Cantwell. Islam in Modern History. Princeton (N. J.): Princeton University Press, 1957.
Soe, Niels H. The Theological Basis of Religious Liberty. Article in The Ecumenical Review, October, 1958.
Soper, E. D. The Philosophy of the Christian World Mission. New York: Abingdon-Cokesbury Press, 1943.
Speer, Robert. Missionary Principles and Practice. Chicago: Fleming H. Revell, 1902.
The Study of Foreign Missions in Hartford Theological Seminary. Hartford: Hartford Seminary Press, 1902.
Tillich, Paul. Biblical Religion and the Search for Ultimate Reality. Chicago: University of Chicago Press, 1955.
————. The New Being. New York: Scribners, 1955.
Toynbee, Arnold J. An Historian's Approach to Religion. New York: Oxford University Press, 1956.
Trueblood, D. E. Philosophy of Religion. New York: Harpers, 1957.
Warren, M. A. C. The Christian Imperative. New York: Scribners, 1955.
White, Hugh Vernon. A Theology for Christian Missions. New York: Willett Clark, 1937.
————. A Working Faith for the World. New York: Harpers, 1938.
————. One Gospel for Mankind. New York: Friendship Press, 1939.

E
SOCIAL ACTION PROJECTS OF THE AMERICAN BOARD

AFRICA

Coles, Samuel B. Preacher and a Plow. Boston: Houghton Mifflin, 1957
Tucker, John T. Currie of Chisamba. Toronto: United Church of Canada, 1945.
Annual Report, Currie Institute, Extracts — Trade Training and Industrial Work — 1935. American Board Library, AFR 64, C 9329, Pm bx.
Phillips. Ray E. The Bantu Are Coming. American Board Library, AFR 20-P 54 B.
————. Jan H. Hofmeyer School of Social Work. American Board Library, AFR 24 H 6729.
Brookes, Edgar H. Adams College — 1936. American Board Library, AFR 24 Ad. 129P2.
Mt. Silinda Industrial Department. Annual Report Agricultural Department — 1935. (Typed) AFR 42 Z9 — Pm bx. Annual Report Agricultural Department. (Typed) AFR 43 Z9 — Pm bx. Report Manual Training Department — 1935. American Board

Library AFR 44 M 86 Z9 – Pm bx. The White African –
Story of Mafavuk (Rev. George A. Wilder), Chapter XII.
Efforts at Mt. Silinda AFR 5465 W.

INDIA

Manshardt, Clifford, Ph.D. The Social Settlement as an Educational
Factor in India. Calcutta: Association Press, 1931.
————. Bombay Looks Ahead. Bombay, DB.: Taraporewah Sons &
Company, 1934.
————. Nagpada Neighborhood House Reports. American Board
Library, Ind 24-N14R-N 14 Z 9 Pm bx.
Holt, Arthur E. Social Action in Bombay-Nagpada Neighborhood House.
American Board Library, Ind 24-N 14 Z9 Pm bx.
Clark, Alden H. Deccan Industrial Institute. (American Board Library.)
Centennial Souvenir. Workshop for Blind.
Jones, J. P. Pasumalai, A Half-Century Record of a Mission Institution.
Madura: Lenox Press, 1895. Ind 64 P 26 P. Pasumalai pam-
phlets, Ind 64 P 26 Z9 Pm bx. Pasumalai Catalog-1908, Ind
64 p 36 HL. Pasumalai High Training Schools, Ind 64 P 26 Z9.
Annual Reports 1932, 1934, 1937 (Printed booklets 1901,
1903. (Industrial Reports.)

NEAR EAST

Nankivell, J. M. A Life for the Balkans – The Story of John Henry House
of the American Farm School, Thessaloniki, Greece. New York:
Fleming H. Revell Company, 1939.
Annual Report – Thessalonica Agricultural and Industrial Institute.
American Board Library NE9-Am. 5Z9, Pm bx.
Barton, James L. Autobiography, Relief in Near East, pp. 246-262.
American Board Library AB 55, B 28.
Peabody, Emily C. (W.B.M.I.) Corinna Shattuck, Missionary Heroine.
American Board Library, NE 26, Sh 2 P.
Gracey, George. Corinna Shattuck, The Heroine of Oorfa. American
Board Library, Mimeo. NE 26-Sh 2.

JAPAN

Pettee, James H. Mr. Ishii and His Orphanage – His Asylum at Okayama.
American Board Library, Jap. 26-IS3P.
Okayama Orphanage. Reports 1902, 1903, 1906, 1912. Jap. 14-OK
1Z9, Pm bx.
Cushing, Dorothy P. A House by the Side of the Road. Yodogawa
Neighborhood House, (Pamphlet), American Board Library,
Jap. 14 Y7Z9.
Moran, Sherwood F. Cary, Alice E. Yodogawa Neighborhood House –
Osaka Dedication, November 10, 1925, Illustrated. Also special
articles – Jap. 14 Y 7Z9.

Japan Mission News, April, Fall, 1925, Sept. 1926, May 1929. American Board Library.

CHINA

Hartwell, Emily S. Foochow Christian Woman's Industrial Institute, Report 1931. American Board Library, Ch 9-F73Z9 Pm bx.
Fan Village Project:
Hubbard, Mrs. Mabel. New Life in Fan Village. Printed pamphlet, illustrated, Ch 78 H86Z Pm bx.
Hubbard, Hugh W. (Miscellaneous writings 1930-1931) (Diary 1937, 1938) Ch 78 H86Z Pm bx.
————. The Healthy Village — An Experiment in Visual Education in West China, UNESCO, Paris — 1951. Ch 78 H86Z Pm bx.

F
FIELD STUDIES

Alden, John Eliot. A Press in Paradise. New York: Papers of the Biographical Society of America. Volume 38, No. 3, 1944, pp. 269-283.
Badeau, John S. The Lands Between. New York: Friendship Press, 1958.
Baly, Dennis. Multitudes in the Valley. Greenwich (Conn.): Seabury Press, 1957.
Bowles, Cynthia. At Home in India. New York: Harcourt Brace, 1956.
Calverly, Eleanor T., M.D. My Arabian Days and Nights. New York: Crowell, 1958.
Ceylon Mission. Minutes of Special Meeting, April 1955. Printed in Ceylon by American Mission.
Chandler, John S. Seventy-five Years in the American Madura Mission. Madras: American Madura Mission, 1909.
Considine, John J. New Horizons in Latin America. New York: Dodd, Mead & Company, 1958.
Davidson, Basil. The African Awakening. New York: Macmillan Company, 1955.
Davis, J. Merle. Publications written by J. Merle Davis for the International Missionary Council, New York. See list Chapter 7, Page 86 n.
Delpech, Jacques. The Oppression of Protestants in Spain. Boston: Beacon Press, 1955.
Dennett, Tyler. Americans in East Asia, A Critical Study of the Policy of the United States with reference to China, Japan and Korea in the 19th Century. New York: Macmillan Company, 1922.
Egerton, F. C. C. Angola Without Prejudice. Lisbon: Agency-General for Overseas Territories, 1955.
Farson, Negley. Last Chance in Africa. New York: Harcourt, Brace & Company, 1950.

Fernswerth, Lawrence. Spain's Struggle for Freedom. Boston: Beacon Press, 1957.

Fisher, Sidney N. Social Forces in the Middle East. Ithaca: Cornell University Press, 1955.

Garratt, G. T. The Legacy of India. Oxford: Clarendon Press, 1937.

Gasset, Jose Ortega y. Inverterbrate Spain. Translation and Foreword by Mildred Adams. New York: W. W. Norton, 1937.

Gibb, H. A. R. Mohammedanism, An Historical Survey. New York: New American Library, 1955.

Groves, C. P. The Planting of Christianity in Africa. London: Lutterworth Press. 3 Vols. Vol. I, 1948; Vol. II, 1954; Vol. III, 1955.

Hazen, William. A Century in India. Bombay: American Marathi Mission, 1913.

Hewat, E. G. K. Christ and Western India, A Study of the Growth of the Indian Church in Bombay City from 1813. Bombay: Wilson College, 1950.

Heyd, Uriel. Foundations of Turkish Nationalism: The Life and Teachings of Ziya Gök Alp. London: Luzac & Company, 1950.

Hume, R. A. An Interpretation of India's Religious History. New York: Revell, 1911.

Hunter, William C. Bits of Old China. Shanghai: Kelly and Walsh, Ltd., 2nd ed. 1911.

Ingham, Kenneth. Reformers in India 1793-1833. Cambridge: Cambridge University Press, 1956.

Jurji, Edward J. The Middle East: Its Religion and Culture. Philadelphia: The Westminster Press, 1956.

Latourette, Kenneth Scott. A History of Christian Missions in China. New York: Macmillan, 1929.

————. The Development of China. Boston: Houghton Mifflin, 1917.

Laubach, Frank C. The Silent Billion Speak. New York: Friendship Press, 1943.

Lazaron, Morris S. Olive Trees in Storm. New York: Thompson Hopkins, 1955.

Madariaga, Salvador de. Spain. London: Jonathan Cape, 1942.

Malinowski, B. Dynamics of Culture Change. New Haven: Yale University Press, 1945.

Malone, H. T. Cherokees of the Old South. Athens (Georgia): University of Georgia Press, 1956.

Manikam, Rajah B. (Ed.) Christianity and the Asian Revolution. New York: Friendship Press, 1954.

Mellen, K. O. The Gods Depart, A Saga of the Hawaiian Kingdom. New York: Hastings House, 1956. (Third volume of a history of Hawaii.)

Mooney, James. Myths of the Cherokee. Washington: Government Printing Office, 1900. (Part of the Nineteenth Annual Report of the Bureau of Ethnology of the Smithsonian Institution.)

McCord, James B. (with J. S. Douglas). My Patients Were Zulus. New York: Rinehart & Company, 1951.

Morison, Samuel E. By Land and Sea. New York: Knopf, 1953.

Nida, E. A. Customs and Cultures: Anthropology for Christian Missions. New York: Harpers, 1954.

Oliphant, J. Orin, (Ed.) Through the South and West with Jeremiah Evarts in 1826. Lewisburg (Pa.): Bucknell University Press, 1956.

Oliver, Roland. The Missionary Factor in East Africa. London: Longmans, Greene & Company, 1952.

Overstreet, Harry and Bonaro. What We Must Know About Communism. New York: Norton, 1958.

Pannikar, K. M. Asia and Western Dominance, A Survey of the Vasco Da Gama Epoch of Asian History, 1498-1945. New York: John Day Company, no date.

Pettee, James H. A Chapter of Mission History in Modern Japan (1869-1895). Okayama: Printed at the Tokyo Seishibunsha, 1895.

Radhakrishnan, Sarvepalli. East and West: Some Reflections. New York: Harpers, 1956.

Rondot, Pierre. Les Chretiens d'Orient. Paris: Peyronnet & Cie, 1955.

Scott, Roderick. Fukien Christian University, A Historical Sketch. New York: United Board for Christian Colleges in China, 1954.

Shepherd, George W., Jr. They That Wait in Darkness. New York: John Day Company, 1955.

Smith, Bradford. Yankees in Paradise. New York: J. B. Lippincott, 1956.

Somervell, T. Howard. Knife and Life in India. London: Livingstone Press, 1956.

Starkey, Marion L. The Cherokee Nation. New York: Knopf, 1946.

van der Post, Laurens. The Dark Eye in Africa. London: Hogarth Press, 1955.

Varg, Paul A. Missionaries, Chinese, and Diplomats. Princeton (N. J.): Princeton University Press, 1958.

Wilder, Harriet. A Garland for Ashes, The History of the Madura Mission 1834-1934. (MS loaned to writer by the author).

Wilder, R. G. Mission Schools in India of the ABCFM (with sketches of missions among the North American Indians, the Sandwich Islanders, the Armenians of Turkey, and the Nestorians of Persia). Boston: Crocker and Brewster, 1861.

Winslow, Miron. Hints to Missions to India. New York: M. W. Dodd, 1856.

Wright, Louis B. Fry, Mary Isabel. Puritans in the South Seas. New York: Henry Holt & Company, 1936.

Yale, William. The Near East: A Modern History. Ann Arbor: University of Michigan Press, 1958.

Zeine, Z. N. Arab Turkish Relations and the Emergence of Arab Nationalism. Beirut: Hayats, 1958.

G
MISCELLANEOUS

Allen, Roland. Missionary Methods, St. Paul's or Ours. London: World Dominion Press, 1910.

Bodo, John R. The Protestant Clergy and Public Issues 1812-1848. Princeton (N. J.): Princeton University Press, 1954.

Bowles, Chester. American Politics in a Revolutionary World. Cambridge: Harvard University Press, 1956.

Bruce, Maurice. The Shaping of the Modern World: 1870-1914. New York: Random House, 1959.

Cox, E. B. Following in His Train. Nashville (Tenn.): Boardman Press, 1938.

Goodall, Norman. (Ed.) Missions Under the Cross. New York: Friendship Press, 1953.

Hoenigswald, Henry M. (Ed.) The Idea of History in the Ancient Near East. New Haven: Yale University Press, 1955.

Holmes, James S. (Translator) A World on the Move. Amsterdam: International Publishing House, 1956.

Latourette, Kenneth Scott. The History of the Early Relations Between the United States and China. New Haven: Yale University Press, 1917.

Laurie, Thomas. The Ely Volume, or The Contribution of Foreign Missions to Science and Human Wellbeing. Boston: Congregational House, 1885.

Lerner, David. The Passing of Traditional Society: Modernizing the Near East. Glencoe (Ill): The Free Press, 1958.

Lerner, Max. America as a Civilization. New York: Simon & Schuster, 1957.

Lippmann, Walter. The Communist World and Ours. Boston: Little, Brown, 1958.

Missionary Responsibility in Our Time. New York: Division of Foreign Missions, 1957.

Morton, H. V. In the Steps of St. Paul. New York: Dodd, Mead & Company, 1955.

Muller, Herbert J. Uses of the Past. New York: Oxford University Press, 1952.

Niebuhr, H. Richard. The Social Sources of Denominationalism. New York: Henry Holt, 1929.

North, Eric M. The Book of a Thousand Tongues. New York: Harpers, 1938.

Patton, C. H. The Business of Missions. New York: Macmillan, 1924.

Price, Thomas. African Marriage. London: SCM Press, 1954.

Riesman, David. The Lonely Crowd. New Haven: Yale University Press, 1950.

Seelye, Julius H. Christian Missions. New York: Dodd, Mead & Company, 1876.

Seabury, Ruth Isabel. So Send I You. New York: Christian Education Press, 1955.

Stocking, Jay T. Immortal Money. New York: Missions Council, 1956 (reprint).

Tavard, George H. The Catholic Approach to Protestantism. New York: Harpers, 1955.

Unamuno, Miguel de. The Tragic Sense of Life in Men and Peoples. (Translated by J. E. Crawford Flitch.) London: Macmillan, 1921.

Whyte, William H., Jr. The Organization Man. New York: Simon & Schuster, 1956.

The World Mission of the Church. New York: International Missionary Council, 1939.

Reports of World Missionary Conference, Edinburgh, 1910. (9 vols.) London: Oliphant and Ferrier, 1910.

Reports of the Jerusalem Meeting of the International Missionary Council, 1928. (8 vols.) London: Oxford University Press, 1928.

Reports of the Tambaram Meeting of the International Missionary Council, 1938. (7 vols.) London: Oxford University Press, 1928.

Addresses and Papers of John R. Mott. (6 vols.) New York: Association Press, 1946.

H
PERIODICALS

Advance. Fortnightly Publication of the Board of Home Missions. New York: 287 Fourth Avenue.

Goodall, Norman. Evangelism. The Frontier. London: January, 1958, pp. 66-70.

International Review of Missions. Publication of the International Missionary Council. Quarterly. New York: 156 Fifth Avenue.

Krutch, Joseph W. How To Taste a Book. New York: Saturday Review, September 21, 1957, p. 22.

Missionary Herald. Boston: American Board Publication 1820 to 1949. Monthly Magazine.

Missionary "Papers". American Board Archives: December 3, 1898.

The Muslim World. Published by Hartford Seminary Foundation. Quarterly. Hartford, Conn.

Nevins, Allan. Should American History Be Rewritten? New York: Saturday Review, February 6, 1954.

Walker, Mary A. The Archives of the American Board of Commissioners for Foreign Missions. Harvard Library Bulletin, Vol. VI, No. 1, Winter 1952, pp. 52-68.

Appendix II
A: Instructions to Missionaries

It was the custom of the Prudential Committee, usually through one of the secretaries, to "instruct" outgoing missionaries. These "instructions" form an interesting body of source material. The following references come from the first three decades of Board history.

Annual Report, 1812, pp. 11-15
 Instructions to Judson, Nott, Newell, Hall and Rice (India)
AB 12 AM 23 (ABCFM Archives), 1819
 Instructions to first missionaries to the Sandwich Islands
AB 12 OR2Z9 (ABCFM Archives), 1819
 Instructions to Parsons and Fisk (Palestine Mission)
 Instructions to Parsons and Fisk (Near East)
Annual Report, 1823, pp. 194-196
 Instructions to missionaries to the Sandwich Islands
Annual Report, 1827, Appendix III, pp. 12-26
 Instructions to missionaries to the Sandwich Islands
Annual Report, 1829, pp. 92-96
 Instructions to Bridgman (first missionary to China)
Missionary Herald, 1830, pp. 300-303
 Instructions to missionaries to Marathi Mission (India)
Annual Report, 1831, pp. 96-98, 114-119
 Instructions to missionaries to the Sandwich Islands
Annual Report, 1832, pp. 149-169
 Instructions to missionaries going to various missions.
Annual Report, 1833, pp. 90, 91
 Instructions to Wilson (first missionary to West Africa)
Annual Report, 1834
 pp. 60, 61 Instruction to Merrick (first missionary to Muslims)
 pp. 100, 104 Instructions to Arms and Coan (Patagonia)
 pp. 45-148 Instructions to missionaries to Africa (Zululand)
Missionary Herald, 1835, pp. 275-281
 Winslow's Address to missionaries to various fields
Annual Report, 1836, pp. 127-134
 Instructions to missionaries in "Indian Archipelago"
Missionary Herald, 1837
 pp. 83-93 Instructions to missionaries to Madura (India)
 pp. 168-173 Instructions to missionaries to Sandwich Islands
Missionary Herald, 1838, pp. 278-283
 Instructions to missionaries to the "Indian Archipelago and to the American Indian Missions West of the Rocky Mountains"
Annual Report, 1839, pp. 170-175
 Instructions to Dibble (Sandwich Islands)

Missionary Herald, 1839
> pp. 39-44 Instructions to Cyrus Hamlin (Turkey)
> pp. 217-221 Instructions to missionaries to Marathi (India) and Siam
> pp. 361-365 Instructions to missionaries to Near East

B: "Papers" by Secretaries and Others (a selected list)

(Page numbers shown indicate place in Board's printed annual reports for the years indicated.)

1810 Farmington	Address to the Christian Public	
	pp. 13, 14	
1811 Worcester	Address to the Christian Public	
	pp. 25-30	
1812 Hartford	Address to the Christian Public	
	pp. 29-36	
1813 Boston	Address to the Christian Public	
	pp. 25-38	

These four "Addresses" were prepared by a Committee consisting of Jedediah Morse, Jeremiah Evarts, and Secretary Worcester.

1818 New Haven The Conversion of the World (Gordon Hall and Samuel Newell)
pp. 30-32

1828 Philadelphia A Notable Conclusion
pp. 113-119

1844 Worcester The Present Duty of the Church to the Heathen World (Treat) pp. 48-56

1846 New Haven Tokens of the Divine Presence in Missions (Anderson) pp. 61-72

1851 Portland Urgent Claims of the Armenian Reformation
pp. 19-23

1852 Troy The Grand Motive to Missionary Effort (Pomeroy)
pp. 21-25

1865 Chicago Obligations of American Christians to Foreign Missions (Treat) pp. 27-38

1871 Salem New Work in Nominally Christian Lands (Chapin)
pp. xxi-xxiii

1873 Minneapolis The Developing Power of the Gospel (Clark)
pp. vi-xii

1877 Providence Shall We Have a Missionary Revival (Alden)
pp. xii-xix

Providence Claims of the Unevangelized Upon the Christian Church (Clark) pp. xix-xxvi

1881 St. Louis Our Great Trust (Clark)
pp. xii-xviii

1884 Columbus   The Historical Argument for Foreign Missions
                    (Smith)   pp. xxiv-xxix
1890 Minneapolis   Higher Christian Education as Related to Foreign
                    Missionary Work (Clark)
                                               pp. xxxii-xxxvi
1906 Williamstown   (The Volume reporting the 1906 Annual Meeting
                    contains several articles and addresses bearing
                    on the general subject of the theological basis
                    for foreign missions)

Appendix III
Toward a Theology of Mission

(The following pages are an attempt to interpret the thought and attitude of many missionaries of the American Board with whom the writer has discussed this subject. It is cast largely in the form of a personal statement in order to allow for differences of opinion.)

Christianity and the Non-Christian Religions

No missionary movement of abiding value can escape the obligation to lay solid foundations in theology. A theology of mission is essential to prolonged missionary operations, that is, prolonged over centuries. Action in any sphere, undirected by sober thinking, is usually either futile or fateful. Thought can articulate scattered reflections, clarify purpose, purify and regiment emotions, give at the same time a sense of stability and of direction and enrich the total personality of a dedicated servant of Truth. This is as true of Buddhism and Islam as it is of Christianity — the three historic, distinctly missionary religions of the human race. This applies in high degree to the attitude to be taken by Christian folk toward alien systems of theological thought and religious practice and to their adherents. Roman Catholicism is far ahead of Protestantism in this matter. The Roman Catholic hierarchy knows what it wants done and why.

It must be confessed that within the Protestant Christian community across the centuries there has been all too little conclusive thinking as to the nature and conduct of the Christian mission. In countless instances, there has been genuine experience of the power of Christ in the lives of men and nations. Out of this experience have sprung passionate convictions as to the need of all men for the Evangel. But it is when experience is analyzed and convictions scrutinized that clearer, common understanding of what should be attempted in the name of Christ is likely to emerge.

In the background of the missionary operations of the American Board for a century and a half are to be found the elements of a theology of mission.[1] In general, these elements have reflected the contemporary thinking on all relevant subjects of the majority of the pastors, theological professors and alert laymen of the churches. But seldom, if ever, in the history of the Board has the attempt been made to prepare a systematic statement of the theological basis of missions to the adherents of other religions.[2] Why has this not been done? It has not been done for various reasons: partly because of more or less naive confidence on the part of American Board folk in the power of authentic

---

[1] The most relevant and accessible source of American Board theological thinking during the nineteenth century is to be found in the series of "instructions" to missionaries, and "papers" by secretaries of the Board presented to successive annual meetings from 1810 to 1900. (For lists see Appendix II.)

[2] The nearest approach to a systematic statement in the earlier period is Rufus Anderson, *Foreign Missions, Their Relations and Claims*, (New York, Scribners, 1869).

Christian experience and witness; partly because, in Congregational circles especially, there has been no inclination to regiment thinking on the subject; and partly because the impact of the non-Christian religions on Christian life and western civilization has been largely ignored by Christian theologians. Beneath all fragmentary formulations of thought has been the common conviction that all men and nations stand in need of what Christ can do when released through vital witness. But the modern missionary movement in general and the American Board in particular throughout its one hundred and fifty years has been on a starvation diet theologically. It has done what it has done largely because of innate vitality in which theology as such has played a minor part. It has been more like adventitious jungle growth than like a garden, intelligently cultivated. Here again, we have already done too much, if we are not willing and determined to do more.

Thoughtful Christians should note with deep satisfaction that the Willingen meeting of the International Missionary Council in 1952 seems to be a turning point in this matter. The topic of that meeting, "The Missionary Obligation of the Church," has inspired serious and widespread thinking as to the theological basis of Christian missions.[1]

There is probably no point on which theologians interested in missions have more frequently focussed their thought recently than the Christian attitude toward other religions.[2] There is no item in the program of the world mission of the Church today on which incisive thinking is more urgent. The old era of theological isolation is drawing to a close. Accelerated intercourse between all the people and races of the world is a very present fact and will rapidly become a greater factor. Not only scholars but also laymen who are adherents of non-Christian religions will still more insistently challenge the truth of the Christian religion and the presuppositions, motives, policies and methods of Christian mission boards.[3]

This is not the place to enter upon an historical resume of the attitude of Christians, both spokesmen and the masses, toward the adherents of non-Christian religions during the early centuries of the Christian movement and its development in mediaeval times and up to the beginning of the nineteenth century. Suffice it to say that a common characteristic of the attitude of the adherents of the Christian faith during the eighteen centuries had been the belief that the principles of Christianity had only to be expounded to the "heathen" to win them to Christian discipleship. The records of the past dealing with this matter strike modern ears as very strange, with overtones of self-delusion, ignorance, and an inflated

---

[1] See Wilhelm Andersen, A Theology of Mission, (London, SCM Press, 1955.)
[2] A selected bibliography on this subject would include Hendrik Kraemer's recent book: Religion and the Christian Faith, (London, Lutterworth Press, 1956.) See especially chapters 10, 11.
[3] Supporting evidence for this statement can be found (1) in K. M. Panikkar, Asia and Western Dominance, (New York, John Day, no date), especially pp. 455, 456 where the author states the reason for the failure of Christian missions as he understands and interprets the facts; (2) Norman Goodall (Ed.), Missions Under the Cross, (New York, Friendship Press, 1953), especially p. 213; (3) Recent articles in the International Review of Missions.

sense of superiority.[1] A recent trace of this attitude was in evidence when some Christians believed that the Emperor of Japan, following the second World War, was about to adopt the beliefs of one or another of the Protestant denominations.

After the modern Protestant missionary movement began to attain some momentum in the seventeen hundreds, following three centuries of apathy and in some cases hostility, the prevailing view of the non-Christian religions among Protestant Christians was that all other religions are false and Christianity alone is true.

During the nineteenth century under the influence of the liberal movement in Christian theology and intimately related cultural trends, the subject of comparative religion was accorded a place in theological studies. Not only acquaintance with the systems of religious thought and the total cultural heritage of non-Christian peoples was emphasized but also students were encouraged to explore and discover the values in non-Christian scriptures and theologies with a view to establishing contacts and, to some extent, to making common cause with all religions in opposition to agnosticism, atheism and secularism. As far as the major Protestant Christian missionary bodies were concerned this trend reached its climax in connection with the Jerusalem meeting of the International Missionary Council in 1928.[2]

The leaders of some mission boards were alarmed by this development. They warned their constituencies against the perils of syncretism. They guided the thinking of their colleagues and supporters into conservative channels. During the decade 1928 to 1938 the focus of attention shifted from a possible fellowship of all faiths to the nature and function of the Christian Church in a secular world. Missions became Church-centric. The International Missionary Council at Madras, India in 1938 echoed the voice of the great conference at Lausanne in 1935 and at Oxford in 1937 with the slogan "Let the Church be the Church."

Interestingly enough, the theologian and philosopher on the staff of the American Board during the nineteen-thirties, Rev. Hugh Vernon White, D.D., took a mediating position. His thought was summarized in various addresses and statements. In his three books[3] he gave a lead which on the one hand discounted the value of comparative religion as a theological discipline and on the other welcomed the most searching inquiry by all thinkers as to the major affirmations of liberal Christian theology. He rejected the ideas that one religion is as good as another,

---

[1] See, for instance, K. M. Panikkar, *Asia and Western Dominance*, (New York, John Day, no date), *passim*.
[2] Studies made in preparation for the Jerusalem meeting included these titles:
Christianity and Hinduism, Nicol McNicol
Christianity and Confucianism, John Leighton Stuart
Religious Values in Confucianism, D. Willard Lyon
Christianity and Buddhism, Kenneth J. Saunders
Christianity and Northern Buddhism, A. K. Reischauer
Christianity and Islam, W. H. T. Gairdner
Secular Civilization and the Christian Task, Rufus M. Jones
See *The Christian Life and Message in Relation to Non-Christian Systems of Thought and Life*, (New York, International Missionary Council, 1928).
[3] See page 122.

that it is a matter of indifference to what household of faith a person belongs, and that America should become a genuinely Christian land before thinking of Christian witness abroad. While admitting the weaknesses of the actual Christian community he asserted the fitness of Christianity to be a world faith.

At this point a distinction must be made between the relation of Christianity as a system of thought to the non-Christian religions as systems of thought on the one hand, and the Christian attitude toward the adherents of non-Christian religions on the other. It is one thing to theologize on the relation of Christianity to non-Christian religions and another thing to maintain an authentic Christian attitude under all circumstances toward the adherents of non-Christian religions or those who profess no religion. Whatever conclusions a Christian may reach regarding theological problems, one is never free from the obligation to maintain a truly Christian attitude toward non-Christian people. Too often intellectual trends or conclusions warp or stain Christian character or conduct. It was said in olden time: "Abhor the sin but love the sinner." Something approaching that position needs to be said today to those who are tempted to go to extremes, either of tolerance or of fanaticism. We cannot expect every missionary of the Board to be an accomplished theologian; we can reasonably demand the fulfillment of at least two conditions of a successful and satisfying missionary career: First, the Board should require a period of serious study of the theological basis of the missionary enterprise as a part of the training of a candidate for career service. Second, the Board should be concerned to see that some career missionaries are prepared to focus the attention of their colleagues on the need for sensitivity to their cultural environment and to give them a lead or a frame of reference within which they can find increasing satisfaction, intellectually and emotionally, as they deal with questions of truth and value which inevitably arise. This does not mean regimentation but vitality.

Christian Attitude and Practice

Insofar as one analyzes, systematizes or explicates the teachings of religions, he is acting as a theologian. That being the case, it is quite necessary to remember that the Christian life or attitude is not exhausted by thought; there is more to Christian piety than even the richest thought.

The Christian attitude toward non-Christians will take full account of Jesus' own attitude and teaching. It is inconceivable that he should not have given his followers a lead in this matter even though his major relations were almost exclusively with the Jewish people.[1] New Testament records, chiefly the writings of Paul, are the chief basis for an understanding of the ideal Christian attitude toward non-Christians.

[1] For a brief but very useful summary of Jesus' attitude toward his compatriots as well as toward non-Jewish people see E. D. Dewick, *The Christian Attitude Toward Other Religions*, (Cambridge, Cambridge University Press, 1953), pp. 61-95.

A double standard in this matter is inexcusable. Christians generally and missionaries are under the same obligation to maintain a Christian attitude toward non-Christians. The missionary may well be an expert both in understanding and in action with reference to the adherents of other religions but certainly there should be no contradiction between the attitude of missionaries and of those who send and support them.

Differences of opinion are inevitable but it would seem that the standards of *Christian* attitude and conduct toward non-Christians should be universally accepted and widely upheld.

The essential characteristics of the Christian attitude and behavior toward non-Christians are respect and goodwill.

The Christian respects his fellowmen, one by one, acknowledging that each person is created in the image of God, regardless of racial origin or creed, economic or social status. Respect means recognition of worth, actual or potential. Each human being is a child of God, worthy of treatment by other humans as of real and distinctive value in the sight of God. Goodwill means an attitude of sincere concern for the physical and spiritual welfare of a human being whether closely related by circumstances of life or so indirectly related as to seem at first glance to be entirely remote. Goodwill does not mean what is usually conveyed by the term fondness or personal congeniality. To desire anything less than the physical and spiritual welfare of a fellow human being is to violate the second great commandment which Jesus emphasized: Love your neighbor as yourself. The world is a neighborhood and always has been.

These two aspects, respect and goodwill, of the Christian attitude toward other human beings are fundamental. Out of them, separately or in combination, grow all other aspects of a Christian attitude toward non-Christians. Consider some of the derivative aspects.

Tolerance. By tolerance is meant patient endurance of thought or action which obstructs or denies in some way the freedom of a fellow human being. This patient endurance rests upon respect for the personality of the other and upon the sincere desire for the personal welfare of that other. This patient endurance has limits, but they are the limits of social welfare not of personal whim or caprice.

Humility. A humble person is not a weak acquiescent. True humility adds strength to personality, for together with patience it enables a Christian to await the operation in another person of the influences released by respect and goodwill. Humility is an element of strength because it takes account of worth in personality but eliminates pride.

Courtesy. There is no substitute in human intercourse for true courtesy. Courtesy is a practical expression of respect for personality. When fully sincere it carries the intention to serve in every possible way the welfare of a neighbor.

Courage. A Christian seeks to know and live by Truth. What is Truth? It is chiefly related to the meaning of life for a human being. The Christian has convictions as to the meaning of life, received from the life, teaching, death and resurrection of Jesus. He cannot wilfully

conceal these convictions without disloyalty to his Lord. He will therefore, when led by the Holy Spirit, witness to what he believes to be the
truth as to the meaning of life and conduct in accordance with that
meaning.

Service.   By service is meant desire or impulse leading to action in
the effort to do whatever may be done to enhance the welfare of another
human being. This desire rests upon the conviction of the worth of each
individual and upon the concern for his welfare, physical and spiritual.
It should be utterly free from prejudice due to circumstances of racial
origin, social or economic status, intellectual prowess or lack of the same.
The disposition to serve is eagerness to help an individual or a group
in need of something essential to human welfare. When ideas of what
is essential differ or clash, the desire to serve will be limited or obstructed
by the willingness of the individual or group to receive such help as is
offered. No service will be imposed, for to impose help is to violate the
principles of respect and goodwill.

The Missionary at Work

Note now the bearing of these principles upon the attitude and work
of a Christian missionary, set down in the midst of adherents of a non-
Christian religion or of those who profess no religion.

A· Christian — missionary or non-missionary — is convinced that in his
Christian faith he has an inestimable treasure. He is a Christian because
he is persuaded that through his relation to Jesus Christ he has entered
upon realms of experience which promise eternal welfare, beginning
with the present moment. He is a new creature, with new horizons, new
ambitions, new attitudes, new moral and spiritual power. In relation
to one who does not know Christ, his instinctive or uninhibited desire is
to tell of his new experience, to communicate his new knowledge, to
share his treasure. The New Testament words for this outgoing desire
are witness, testimony.

In his desire to share his new knowledge, the Christian by his very
nature as a Christian will refrain from everything that savors of coercion,
that is, violation of another's personality. Just as his witness is voluntary, so will the acceptance or rejection of it depend upon the will of
the one who listens or observes. This means among other things that
proselytism, as that word is commonly understood today, is offensive to
the Christian spirit, as offensive to the Christian as it should be to the
ardent disciple of any other religion. Proselytism usually violates personality in one way or another. Coercion and deception are often accom-
paniments of proselyting effort. With these the Christian will have
nothing to do.

Further, in his desire to share his new knowledge, the Christian will
rely both upon the activity of the Spirit of God within the heart and life
of the one who listens or observes and especially upon the ministry of
the Holy Spirit in his own life. This means that the Christian will be

humble, patient, courteous and expectant; humble because he knows his own inadequacies, patient because he knows that faith in Christ and real acquaintance with him is often a matter of slow growth, courteous because discourtesy is violation of respect for another's personality, expectant because he knows that God never deserts his responsive children.

If it be objected that these characteristics of the Christian attitude present an ideal beyond the possibility of fulfillment, the only adequate reply is to point to the teachings and life of Jesus. Nothing less than progress toward fulfillment of the ideal does honor that is due to him.

The Christian occasionally finds himself in circumstances or situations where his freedom to witness by word is more or less restricted. This happens frequently in the life and work of our missionaries abroad. This does not mean that no witness is possible. It rather means that the Christian attitude is all the more in demand because witness is restricted to actions which, we say, always speak louder than words. A life of true witness can be more effective than many sermons or testimonies, however desirable freedom of speech may be.

Nothing that has been said so far should be interpreted as disparagement of the effort to understand the thought-basis of any non-Christian religion or anti-Christian philosophy. Theology is as natural as breathing. But just as it is unnecessary to understand the anatomical and physiological conditions for breathing in order to continue to be a normal breathing organism, likewise it is unnecessary to understand the theology of a religion, Christianity or any other, in order to be a Christian or an adherent of a non-Christian religion. Nevertheless it is of prime importance to define or describe as clearly as possible the Christian position in relation to non-Christian religions and philosophies. Competent scholars, including some missionaries, render great service in their attempts to clarify and direct the thinking of the Christian community in these matters.

It is not difficult to outline alternatives.

1) One may take the position that all religions are expressions of the human search for God and knowledge of his relation to humanity. Each religion represents one way of approach to God. Religions are of equal value or at least worthy of study as possible ways to know God. Times without number the missionary encounters this position, one favorite simile being that different religions are like different trails to the summit of the same mountain.

2) One may take the position that only one religion is or can be true. All others are false. Some ardent souls throughout the history of Christianity and of other religions have passionately held and promulgated this view.

3) One may take the position that the highest and best religion will incorporate the truth of all religions, that mankind in the search for God has not yet attained the final religion and may never reach finality, but is destined to make a continual search for the highest and best through synthesis of the insights of all religions.

4) One may take the position, closely allied to that just mentioned, that human understanding involves constant reformulation and reconception of the truth about God and his relation to humanity. Christianity and all other religions are subject to reinterpretation from age to age. Practice is never perfect but sincere practice of a faith leads to reconception of what that faith really is or asserts.

5) One may take the position suggested by the story of the blind man in the ninth chapter of the Gospel of John. That man had an experience of healing which he could not explain but of whose reality he had no doubt. "One thing I know, that though I was blind, now I see" (John ix 25). No threat of inability to explain how he recovered his sight could persuade him that he was still blind. He knew the person who had healed him but he didn't know how he did it or what his power to heal implied as to his nature or relationships. He did not try to point out the inadequacies in the belief of his interrogators or accusers. He did not know much about their theology but he knew what had happened to him and the person to whom he owed his new sight.

This position involves nothing that can be called disrespect or lack of goodwill. It does involve the willingness to acknowledge the source of blessing. It does involve a lively sense of gratitude and loyalty to him to whom one owes his sight. It does involve loyalty to the truth as one knows it through various stages of a testing experience. It does involve courage to assert the nature of the blessing in the face of opposition.

A Personal Testimony

The time has come when Christians, Christian theologians and Christian missionaries should steadily put witness and theology in the sequence suggested by the story in John ix. Witness to what God in Christ has done for individuals and societies is a continuing imperative. "You shall be my witnesses . . . to the ends of the earth" (Acts i 8). It is very difficult to see how any reasonable objection can be made to honest, voluntary witness in matters of faith. When unreasonable objections or restrictions are made, the Christian attitude is patient tolerance and firm adherence to the truth as one sees it without arrogance or discourtesy.

Theology is the effort to explain the "how" of the new creation which results from any encounter with God in Christ. Theology is not religion. Theological systems may conflict but Christians loyal to Christ will never fight in the effort to win an argument. Christians need the stimulus of continuous thought and reinterpretation as to the deeper meaning of their religious experience but unwavering allegiance to any one system of thought is likely to spell stagnation and death to vital religion.

The basic issue in this matter must not be overlooked. It is this: Has there been a prophet or have there been prophets in human history prior to or outside of the Hebrew-Christian heritage who have communicated the authentic, dynamic, redemptive word of God to mankind? This is a theological-philosophical issue of prime importance. It is now receiving much attention in many parts of the world. The resurgence of interest in the non-Christian religions, both among their adherents and among Western scholars, has served to sharpen the issue which has always been implicit in the theology of mission — Buddhist, Christian and Muslim.

The most recent noteworthy protagonists of opposing views are Dr. Hendrik Kraemer of Leyden University, Holland and Dr. William Ernest Hocking of Harvard University, Cambridge, U.S.A. Some of their books[1] are being read by Muslim and Buddhist theologians as well as by Christian. This is not the place even to outline the opposing philosophies. Suffice it to say here that no thoroughgoing theology of mission can ignore the basic issue and fail to seek a satisfying answer.

One cannot deny the wisdom and beauty of many passages in the Scriptures of the non-Christian religions, especially Hinduism, Buddhism and Islam. One cannot deny the wisdom and beauty in the lives of many adherents of non-Christian religions. There is one thing, however, which the Christian can assert, not, to be sure, without contradiction, but without disloyalty to truth: The moral and spiritual transformation that takes place in the life of a person who comes to know Jesus Christ as Lord and Master, God as the loving and forgiving Heavenly Father, and the Holy Spirit as Teacher and Guide is characteristic of a genuine Christian community. It is seldom, if ever, seen elsewhere. It is in the realm of the will even more than in that of the mind that faith in Christ merits attention. Redemption from sin and a sinful life is a fact of experience so often demonstrated in the Christian community that it assumes the character of proof of God's search and concern for man rather than man's search for God.

Paul hit the nail on the head when he said: "I am not ashamed of the gospel; it is the power of God for salvation to every one who has faith" (Romans i 16). Add to this the fact that ethical principles which derive from Christ's teaching, when released in society through the transformed lives of individuals and in other ways, start processes of moral and spiritual reformation and set up standards of action which under favorable circumstances work toward moral regeneration on community levels. In other words, the Christian Gospel is both individual and social.

It is easy to claim too much for one's convictions or to reach illegitimate conclusions from limited experience. The Christian faith has a record of demonstrated moral and spiritual power, unapproached by any other religion or philosophy. That fact may not be philosophical proof of the uniqueness or finality of the Christian faith but it is in line with the honest testimony not only of first century Christians but of

---

[1] See especially William Ernest Hocking, *The Coming World Civilization*, (New York, Harpers, 1957) and Hendrik Kraemer, *Religion and the Christian Faith*, (London, Lutterworth Press, 1956).

multitudes of Christians in many lands from the first century to the present time. Perhaps there are other ways of redemption from sin and evil. If so, the evidence is not abundant, whereas the experience of men and women of many races in every century of the Christian era points to Christ as the Way, the Truth and the Life.

The Christian missionary need not depend entirely on any claim for Christ purely on an intellectual basis. Certainly he should refrain from verbal arguments which experience has shown seldom result in convincing an opponent of their validity. The Christian at home and abroad, missionary or non-missionary, should be willing and ready and able to say to his fellowmen: "Let me live in your midst, let me pursue some useful occupation, let me interpret as best I can by my life what Christ and the Christian faith means." Let those who have this experience of Christ demonstrate the reign of brotherhood and justice in their individual lives and in their midst as a community, leaving no area of human concern out of their minds and hearts and practice. As this process of acquaintance and witness goes on, indubitably discriminating observers will say as of old "They have been with Jesus."

Appendix IV
Christ and Culture

The American Board has proved its ability to grow and to adjust itself to changing circumstances and to proclaim the truth as it is in Jesus effectively to many peoples of non-Anglo-Saxon cultural backgrounds. The stiffest scientific challenge that the Board must continue to meet throughout the next century or more as the world becomes more compact and unified is the charge of "cultural murder," as one sociologist expresses it. An interpretation, therefore, of the Board's attitude on this matter is appropriate.

A scholar has recently translated a word of Paul's in this fashion: "Don't let the world around you squeeze you into its own mould, but let God re-mould your minds from within, so that you may prove in practice that the Plan of God for you is good, meets all His demands and moves toward the goal of true maturity."[1] These words of wisdom embody the truth which it is hard for passionate partisans of specific cultural systems to receive. The basis of the Christian conviction is the need of man, universally, for spiritual regeneration whatever his cultural tradition. Jesus was a Hebrew to the Hebrews and stood in the tradition of Moses and the great prophets of Israel. In his own mind, he purposed not to destroy but to fulfill, that is, to enrich, that great tradition which he loved. He understood its weaknesses but he gloried in its wisdom as far as it went. The law, even when interpreted in the lofty spirit of an Isaiah or a Micah, fell short of man's deepest need — salvation from sin, redemption from the impotence of unfulfilled aspiration to the strength and freedom of a true child of God. He conceived of love which fulfilled the law as power transforming power.

The conviction of the Christian disciple, implicit in his faith, is that Christ is ready and able to enter every culture without destroying any values that enrich human life. At the same time it must be maintained that the concept of fulfillment does not adequately complete the description of the relation of Christ to every human being, to every society and to every system of culture. The unique quality of the Christian faith, the quality which sets it apart from all other faiths and makes it worthy of acceptance by all men everywhere in all ages, is intimately personal. Christ as a person in his life, teachings, cross and resurrection reveals God and his love for the world of human beings. In revealing God's love, Christ also reveals God's ideal for man and for human relations. The quaint language of the writer to the Hebrews attempts to express the essential truth to which the Christian disciple would bear witness:

In many and various ways God spoke of old to our fathers by the prophets; but in these last days He has spoken to us by a Son,

[1] Emile Caillet, *The Christian Approach to Culture*, (New York, Abingdon-Cokesbury Press, 1953), title page, Romans xii 2.

whom he appointed the heir of all things, through whom also he
created the world. He reflects the glory of God and bears the very
stamp of his nature, upholding the universe by his word of power.
When he had made purification for sins, he sat down on the right
hand of the Majesty on high, having become as much superior
to angels as the name he has obtained is more excellent than theirs.[1]

This faith is not only worthy of acceptance by all men, it is possible
for any man in any culture to accept it and in so doing to enrich rather
than to destroy the values of the cultural tradition in which he stands
just as Jesus the Christ enriches without harm the Hebrew tradition in
which he stood.

These are large claims, ambitious assertions, affirmations of a faith
which can be proved and communicated not by logic or philosophy but
which can commend itself to men of all cultures only as an experience
in which love, primarily as good will, is demonstrated in the affairs of
daily living; an experience in which integrity, that is, honesty, is incarnate in personal dealings of all kinds; an experience which reveals
unalloyed allegiance to purity of motive and mastery of all human
passions; an experience which humbly acknowledges human weakness
and failures but falls only to rise in the might of a Heavenly Father who
is like Jesus.

This faith, because it is based upon the needs of man as man, because
it is a personal disclosure of God's purpose and love for all men, because it patiently relies upon living, daily witness to its redeeming, transforming power in individuals and in society and refuses to accept
coercive methods which violate personality — for these basic reasons this
faith seeks to lift up Jesus the Christ who has the power to draw all
men unto himself as the revealer of God.

---

[1] Hebrews i, 1-4.

Appendix V
Record of Missionary Appointments

The actual record of missionary appointments by the American Board from 1810 to the present deserves more careful study than has yet been given to it. It would entail scrutiny of the records of 4800 men and women in thirty-four fields. At various times lists of missionaries have been published with indication of their fields and years of their service. For instance, in 1877, the annual report of the Board (pp. 97-104) gives the names of 375 active missionaries as of that year, by fields.

Field	Number of Missionaries
Zulu Mission, South Africa	24
European Turkey Mission	19
Western Turkey Mission	60
Central Turkey Mission	19
Eastern Turkey Mission	36
Mahratta (Marathi) Mission, India	27
Madura Mission, India	27
Ceylon Mission	14
Foochow Mission, China	15
North China Mission	29
Japan Mission	34
Micronesia Mission	15
North Pacific Institute, Honolulu, S. I.	2
Western Mexico	4
Mission to Spain	4
Mission to Austria (Czechoslovakia)	8
Dakota Indians Mission	14
Missionaries (retired) resident in the Sandwich Islands	24
Total missionaries in 18 fields	375

In the archives of the Board there are two large notebooks, called the Vinton Books,[1] which give names and biographical data regarding missionaries appointed by the Board from 1810 to 1910. In 1910 a card catalogue was substituted for a continuation of the Vinton Book record. This has been carefully kept since that date. In 1886 the Board began the publication of an annual "Almanac" which, in addition to miscellaneous information regarding the Board and foreign missions generally, gave a list of all active missionaries with their field addresses. In 1917 the annual Almanac became the "Yearbook" with expanded contents

---

[1] Because originally compiled by Rev. John Adams Vinton in 1869.

including more biographical data regarding active missionaries. The Yearbook is currently published as *The American Board Directory and Calendar of Prayer*.

The first "Almanac" (1886) states that during the first seventy-five years the Board sent out 1866 missionaries, 786 men and 1080 women. On the active list at the seventy-fifth anniversary (1885) were 156 ordained ministers, six of whom were physicians, twelve other physicians (eight men and four women), six men assistants, 147 wives and 101 unmarried women, a total of 422 appointees.

The centennial report of the Board (1910) gives a list of 595 active missionaries according to the twenty missions in which they were located:

Zulu Mission	24
Southern Rhodesia Mission	15
West Central Africa Mission	27
European Turkey Mission	30
Western Turkey Mission	80
Central Turkey Mission	35
Eastern Turkey Mission	46
Marathi Mission	52
Madura Mission	39
Ceylon Mission	11
Foochow Mission	41
South China Mission	8
North China Mission	62
Shansi Mission	16
Japan Mission	69
Micronesian Mission	14
Mission to the Philippines	4
Mexican Mission	13
Mission to Spain	5
Mission to Austria	4
Total missionaries in twenty missions	595

A proper study of the missionary personnel sent by the American Board since 1810 would naturally include, among other items, information regarding the origin and denominational connections of all missionaries. Such a study has not been made but an estimate based upon such records as have been studied with care leads to the following conclusions:

During the years when the American Board was the agent in foreign missions of the Presbyterian, the Dutch Reformed, the German Reformed, and the Congregational Churches approximately fifty percent of the missionary personnel were of non-Congregational connections. In addition to members of the denominations noted, there were many Episcopalians, Methodists, Baptists and others among the active missionaries. As already stated, the Board never has required and does not now require membership in a Congregational Church when the candidate accepts appointment as a missionary of the Board, provided he is a member in good standing of some other evangelical church. Probably the same proportion (50% Congregational, 50% other) prevails today.

The number of missionaries (counting all categories) has varied greatly through the years. Conditions on the fields, the financial resources of the Board and the growth of national leadership in mission areas have been the main factors determining the record year by year. It is one of the ABC's of mission administration that as national Christian leaders emerge in an area, the number of foreign missionary personnel normally decreases. With these facts in mind the following graphs (pages 290, 291) may be studied with interest.

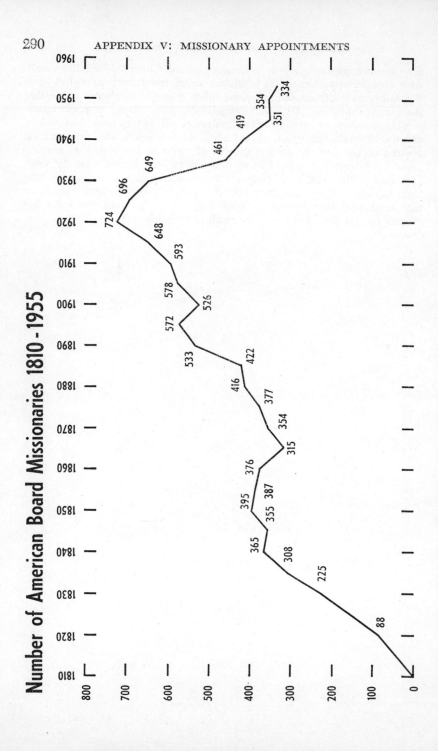

Number of American Board Missionaries 1810 - 1955

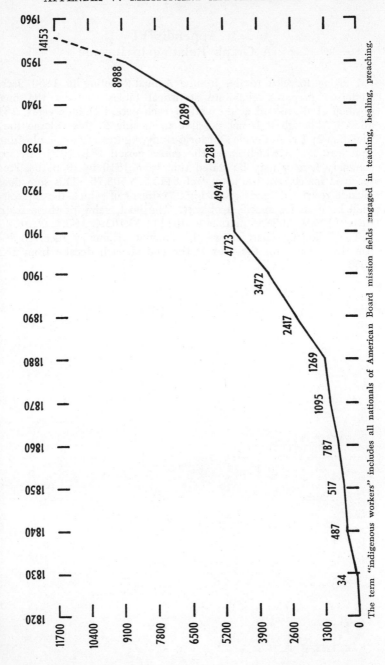

Number of Indigenous Workers Related to American Board Missions 1830-1956

34, 487, 517, 787, 1095, 1269, 2417, 3472, 4723, 4941, 5281, 6289, 8988, 14153

1820, 1830, 1840, 1850, 1860, 1870, 1880, 1890, 1900, 1910, 1920, 1930, 1940, 1950, 1960

0, 1300, 2600, 3900, 5200, 6500, 7800, 9100, 10400, 11700

The term "indigenous workers" includes all nationals of American Board mission fields engaged in teaching, healing, preaching.

Appendix VI
A Graph Relating to Income

Looking forward to the Jubilee Annual Meeting in 1860 Secretary Anderson prepared elaborate statistical tables showing the financial position of the Board at the end of each period of four years, 1810 to 1859.[1] Although it is not possible to include in this volume the continuation of Dr. Anderson's historic study, figures are available from the American Board which cover the entire period 1810-1956. By way of summary here it may be stated that from 1810 to 1956 the Treasury received for current use a total of $115,573,508.75. This sum does not include restricted funds given for investment of which the interest only shall be used for specified objects. The book value of these restricted funds (1956) — 585 in number — stood at $3,103,409.98,

The following chart shows the amount of money received by the American Board for the year at the end of each decade from 1820 to 1956.

[1] AR, 1862, p. 38.

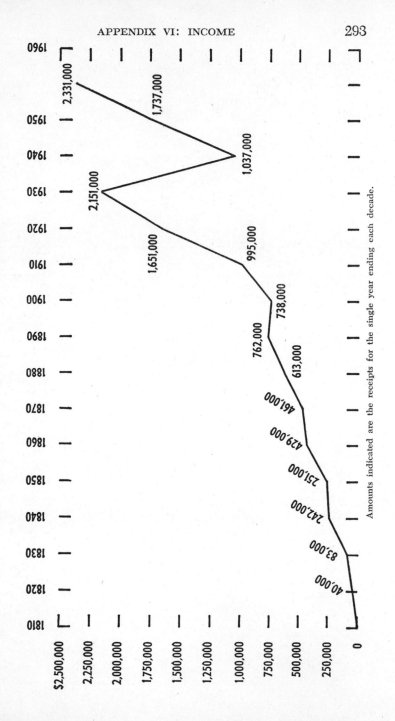

Total Receipts of the American Board at the End of Each Decade 1820-1956

Amounts indicated are the receipts for the single year ending each decade.

INDEX

Index

A

Abeel, David: 133, 156
Abeih (Syria): 38
Adams, Mrs E B: 207n
Adams, Newton (M D): 64
Adaptation: 242
Africa: 2, 65, 68, 143, 159, 252
  Angola (PWA): see Interlude
    I, pp 41-48, 192, 193, 219
    Bailundo 191
    Chilesso 44
    Church Council 44
    Dondi 44, 47
    Elende 45-47, 191
    Galangue 44, 191, 192
    Indigenous churches 20, 41-48
    Mission 16, 41, 44
    Ovimbundu people 16, 20, 41,
      42, 191
    Primitive cultures 20, 41
    Umbundu church 45-48
  Cape Palmas Mission: 15, 190,
    193
  East Central Africa: 190, 193
  Gaboon Mission: 16, 131, 190,
    193
  Liberia: 190
  South Africa:
    Adams College (Amanzim-
      tote) 59
    Inanda Seminary 159
    Mission 15, 194
    Natal 177
    Zululand, Zulu People, Zulu
      Mission 15, 20, 28, 84, 91,
      107, 156, 177
  Southern Rhodesia Mission 16,
    219
Agnew, Eliza: 183
Agricultural Missions: 83, 85, 192
Ahmednagar (India): 111; Col-
  lege 63n

Aintab: (see Gaziantep)
Alcorn College: 190
Alden, E K: 68, 71, 112, 113, 114,
  206n; re medical work 68, 69
Allen, Roland: 38
Amanzimtote: (see Africa)
American Board:
  Address to Christian Public 8,
    9, 10, 208, 209, 210
  Administration 200, 205-207,
    253
  Andover Controversy 110, 114,
    115, 116, 122, 184, 219
  Annual Meetings, first, 8; sec-
    ond, 9; third, 11; 51, 24, 36,
    108; (1886) 112; (1870) 131,
    141, 139n; (1849) 103; (1925)
    170; (1885) 68; (1907) 60,
    205, 216
  Annual Report (1848) 102, 205;
    (1860) 238; (1861) 213, 235,
    236; (1877) 238; (1910) 227
  Archives 204
  Attitude to "Rethinking Mis-
    sions" 118, 119
  Charter 132
  Commissioners 7, 8, 9, 10, 11,
    198
  Communication to Nat'l Coun-
    cil 1913 146
  Constitution and by-laws 8, 9,
    104, 124, 226
    "A national institution" 128,
      198
  Cooperation other foreign boards
    125, 127, 207
  Deputations 206, 207, 252
    India, Ceylon and Near East
      (1854-1855) 53, 54, 55,
      57, 67, 95, 108
    India and Ceylon (1901) 73

Doctrine (see Chapter 9) 184, 206

Ecumenical spirit of (see Chapter 10)

Executive Vice-President 200, 201

Extent of responsibility 106, 205

Finances, Financial support (see Chapters 15, 16 *passim*) 10, 12, 213, 214, 236, 250; see Appendix VI

Appeals for support 10, 59-63, 208, 209, 210, 212, 231

Deficits, deficit financing 211, 227-231

Endowments, Higher Education 60-63

Funds: General Permanent 217, 218, 237

Permanent Fund for Officers 218

Twentieth Century Fund 220-224, 229

Conditional Gift Fund 220-226, 229

Legacy Equalization Fund 225

Missionary Education 149

Unified Promotion, united promotion 148, 152

Foreign Secretary 201, 228

History 1-4, 245

Home Office 200, 202

Home Secretary 111, 200, 201

Incorporation 11, 198, 209, 210

Indemnities 230

Institutions 244, 251, 252

Interdenominational 198

Intern'l Seminar 28

Legacies 218, 229, 230, 230n, 237

Norris 154

Otis 215, 219

Phelps 237

Swett 219

Thomas 154

Membership

Corporate 133, 139, 139n, 144, 147, 198, 199, 202, 212

Corresponding 139

Honorary 12n, 139, 139n, 144, 199, 212

Life 199

Merger 133

Missionaries (see Missionary)

Missions Council 149, 201, 229

Missions (see specific name of mission)

National Workers: see graph, Appendix V

Non-ecclesiastical nature of 106, 128

Objective, purpose, motive, raison d'etre 34, 35, 40, 99, 105, 174, 248

Organization 143, 200, 247, 248, 253

"Papers" by secretaries 205, 216n, 234, App II B

Principles, Policy 74, 101, 102, 104, 105, 108, 109, 193, 205-207, 245, 248, 252, 253

Property 34, 134, 229, 230

Prudential Committee 8, 9, 10, 23, 24, 36, 37, 40, 53, 54, 59, 60, 71, 74, 75n, 164, 183, 188, 198, 202, 203, 214, 229, 236, 245

Enlargement of 170

Measure of experience 101, 103, 104, 106, 107, 114, 117, 124, 140, 142, 158

Second century 227

Social Action (see Chapter 7)

American Foreign and Christian Union: 24, 143, 215

American history: 5, 90

American Indians: 7, 20, 65, 84, 107, 127, 143, 156, 186, 189, 193; Caghnawagas 10; Cherokees 15, 155, 203; Chickasaws

15; Choctaws 15; Dakotas 15; Ojibwas 131; Senecas 131
American Missionary Association: 14, 143
Amherst College: 49, 58, 112, 136
Amoy Mission: (see China)
Anderson, Martin B: 55
Anderson, Rufus: 31, 36, 53-55, 57, 66, 95, 102, 108, 206n, 214, 234, 236, 248
Andover Controversy: (see American Board)
Andover Theol. Sem'y: 6, 58, 112, 186, 204, 208; see also American Board
Andrews, Mary: 159
Andrews, Seth: 64
Anglicans: 96; CMS 31, 243; SPG 243
Anglo-Saxon groups: 188
Angola: (see Africa)
Anthony, Susan B: 157
Anthropology, anthropologists: 41, 185, 247
Arabia: 17, 26, 27; Arabic 26
Archer, John Clark: 187
Arcot Mission: (see India)
Armenians: 16, 21, 22, 26, 58, 188, 188n, 244; Armenian Orthodox Church 21, 22, 25, 188n; Protestant Armenians 22, 54; Armenian and Syrian Relief Committee 61
Armistice: 61
Armstrong, Secretary: 24
Asia: 209, 252
Asia Minor: 2, 23, 58, 72, 229
Associate Reformed Churches: 127, 133
Associated Medical Missions Office: 78, 79, 80
Assyrians: 17
Ataturk: 244
Athens (Greece): 21
Atlantic, Middle (Conference): 188

Atom: 240
Atwood, I J (M D): 73
Auburn Theol. Sem'y: 187
Australia: 189
Austria: 24, 194

B

Bacon, Leonard: 235, 238
Bagster, William W: 41, 190
Bailundo: (see Africa)
Bainton, Roland H: 186
Baldwin, Dwight (M D): 64
Ball, Dyer (M D): 64
Bangor Theol Sem'y: 187
Bantu people: 82
Baptists: 7, 55, 78, 157, 192
Bartlett, Mrs. Homer: 158
Bartlett, Mr and Mrs Samuel C: 114, 159, 214
Bartlett, William: 11, 127n
Barton, James L: 55-60, 61, 62, 73, 86, 116, 206n, 207n, 218, 220, 231, 244
Batticotta (Vaddukoddai): (see Ceylon)
Beach, Harlan P: 187
Beaver, R Pierce: 136n
Bebek (Turkey): 38, 54
Beirut (Syria): 21
Bell, Enoch Fry: 112, 115, 207n
Beloit College: 116
Bengal (India): 155
Benson, Egbert: 127n
Berkeley (Cal): 161
Berry, John C (M D): 72, 207n
Bible: references to, 1, 18, 24, 43, 44, 52, 66, 83, 92, 173, 180, 253; translations of, 26, 29; use of, 185
Biography (autobiography): 1
Birman Empire (Burma): 10
Blaisdell, James A: 207n
Blatchley, Abraham (M D): 64
Blockwelder, O F: 173n
Board of Home Missions (Cong'l): 151, 193n, 201

Bombay (India): 53, 67, 243
Borneo: 2, 15, 29, 134, 194
Boston: *passim,* Cornhill, Hanover, Pemberton, Somerset 197
Boudinot, Elias: 127n
Bowdoin College: 116
Bowker, Mrs Albert: 157, 158
Boxer Indemnity Fund (China): 82
Bradford, A H: 206n
Bradford (Mass): 7, 110, 126, 138
Bradley, Dan B (M D): 64
Brainerd, David: 7, 186
Bridgman, F B: 207n
Bridgman, H M: 177
Brigham, John C: 23
British Miss'y Societies: 10
Brooklyn (N Y): 139, 141
Brousa (Turkey): 136
Brown, A J: 128
Brown, Jean: 180
Buddhism: 19
Buenos Aires (Argentina): 23
Bulgaria: 16, 22, 23, 57, 58
Bunker, Mr and Mrs Fred: 190
Burder, George: 9
Bushnell, Horace: 114
Butler, Mrs William: 158

C

Calcutta (India): 7, 11, 243
Calkins, Raymond: 61
Cambridge Platform: 105
Canada: 137, 189
Candidates: 194, 195, 196
Canton (China): 14, 65, 193
Canton Mission: (see China)
Cape Palmas Mission: (see Africa)
Capen, Samuel B: 60, 116, 207n, 220, 221, 223
Capron, Mrs William B: 180
Caravan (ship): 7
Carey, William: 7, 240
Caroline Islands: 16
Central America: 25
Central English High School: (see Ceylon)

Ceylon: 14, 53, 57, 58, 64, 66, 67, 73, 156, 158, 194, 243
  Batticotta (Vaddukoddai) 38, 53, 57, 58
  Caste as a social issue 92-94
  Central English High School 53
  Churches 36, 100, 107
  Jaffna College 57, 58
  Mission 14
  Plan for College 51-53
Chambon-sur-Lignon (France): 17
Chandler, John S: 67n, 95
Chapin, A L: 206n
Chapin, Alonzo (M D): 64
Chapin, Calvin: 8, 11, 127n
Chase, Judith: 155
Cherokees: (see American Indians)
Chester, Edward (M D): 72
Chicago: 201; Theol Sem'y: 187; Univ: 191
Chickasaws: (see American Indians)
Chilesso: (see Africa)
China: 18, 57, 58, 133, 137, 156, 176, 231
  Missions: Amoy 14, 15, 133, 134, 194; Canton 14, 65, 68, 193; Fenchow 15; Foochow 14, 15, 59, 156, 179; North China 14, 73, 193; Shanghai 14; Shansi 15; Shaowu 15, 193; South China 15
  Schools: Foochow College 59; Foochow Girls' College 60
  Villages: 176
Chissamba: (see Africa)
Choctaws: (see American Indians)
Christ: 1, 12, 13, 18, 19, 30, 33, 40, 41, 43, 73, 74, 111, 246; see Appendix IV
Christian Church: 137
Christian communities: 2, 32, 43, 44, 49
Christian Medical Council for Overseas Work: 79, 80
Church (in America): 3, 235

Church Miss'y Society: (see Anglicans)

Church of South India: (see India)

Church (Overseas): planting, nurturing and maturing of indigenous churches 1, 13, 30, 31, 43, 48, 59, 207, 248, 250; see chap. 8; ecclesiastical independence of 100-105, 108, 109; native pastors of 46, 104; structural changes of 20; primary purpose of their mission 35, 36, 37, 38; Mission and Church see chap. 8, 189; older and younger churches 241, 248; see also Church of South India

Church Union: 3, 207, 248

Church Universal: 235, 236, 239, 241, 249, 253

Civilization: 84

Civil War: 213, 214

Clark, Alden Hyde: 118, 120, 207n

Clark, N G: 108, 140, 157, 158, 206n

Cleveland (Ohio): 60

Coe, Mr and Mrs A B: 207n

Coghill, Patty Lee: 207n

Cole, Mrs R E: 161

Coles, Mr and Mrs Samuel B: 192

Colleagues: 241

Colleges: (see Higher Education; see American Board)

Collegio Internacional: (see Mexico)

Colombo (Ceylon): 245

Colonialism: 247

Colossae: 105

Commission on Missions: (see Cong'l denomination)

Commonwealth of Massachusetts: 7, 11

Commissioners: (see American Board)

Communism, Communists: 14, 15, 31, 203, 247

Confucianism: 19

Cong'l denomination, Cong'l Christian: 1, 2, 33, 49, 50, 78, 114
  Associations 7, 110, 126
  Benevolences 144
  Churches 3, 17, 24, 63, 126, 144
  Commission of Fifteen 146
  Commission on Missions 147, 148, 149, 151, 152, 201, 229
  Commission of Nineteen 146
  Committee of Seventeen 144
  Cong'lism 141, 142, 143, 144, 147, 149, 251
  Consolidation of Miss'y Magazines 143
  Consolidation of Miss'y Societies 142
  Councils (Nat'l) (General) 115, 137, (1865) 140, (1871) 140, (1874) 142, 143, (1892) 150, 152, 169, 199, 201, 205, 216, 238
  Expansion of 144
  General Convention (1852) 139
  Home Mission Societies 139, 144, 150, 151
  Mid-Winter meetings 152, 153
  Plan of Union 139
  Relation of ABCFM to Churches 145, see chap 11
  State Conferences 143, 144, 145, 216
  State Women Presidents 152
  Theol Seminaries (see Andover Theol Sem'y)
  Union Congregational and Christian Churches 137

Connecticut Gen'l Conference: 145

Connecticut Home Miss'y Soc: 7

Constantinople (Turkey): see Istanbul

Converts, conversions: 30, 33, 34, 49, 50, 83

Corinth (Greece): 105

Cornish (N H): 154, 155

Cornwall School: 188, 189n

Corporate body, members, etc.; see American Board

Council for Social Education and Action: 152
Cowles, Mrs. Amy: 177, 178
Cox, Ethelene Boone: 157n
Crusades: 25
Culture: Christ and Culture, see Appendix IV
Currie, W T: 41
Cyprus: 194
Czechoslovakia: (see Austria)

D

Daibutsu, Kamakura (Japan): 18
Dakotas: (see American Indians)
Dartmouth College: 112, 116
Davis, Grace T: 156n, 181n
Davis, Henry: 127n
Davis, J Merle: 86
Day, George E — Missions Library: 187
Decatur, Mrs Austin A: 207n
DeForest, J H: 74
Denney, James: 235
Denominationalism: 115, 141, 248, 250, 251
Depression, Great: 78, 220, 227, 230, 231
Deputations: (see American Board)
Des Moines, Iowa: 112
Dindigul (India): 72
Disciples denomination: 17
Disease: 2, 42, 66, 83, 91
Doctrine: (see chapter 9), 110, 184
Dodge, Asa (M D): 64, 65
Dondi: (see Africa)
Doremus, Mrs Thomas C: 157
Dudley, Raymond A: 207n
Dumaguete (Negros, P I): 17
Dunlap, Mrs Mary Uline: 171n
Durban (Africa): 190
Dutch Reformed Church: 14, 125, 127, 132-135
Dwight, Timothy: 8, 11, 127n
Dyer, Frances J: 174

E

East India Company: (see India)
Eastern Turkey Mission: 231
Eastern world: 9, 60, 75
Eaton, Edward D: 116, 206n
Ecumenical Movement: 31, 124, 136, 138, 147
Eddy, David Brewer: 231, 232, 233
Edinburgh Miss'y Conference: 184
Education: 2, 45, 51, 52, 54
　Adult: 47
　Elementary schools: 51
　Higher Education: 49; in Ceylon 51-53, 54, 55; controversy over 53-57; fund raising for 60-63, 232, 252
　Presbyterian schools: 57
　Schools: 27, 29, 30, 34, 35, 42,; in Angola 45-47
　Theol schools: 57, 58
　Vernacular theory of: 52-54
Edwards, Mrs Mary K: 158
Elende: (see Africa)
Eliot, John: 7
Ellison, W I: 206n
Ely, I S: 206n
England: (see Great Britain)
English language: 52, 53
Ennis, Merlin W: 41, 42
Ephesus: 105
Episcopal Church, Episcopalians: 15, 78, 127
Europe: 51, 194
Evangelical Churches: 20-23
Evangelical Reformed Church: 137
Evangelical United Brethren: 17
Evangelism: 5, 6, 26, 33, 34, 35, 40, 44, 49, 50, 51
Evarts, Jeremiah: 127n, 197n, 216
Every Member Canvass: 212
Explorers: miss'y influence on trade, travel, diplomacy 2-3

F

Fagley, F L: 143, 147
Famine: 2, 83
Farrar, Cynthia: 155
Fellowship Center: 197
Fellowship of Those Who Care: 198
Fenchow: (see China)
Ferrier, Mrs W W: 170
First Cong'l Church (Oakland, Cal): 161
Fisk University: 190
Foochow: (see China)
Foochow Mission: (see China)
Fourteen Beacon Street: 197
France: 194
Frear, Walter: 165
Free Church of Scotland: 14
Freedom: 110, 123, 125
Frelinghuysen, Theodore: 135
French Revolution: 31
Fukien: (see China)
Fukuyama, Yoshio: 193n

G

Gaboon Mission: (see Africa)
Galangue: (see Africa)
Galatia: 105
Garrison, William Lloyd: 135
Gates, George A: 116
Gaylord, E D: 207n
Gaziantep: (see Turkey)
General Ass'n of Cong'l Ministers: Bradford meeting 7
General Council: (see Cong'l Denomination)
General Theol Sem'y: 187
Georgia: 203
German Reformed Churches: 125, 135-137
Germany: 189
Getchell, Mrs Dana (Miss S D Riggs): 175
Ghana (see Int'l Miss'y Council)
Gilbert Islands: 16

Gladden, Washington: 114
Golden Rule: 2
Goldthwait, Joel E (M D): 75
Good, James I: 136
Goodell, William: 188n
Grant, Asabel (M D): 64
Great Awakening: 186
Great Britain: 5, 189
Greece:
　Athens: 21
　Greek Orthodox Church: 16, 21, 22
　Greek people: 16, 18, 21
　Missions: 16, 21, 22, 23
Green, Ashbel: 127n, 155
Green, Samuel F (M D): 67, 72
Greene, David: 102
Guadalajara (Mexico): 59, 161
Gulick, Rev and Mrs William H: 24

H

Hall, Bishop: 242
Hall, George A: 207n
Hall, Gordon: 11
Hamlin, Cyrus: 53, 54, 55
Hardy, Alpheus: 115, 158
Hardy, Mrs. Alpheus: 158
Harmony (sailing ship): 11
Harpoot (Turkey): 58, 232
Hartford (Conn): 11, 12, 185; Theol Sem'y 185, 191
Harvard College: 187
　Center of Unitarianism 6, 50, 111
　Librarian quoted 204
　Library (Houghton) 204
Hastings, Mr and Mrs Daniel: 191
Haystack prayer meeting: 6, 7, 116, 208
Haute Loire (France): 17
Hawaii (Sandwich Islands): 50, 64, 107, 156, 189
　Church 100, 105
　Hawaiian Mission 15, 29, 34, 36, 194, 203

Primitive cultures 20, 84
Roman Catholics 21
Status of women 91
Heebner, Flora: 137
Heresy trial: 114
Higher Education: 49-63, 232, 252
Higher Educational Work Endowment Fund 60-63; statistics 62; see Education
Hinduism: 19, 72, 94, 111, 240
Hingham (Mass): 50
Hitchcock, A N: 165
Hocking, William Ernest: 117
Holbrook, Mary A (M D): 73
Holland, George A: 61
Holman, Thomas (M D): 64
Holyoke, Mt, College: 116, 157
Hongkong: 194
Hooker, John: 11, 127n
Hope, Mather B (M D): 64
Hopkins, Col Charles A: 60, 206n
Hopkins, Henry: 116
Hopkins, Mark: 112
Hotel Roosevelt, New York: 117
Howe, Julia Ward: 157
Hubbard, Mrs (of Foochow): 179
Human welfare: 2; chapter 7 passim
Hume, Robert A: 111, 113
Huntington, Gen: 8, 11, 127n
Hyde lecture (see E F Bell)
Hyde, William D: 116

I

Iberian Evangelical Union: (see Spain)
Ignorance: 50, 65, 91
Inanda Seminary: (see South Africa Mission)
India: 3, 12, 53, 57, 65, 68, 73, 95, 107, 158, 240
Ancient non-Christian civilizations 107
Arcot Mission 14, 134, 194
Caste, (as social issue) 92, 95-98; Indian Constitution regarding 98

Churches 18, 105
Church of South India 104
East India Company 243
Madras Mission 14
Marathi Mission 13, 194
Ahmednagar College 63n
Churches 36
Pastors 36
Madura Mission 14, 180, 194
Churches 36
Colleges Lady Doak College 63n; Pasumalai College 38, 58
Pastors 36
Tamil people 14, 52, 95
Marriage customs 97, 98
Missions 13, 14
Missionaries 7, 11, 18
Indonesia: 133, 134
Industrial Missions: 83, 84, 85
Ingram, J H (M D): 73
Inhambane (Portuguese East Africa): 16, 190
Institute of Religious and Social Research: 116
Intern'l Institute for Girls: (see Spain)
Intern'l Miss'y Council:
Accra (Ghana) Assembly 241
IMC and economic problems 85
Jerusalem Assembly 27, 32, 246, 249, 252
Madras Assembly 85, 195, 240, 241
Whitby Assembly 241
Willingen Assembly 241, 249
Intern'l relations: miss'y concern for 2
Intern'l Review of Missions: 241n
Interracial Policy: 193
Ipswich (Mass): 157
Islam:
Religion 22
Muslim peoples 17, 18, 25-27, 187, 244
Muslim reaction to medical work 83

Muslim women 176
Muslim youth 244
Qur'an 25
Istanbul (Constantinople) (Turkey): 53, 54, 58, 136, 188n
Italy: 16, 24, 194

J

Jaffna (Ceylon): 14, 53, 57, 243
Jamaica, Jamaicans: 191
James, Arthur Curtiss: 61
James, Benjamin V: 190
James, D Willis: 61, 220, 221, 223
James, Mrs D Willis: 61
Japan: 68, 72, 73, 74, 194, 251
Church 18
Church of Christ 3
Church Union 3
Kumiai Churches 104
Mission 14, 104
Schools 57
Doshisha University 58
Kobe College for Girls 58
Java: 194
Jay, John: 127n
Jerusalem: 21, 26, 32, 246
Jewett, Mrs H E: 161
Jews: 14, 18, 25, 26
Johannesburg (Africa): 82
Johnson, J G: 206n
Jones, Nancy: 190
Jones, Rufus: 27
Jones, William: 127n
Josephus, Flavius: 172
Jubilee Year: 213
Judd, Gerrit P (M D): 64
Judson, Mr and Mrs Adoniram: 9, 11

K

Kamakura (Japan): 18
Kamundongo (see Africa): 44
Kennedy School of Missions: 185
King, Henry Churchill: 116
King, Robert: 193n

Kobe (Japan): 14, 58
Kopf, Carl H: 207n
Kraemer, Hendrik: 122
Kumiai Churches: (see Japan)
Kusaie (Micronesia): 179
Kyoto (Japan): 14, 58, 72

L

Lackey, Mrs: 67
Lady Doak College: (see India)
Lafon, Thomas (M D): 64
Lahainaluna (Hawaii): 38
Lamson, Charles M: 186
Lamson, Kate G: 156n, 176n
Langdon, John: 127n
Latin America: 23, 24, 252
Latourette, Kenneth Scott: 187
Lausanne (Switzerland): 244
Laymen: 199
Laymen's Foreign Missions Inquiry: (see "Rethinking Missions")
Laymen's Miss'y Movement: 60
Leaders, leadership: 2, 46, 55, 56, 59, 189, 100
Lebanon: 17, 63n
Legacies: (see American Board)
Lemoyne Institute: 190
Liberia: (see Africa)
Library Missions, George E Day: 187
Lindsay Commission (India): 63
Linguistics: 185
Lippmann, Walter: 28
Literature: 27, 29-30, 65
Loba, J F: 73, 206n
London Miss'y Soc. 7, 9, 16, 241n
Lull, Raymond: 25
Lutherans: 96
Lyman, Joseph: 8, 11, 127n
Lyon, Mary: 157

Mac — Mc

MacCallum, Frederick W: 137
MacDonald, Duncan B: 187

MacLachlan, Alexander: 137
McDowell, Mr and Mrs Henry Curtis: 45-48, 191
McLean, Mrs J K: 161
McMillan, Aaron and Mrs (M D): 192

M

Madras (India): 66, 122, 134, 240, 241
Madras Mission: (see India)
Madura (Mathurai) (India): 14, 53, 243
Madura Mission: (see India)
Malta: 194
Manila (P I): 17
Marash (Turkey): 58
Mardin (Turkey): 159
Marlboro (N H): 155
Marshall Islands: 16
Marsovan (Merzifon) (Turkey): 58, 175
Martyn, Henry: 25
Massachusetts: 209, *passim*
Matterhorn (Switzerland): 240
Mead, C M: 206n
Medical Work: 27, 35, 45, 74, 83, 192; see chap. 6
    Clinics 47
    Dispensaries 30, 73, 184
    Function of Medical Miss'y personnel 66, 67, 68
    Hospitals 27, 72, 184
    In Villages 72
    Medical Schools, at Aintab 72; in Ceylon 72; in Madura 72; in Japan 72
    Medical text books 72
    Nationals as physicians and nurses 72
    Nurses' Training Schools 72, 73n
    Physicians 64; (as ordained ministers) 65
    Public health 47, 81
Memorial Volume (1860:) 156, 236

Mercersburg movement: (see German Reformed Church)
Methodist: 78
Mexico: 63n
    Churches 25
    Mexico City 16
    Mexico Mission 16, 24, 25, 194
    Schools 57; Collegio Internacional 59
Micronesia: 16, 20, 28, 65, 178, 194
Mid-Winter Meeting: (see Cong'l denomination)
Miller, Samuel T: 127n, 190
Mills, Samuel: 6, 7
Mindinao (P I): 17
Missiology: 187
Mission: 1, 2; see chap. 8
Missionary Education: (see American Board)
Missionary Herald: 163, 200, 211
Missionary, Missionaries: 36, 41, 42, 55, 206
    Appointment 111, 125, 132; see Appendix V
    As pastors 37, 100, 101
    As preachers 50, 52, 55
    Attitudes 18, 19, 21, 29, 52
    Characteristics 2, 3, 19
    Compassion 2, 19
    Correspondence 18, 19, 26, 45, 46, 47, 48, 51-53, 54
    Distribution 193, 194, 205
    Ecclesiastical liberty 103
    Evangelistic zeal 2, 5, 6, 26, 33, 192
    First volunteers 6, 7, 11
    Function 102, 108, 207, 242, 249, 250
    Health 29, 64, 65
    Instructions to, see Appendix II
    Internat'l ambassadors 2, 3
    Language study and use of vernacular 42, 102
    Living conditions 29
    Negro missionaries 191

Preparation 183-185, see chap 13
Qualifications of 125, 182
Recruitment of 185, 188
Status 71, 182, 193, 194
Teaching 106
Missionary Movement (in America):
Relation to American History 90
'The nerve of missions" 113
Mission of Fellowship (France): 17, 28
Missions Council: (see American Board)
Mississippi: 203
Mobility: 242
Money, Immortal: 238
Moore, Edward C: 60, 61, 207n
Morrison, Robert: 14
Morse, Jedidiah: 11, 127
Mott, John R: 185, 245
Mt. Silinda: (Southern Rhodesia; Africa): 69
Munger, Theodore S: 114
Murdock, Virginia C (M D): 73, 176
Museum (missionary): 204
Muslim peoples: (see Islam)
Mustafa Kemal: 244

N

Nat'l Council (Churches of Christ USA) United Church Women: 117
Nat'l Council of Cong'l Christian Churches: (see Cong'l denomination)
Nationalism: 31, 247
Ndau people: 16, 206
Near East: 17, 25, 29, 36, 53, 55, 188, 194, 244
Near East Foundation: 61
Near East Relief: 61, 86
Neesima, Joseph Hardy: 58, 72
Negroes (American): 189, 190, 191, 192, 193; Negro Cong'l Churches 192

Nestorian Mission: 64
Netherlands, Government of: 15
Netherlands India: (see Indonesia)
Nevin, John W: 136n
Newell, Mr and Mrs Samuel: 11, 243
New England: 1, 49, 50, 188
New Hanover (Pa): 136
New Haven (Conn): 235
Newton Center (Mass): 204
New York: 201, passim
Norris, Mary: 154
Norristown (Pa): 136
North China Mission: (see China)
Northfield (Mass): 185
Nott, Eliphalet: 127n
Nott, Mr and Mrs Samuel: 11
Noyes J T: 97
Noyes, William: 112
Nurses: (see Chap 6)

O

Oberlin College: 116, 140, 187
Ojibwas: (see American Indians)
Okuma, Thomas: 193
Old South Church (Boston): 158
Opium War: 14
Orient, Orientals: 193
Orthodox Churches: 18, 21, 22, 23
Osaka (Japan): 14
Ottoman Empire: 16, 21, 64, 107, 136, 230, 244
Ousley, Mr and Mrs Benjamin F: 190
Outer Space: 240
Ovimbundu, Umbundu: (see Africa)

P

Pacific School of Religion: 161, 187
Pacific States: 160
Pacific Theol Sem'y: (see Pacific School of Religion)
Padelford Commission (Japan): 63
Paganism: 106
Pangchuang (China): 73

Panoplist: 210, 211
"Papers" by Board Secretaries: (see American Board)
Parker, Peter (M D): 64, 65
Park Street Church, Boston: 100, 203
Parmelee, Olive L: 159
"Partners in Obedience": 241
Parvin, Theophilus: 23
Pasumalai, Pasumalie: (see India)
Patagonia: 2, 23, 194
Patton, Cornelius H: 115, 116, 207n, 220, 232
Paul, Saint: 38, 172
Payson, Seth: 127n
Peck, A P (M D): 73
Peet, W W: 229, 230
Peking (China): 18, 159
Penrose, S B L: 73
Perkins, Mrs H P (M D): 73
Perry, Arthur: 61
Persia, Persians: 17, 26, 27, 57, 107, 131, 156, 194
Phelps, Anson G: 237
Philadelphia (Pa): 243
Philippine Islands: 194
  Church, union 3, 251
  Missions 17
  Muslims 17
  Pagan tribes 28
  Schools, Dansalan Junior College 63n; Southern Christian College 63n; Silliman University 17
  United Church of Christ 17, 135, 153
Phillips, Ray: 82
Phillips, William: 11
Philosophy: 247
Physicians: (see Chap 6)
Pierce College (Greece): 63n
Plan of Union: (see Cong'l denomination)
Plunket, William B: 227
Polynesians: 16
Pomona College: 116

Ponasang (China): 180
Porter, H D (M D): 73
Porter, Mary H: 159
Porter, Noah: 8
Portugal: 23, 41
Portuguese East Africa: 15 (see Africa)
Portuguese West Africa: 16 (see Africa: Angola)
Potter, Rockwell Harmon: 207n
Poverty: 2, 34, 83, 91
Prayer: 197
Preachers, Catechists: 30, 46, 55
Preaching: 34, 55, 56, 67, 83, 102
Presbyterians, Presbyterian Church· 14, 57, 78, 136, 215, Chap 10 passim
  General Assembly 126, 130, 141
  "New School" "Old School" 131, 132, 141, 142, 215
  Plan of Union 139
  Presbyterian Board 16, 17
  Presbyterians and Congregationalists 125-132
  Synod of Pittsburgh 128
  Syria and Persia Mission 17
Pressure for change: 247, 248
Primitive cultures: 15, 19-20, 28, 84
Princeton College: 127n, 155, 187
Principles of policy: (see American Board)
Printing presses: 2, 29
Protestantism, Protestants: 5, 17, 32, 38, 242
Protestant Reformation: 20
Providence (R I): 192, 215, 238
Psychology: 247

Q

Quakers: 27

R

Rabbit Rock: 208
Ralston, Robert: 127n

Recruits, Recruitment Office: 194
(see Chap 13)
Regional Meetings: 205
Reiff, Mabel H: 137
"Rethinking Missions": 116-123
Revivals: 33
Rice, Luther: 11
Richards, George (M D): 74
Richards, James: 127n
Richards, Miss Linda: 73n
Riggs, Miss S D (Mrs Dana Getchell): 175
Robert College: 55
Rockefeller, John D Jr: 116, 121
Roman Catholicism: 43
Clergy 24, 54
Counter Reformation 242
Countries 16, 17, 21, 23, 24
Missions 45
Roosevelt, Theodore: 82
Rutgers College: 135

S

St Paul's Institute: (see Turkey)
Salem (Mass): 11, 13, 24, 154, 202, 243
Samokov (Bulgaria): 58, 85
Sanders, Marshall D: 58, 93
Sanders, William Henry: 41, 190
Sandwich Islands: (see Hawaii)
San Francisco: 201
Sanscrit: 52, 53
Schools: (see Education)
Schwenckfelder Churches: 137
Scudder, H M (M D): 66
Scudder, Mrs H M: 67, 158
Scudder, Dr and Mrs John (M D): 64-66, 134
Second Presbyterian Church (Chicago): 159
Secularism: 27, 49
Seelye, Julius H: 49
Seelye, L Clark: 116
Seir (Persia): 38
Senecas: (see American Indians)

Seropyan, Christopher: 188, 189
Service, enlarging concept of: 2, (see Chap 7)
Severinghaus, E L (M D): 81
Shanghai (China): 14
Shansi Mission: (see China)
Shaowu Mission: (see China)
Sheetswa language: 190
Siam: 14, 29, 64, 65, 194
Silliman University: (see P I)
Singapore (Malaya) Mission: 14, 64, 65, 194
Siva (Hinduism): 181
Slavery: 41, 91, 92, 106, 203
Smith, Arthur: 82
Smith, Azariah (M D): 72
Smith College: 116
Smith, Judson: 56, 57, 186, 206n, 232; Re importance of medical work 68
Smith, Mrs Moses: 160
Smyrna (Izmir, Turkey): 21, 58
Smyth, Egbert E: 113
Smyth, Newman: 114
Social Action:
Biblical basis of 83
In American Board fields 82, 89, 90, 91
Organization of Council for Social Education and Action 87, 87n
Role of miss'y confronting social issues 87-90
(See Council for Social Education and Action)
Social Science: 247
Social Work: objectives 34, 40
Society for Promoting Female Education in the East: 157
Society for Propagation of the Gospel: (see Anglican)
Sociology: 247
Solway Hut (Switzerland): 240
South America: 23, 57
South China Mission: (see China)

Southern Christian College: (see P I)
Southern Rhodesia: 16
Spain: 16, 17, 23, 24, 57, 59, 194
Churches 24; Intern'l Institute for Girls 25, 59; Missions 16, 24
Speer, Robert E: 185
Spring, Samuel: 8, 11, 127n
Springfield (Mass): 36
Stamm, R T: 173n
State Conferences: (see Cong'l denomination)
State Women Presidents: (see Cong'l denomination)
Statistics: 76, 77, 193, 194, 198, 218, 219n, 227, 228. See App. V, VI
Stauffacher, A D: 207n
Stewardship, Christian: 238, 249
Stocking, Jay T: 238
Stockton, Betsy: 155
Stoddard, Charles: 115
Stone, Mrs. Andrew: 161
Strong, Caleb: 11
Strong, Elnathan: 207n
Strong, Sidney: 207n
Strong, William E: 116, 207n;
Strong, Mrs W E: 207n
Student volunteer movement: 116, 185, 187
Suffering: 2, 19, 66
Sumatra (Netherlands Indies): 15, 194
Superstition: 29, 50, 114; witch-doctors 44
Swift, Elisha P: 130
Switzerland: 189, 240
Syria: 16, 17, 21, 23, 61, 64, 65, 131

T

Tabernacle (Salem, Mass): 11
Taj Mahal (India): 18
Talas (Turkey): 193n
Talladega College: 191

Tambaram (India): 240, 252
Tamils: 243 (see India, see Ceylon)
Tarsus (Turkey): 61
Tellipallai (Ceylon): 58
Temple of Heaven (Peking): 18
Tennessee: 203
Theological Schools: 34, 185-187
Theology: 110-114, 117, 124; See Chap 9; See Appendix III
Thomas, Sally: 154
Thompson, A C: 53, 186, 206
Thompson, W L (M D): 69-71
Tissera, Gabriel: 100
Torrey, D T: 112
Torrey, Eldridge: 206n
Tracy, Stephen (M D): 64
Transvaal (Africa): 64
Treadwell, John: 8, 11, 127n
Treat, Selah B: 102, 131, 132, 141, 143, 144
Trowbridge, Tillman C: 58
Tucker, William J: 116
Tungchow (see China): 58, 159
Turkey: 17, 21, 22, 57, 68, 136, 156, 188, 229, 244; colleges 58, 61; Gaziantep 22, 58, 72; gov't 230, 245; language 26
Tutors (see Miss'y status)

U

Umzumbe (South Africa): 177, 178
Unified Promotion: (see American Board)
Union of South Africa: 16, 64
Union Theol Sem'y (Manila, P I): 17
Union Theol Sem'y (N Y): 187
Unitarianism, Unitarians: 6, 110, 114
United Church of Canada: 44
United Church of Christ: 17, 135, 153
United Foreign Missionary Society: 127, 128, 133

United Nations: 88
United States: 168, 198
"Unity we seek": 248, 250

V

Vaddukoddai (Batticotta) (Ceylon): 38, 53, 57, 58
Van Rensselaer, Stephen: 133
Venn, Henry: 31
Vernacular: theory of education 52-54
Victorian Age: 218

W

Wagner, E R (M D): 73
Walla Walla (Wash): 73
Walley, Samuel A: 8, 216
Waples, F A (M D): 73
War: 77, 78, 227, 229, 244, 245
War of 1812: 243
Ward, Langdon S: 237
Ward, Mark H (M D): 75; see Chap 6 *passim*
Ware, Henry: 50
Warner, Mrs Franklin Hynes: 169
Warner, L C: 207n
Washington (D C): 169, 170
Watkins, Mrs. David: 161
Webb, Edward: 97
Welcher, Amy: 172, 207n
Wesleyans: 243
West, Far: 115, 145
Western Foreign Miss'y Soc: 129, 130
Wheeler, Charles H: 58
Whitby: (see Intern'l Miss'y Council)
White, Hugh Vernon: 118, 120, 122
Whitman College: 73
Whittemore, W F: 73, 206n
Wilcox, Mrs G B: 160
Wilder, Robert P: 185
Williams College: 6, 112, 116, 208
Williamstown (Mass): 6
Wilson, Alexander E (M D): 64

Wilson, Louise: 178
Winslow, Francis O: 60
Winslow, Miron: 14
Winslow, Mrs Miron: 156, 158
Winston-Salem (N C): 191
Womanhood:
  Degradation of 156
  Purdah (veiled seclusion) in India 91
  Status of women in Muslim countries 91
  Status of women in primitive societies 91
Woman's Boards of Missions: see Chap 12 and Interlude III
  WBM 156-165, 167, 169, 171, 174, 178, 223
  WBMI 159, 160, 165, 171, 180
  WBMP 160, 165, 170, 171, 179, 180n
  Administrative expense of 164
  Bible women 157n, 176, 179
  Branches and auxiliaries 165
  Congregational women 157
  Female Cent Societies 154, 155
  Female Society for Foreign Missions 154, 155
  Fields 163
  Giving (1879, 1899) 165; (1909) 167; (1868-1918) 167
  Ladies Associations 155
  Merger with ABCFM 168-171
  Mission accomplished 168
  Mission Bands for children 159
  Missionary Associations 155
  Personnel statistics 172n
  Relations with American Board 163, 164, 165, 166
  Schools for Girls 157n
  Women in Mission Service 156, 183
Woman's Home Miss'y Federation: 168

Woman's Union Miss'y Society of
N Y: 157, 157n
Women: 12, 210; English ladies
157
Wood, George: 108
Woolley, Mary: 116
Worcester, Samuel: 8, 11, 127,
182, 197n, 202
Worcester (Mass): 9
World Council of Churches: 32
Worship: 197
Wynn, Mr and Mrs Walter C: 192

Y

Yale Band: 233
Yale College: 72, 186, 188
Yale Divinity School: 186, 187

Z

Zenana Work: 157
Zululand, Zulu peoples, Zulu missions: 15, 20, 28, 64, 84, 91,
107, 156